HOWARD
FAST

Howard Fast. Photograph by Maxine C. Gomberg. Used by permission of the photographer.

HOWARD FAST

A Critical Companion

Andrew Macdonald

CRITICAL COMPANIONS TO POPULAR CONTEMPORARY WRITERS
Kathleen Gregory Klein, Series Editor

Greenwood Press
Westport, Connecticut • London

813.52
FAST

Library of Congress Cataloging-in-Publication Data

Macdonald, Andrew.
    Howard Fast : a critical companion / Andrew Macdonald.
      p. cm—(Critical companions to popular contemporary
writers, ISSN 1082–4979)
    Includes bibliographical references (p.   ) and index.
    ISBN 0-313-29493-3 (alk. paper)
    1. Fast, Howard, 1914- —Criticism and interpretation.
2. Historical fiction, American—History and criticism. I. Title.
II. Series.
    PS3511.A784Z7   1996
    813'.52—dc20   95-50458

British Library Cataloguing in Publication Data is available.

Library of Congress Catalog Card Number: 95-50458
ISBN: 0-313-29493-3
ISSN: 1082-4979

First published in 1996

Greenwood Press, 88 Post Road West, Westport, CT 06881
An imprint of Greenwood Publishing Group, Inc.

Printed in the United States of America

(∞)™

The paper used in this book complies with the
Permanent Paper Standard issued by the National
Information Standards Organization (Z39.48-1984).

10 9 8 7 6 5 4 3 2 1

Contents

Series Foreword

The authors who appear in the series Critical Companions to Popular Contemporary Writers are all best-selling writers. They do not have only one successful novel, but a string of them. Fans, critics, and specialist readers eagerly anticipate their next book. For some, high cash advances and breakthrough sales figures are automatic; movie deals often follow. Some writers become household names, recognized by almost everyone.

But novels are read one by one. Each reader chooses to start and, more importantly, to finish a book because of what she or he finds there. The real test of a novel is in the satisfaction its readers experience. This series acknowledges the extraordinary involvement of readers and writers in creating a best-seller.

The authors included in this series were chosen by an Advisory Board composed of high school English teachers and high school and public librarians. They ranked a list of best-selling writers according to their popularity among different groups of readers. Writers in the top-ranked group who had not received book-length, academic literary analysis (or none in at least the past ten years) were chosen for the series. Because of this selection method, Critical Companions to Popular Contemporary Writers meets a need that is not addressed elsewhere.

The volumes in the series are written by scholars with particular expertise in analyzing popular fiction. These specialists add an academic focus to the popular success that these best-selling writers already enjoy.

The series is designed to appeal to a wide range of readers. The general reading public will find explanations for the appeal of these well-known writers. Fans will find biographical and fictional questions answered. Students will find literary analysis, discussions of fictional genres, carefully organized introductions to new ways of reading the novels, and bibliographies for additional research. Students will also be able to apply what they have learned from this book to their readings of future novels by these best-selling writers.

Each volume begins with a biographical chapter drawing on published information, autobiographies or memoirs, prior interviews, and, in some cases, interviews given especially for this series. A chapter on literary history and genres describes how the author's work fits into a larger literary context. The following chapters analyze the writer's most important, most popular, and most recent novels in detail. Each chapter focuses on a single novel. This approach, suggested by the Advisory Board as the most useful to student research, allows for an in-depth analysis of the writer's fiction. Close and careful readings with numerous examples show readers exactly how the novels work. These chapters are organized around three central elements: plot development (how the story line moves forward), character development (what the reader knows about the important figures), and theme (the significant ideas of the novel). Chapters may also include sections on generic conventions (how the novel is similar to or different from others in its same category of science fiction, fantasy, thriller, etc.), narrative point of view (who tells the story and how), symbols and literary language, and historical or social context. Each chapter ends with an "alternative reading" of the novel. The volume concludes with a primary and secondary bibliography, including reviews.

The Alternative Readings are a unique feature of this series. By demonstrating a particular way of reading each novel, they provide a clear example of how a specific perspective can reveal important aspects of the book. In each alternative reading section, one contemporary literary theory—such as feminist criticism, Marxism, new historicism, deconstruction, or Jungian psychological critique—is defined in brief, easily comprehensible language. That definition is then applied to the novel to highlight specific features that might go unnoticed or be understood differently in a more general reading of the novel. Each volume defines two or three specific theories, making them part of the reader's understanding of how diverse meanings may be constructed from a single novel.

Taken collectively, the volumes in the Critical Companions to Popular Contemporary Writers series provide a wide-ranging investigation of the complexities of current best-selling fiction. By treating these novels seriously as both literary works and publishing successes, the series demonstrates the potential of popular literature in contemporary culture.

Kathleen Gregory Klein
Southern Connecticut State University

Acknowledgments

Many people had a hand in producing this book. Series editor Kathleen Gregory Klein gave helpful advice and criticism. Howard Fast opened his life and his work to examination by a stranger; his hospitality and generosity went far beyond the conventional, and I shall long remember his Connecticut. Professor Raymond McGowan of Loyola University was a learned, precise, and punctilious editor. And as always, Gina Macdonald was my companion and soulmate, sharing victories and defeats with equanimity and goodwill; her contributions are invisible but enormous, and go beyond thanks.

Introduction

Choosing representative texts for a study of any author's canon is a difficult task; choosing typical works from among Howard Fast's eighty or so publications is enough to induce paralysis of the will to choose. Most writers work one side of the street only; as the following chapters will show, Fast has worked both sides of the street, the roadway itself, and several minor crossroads as well. Historical novel, fictionalized biography, nonfiction biography and history, novel of ideas, short story, poetry, plays, film scripts, detective story, family saga—the types and genres in Fast's canon go on and on. Fast matches versatility with productivity, for his works of any one type or genre typically number at least a dozen, and in some cases many more. Because Fast's career began in 1931, many books, long out of print, are unavailable, even in libraries. Choices made for a critical book of a few hundred pages, then, must reflect a number of criteria, including the quality of the work, its significance to continuing themes and concerns in the canon, its availability, and, perhaps most important, its likelihood of surviving changes of taste and style in future generations of readers.

The Fast enthusiast is likely to be disappointed in not seeing a favorite work covered in the chapters that follow. In fact, many deserving books have been left out. *Power*, for example, an exquisitely shaded fictional biography of United Mine Workers president John L. Lewis, has many of the virtues of Robert Penn Warren's similar portrait of Huey P. Long in *All the King's Men*. Both books trace, with great psychological acumen, the corrosive effects of money and power on idealists, both are told by journalist-narrators caught in the very modern dilemma of observing versus participating, and both capture place and time with great skill. Yet *Power* is difficult to find even in used-book stores and libraries. It also is somewhat anomalous in Fast's canon, for he wrote few books exactly like it—biographies of contemporary leaders from an ambivalent authorial point of view. Thus, availability to the reader was one important criterion of choice, since it seems wrong to point the newly inspired reader toward a book impossible to find. Centrality in the canon was another important criterion, for *Power*, excellent though it is, might not be recognized as a book by Fast on the evidence of its text alone.

Finally, the ultimate critic and judge of value is the passage of time. The survival of a book or an author's canon into a distant future leaves pontifical reviewers and critics behind in the dust of old newspapers and journals; no one will care for very long what professional readers thought if the original work keeps finding new, unpaid readers. Such survival of a book or author reflects some luck, perhaps, but also the enthusiasm of many readers who will not let an author's work die and keep urging it on others. Teachers and book editors may make an author's works available but cannot alone shape reactions; only the single judgments of thousands of intelligent readers can keep a work alive. This criterion for inclusion is precisely as easy to apply as is anticipating the future, but Fast's long career does provide some advantages, since readers are continually exercising their judgments about his earlier books.

The works covered in this study reflect the criteria I have delineated. Chapter 1, a biography of the author, leans heavily on Fast's autobiography, *Being Red*, and on his farewell to the Communist party, *The Naked God*. The latter has mostly ideological interest, but the former will be read as long as people are interested in the fascinating and turbulent events of the mid-twentieth century, for *Being Red* records not only politics but also literary events, social happenings, funny stories, major scandals, gossip, lifestyle changes, and so on. Far from being a simple autobiography, it is a picture of the times that made us. The "early" Revolutionary War novel, *Citizen Tom Paine*, has been included as an example of Fast's best work in that vein, but also one that most clearly represents his politics and thinking about the place of the common man (and woman) in a world controlled by the rich and the aristocratic. Fast edited a modern collection of Paine's works. Perhaps more than any other political figure, Fast's Paine shows us a model of virtuous political behavior, a proletarian, revolutionary thinker-writer uncorrupted and incorruptible. As a revisionist look at the people and forces that created the American Revolution, *Citizen Tom Paine* seems likely to last as a standard reference, for both students of the period and general readers as well. The book is commonly found in public libraries and seems to enjoy a continuing wide readership.

The next two books examined, *Freedom Road* and *Spartacus*, are included for some of the same reasons as *Citizen Tom Paine*. Both express Fast's ideas about repression and revolt, but outside the context of the Revolutionary War. These two books are in fact representative of a whole line of Fast's works about servitude, including *Moses, Prince of Egypt, My Glorious Brothers*, and even *Power*, whose coal miners of West Virginia are little more than chattels of the mining company. Fast sees slavery as taking many forms, from the literal to the wage slavery of factory and mine. *Spartacus* shows the vicious effects on a whole society when it begins to depend on slaves. In Fast's view, Roman decadence and the fall of the empire were inevitable effects of this dependency. *Freedom Road* explores a successful revolt against slavery but shows how reforms are betrayed. Like *Citizen Tom Paine* and *Spartacus* it captures the brevity of revolt, the way the old order quickly reimposes itself. Both books are well known, *Spartacus* in part because of the famous blockbuster film by the same name, and *Freedom Road* because of the enormous praise it garnered when first published. *Spartacus* will long be read for its brilliant pictures of Rome at its most powerful; *Freedom Road* may well capture a new audience because, as a serious attempt to view Reconstruction through the eyes of a freed slave, it addresses modern multicultural concerns.

April Morning and *Seven Days in June* return to the Revolutionary War, a subject that Fast found sustained him throughout his career. *April Morning* came almost two decades after *Citizen Tom Paine*, and *Seven Days in June* more than fifty years after. In spite of the long period intervening, some of the same major themes prevail, the difference lying in the increasing pacifism and disgust with war in later years. Thus we can again see Fast's evolving ideas in these core works. Both books were well received. *April Morning* sold millions of copies and is a classic of its kind; it is a completely adult work but a favorite with young readers as well, which promises well for its future. Reports indicate that it is frequently assigned reading in middle school and high school. *Seven Days in June* garnered favorable reviews and has a nicely modern perspective on the Battle of Bunker Hill, celebrating heroism but never shrinking from the

cowardice and treachery that afflicted both sides and ultimately acknowledging the pointlessness of all battle. Neither has been turned into
a film, although both have great promise for film treatment. Its finest
character is Evan Feversham, the British army surgeon we first meet in
The Hessian at a later point in his career. *Seven Days* is thus a "prequel,"
a later work that covers earlier events in a character's life. Feversham
sums up Fast's ideas on war succinctly and memorably, and his reap-
pearance is an inspired act.

In the extended period between *April Morning* and *Seven Days in June*,
Fast drew, much more than usual, on personal experiences for inspira-
tion. This new emphasis on the domestic and spiritual side of life, as
opposed to the political and historical, is traced in the long chapter on
The Immigrants and the novels that follow it: *Second Generation, The Establishment, The Legacy*, and *The Immigrant's Daughter*. The Immigrants
series was not only a commercial success, selling 10 million copies, but
also a television miniseries. While it is difficult to predict the future popularity of such a long family saga (it totals thousands of pages), The
Immigrants should remain a classic about the American entrepreneurial
spirit, the founding of the great business families of California, and the
establishment of West Coast mores and attitudes. The series is also a
good window on Fast himself, for besides including a number of autobiographical elements recognizable from *Being Red*, it wrestles with
themes both philosophical and social that run throughout the canon. It
thus provides a good way of seeing Fast's life and work in totality.

The last book discussed is *The Bridge Builder's Story*, an excellent evocation of earlier themes and characters, but with twists of point of view
and genre that make it a challenging and gripping reading experience.
Though Fast continues to experiment with his material and returns to
familiar territory, he nevertheless leads the reader to see it from new
perspectives.

One can only hope that the reader, intrigued by the nine chapters of
this book, will read the whole of Fast's works, and explore all of Fast's
themes. If this happens, the injustice of covering so limited a portion of
the author's canon will be ameliorated, and I will be well satisfied.

1

Howard Fast: An American Life

> I've been very fortunate, no question about it, because even during the blacklist years my books were selling by the millions all over the world. There were always enough royalties for us to live decently. I was very lucky, very fortunate. But I was born and grew up in the greatest, the noblest achievement of the human race on this planet—which was called the United States of America.
> —Howard Fast, quoted by Mervyn Rothstein in "Howard Fast in a New Mode," *New York Times*, March 10, 1987.

All writers create out of their life experiences, and their biographies—biographies in the larger sense of what they read, thought about, and learned, as well as what events happened to them—are vital to our understanding of what shaped their fictional work. The influence of life experience clearly varies from writer to writer, with some using the fictional world as an escape from a grim past or present, some following the events of their own lives as a general guide, and others indulging in virtual autobiography disguised as fiction. In the case of a writer like Howard Fast, much of whose early and best work was based on historical research, biographical information may seem beside the point, for surely the overwhelming weight of historical fact and the inescapable patterns of verifiable event must guide the fiction. What chance can the writer's own experience have against the known circumstances of, say, the American Revolutionary War?

In fact, although Fast has said he is "too close" to the incidents of his life "to be able to separate the important from the unimportant" (*Something about the Author* 81), much of his work, even the historical fiction, is autobiographical. When Fast writes from research, he chooses his central characters with great care; protagonists such as Tom Paine, whose life and work have been well established in documented sources, parallel elements in Fast's own personality and worldview, elements clearly related to his personal history. The historical figures thus provide a kind of psychological biography of Fast, a duplication and validation of his own philosophy and personal leanings in someone known to have existed earlier. When the protagonist of a Fast historical novel is purely fictional—an amalgam of real figures, perhaps, but not a historical personality—Fast again puts together a character who is recognizably a product of forces familiar to Fast from his own life. The central figures from books such as *Conceived in Liberty* and *April Morning*, for example, though fictional and very different from their creator in age, education, religion, geographic origin, vocation, and so on, nevertheless share key values, attitudes, and assumptions that firmly link Fast, the urban New York literary figure and political activist, with rural farm boy or uneducated soldier.

In addition, some nonhistorical Fast works are thinly disguised autobiographies. *The Pledge*, a straightforward account of a young journalist's experience in post–World War II India and the United States, culminating in a jail term for contempt of Congress, is virtually true, at least if Fast's accounts of his own experiences are to be trusted. More commonly, echoes and parallels of Fast's life occur throughout the novels—reminders of real characters encountered, locations visited, events and situations experienced, political and social happenings confronted. The lines between biography and fiction are often parallel but at times diverge, depending on the kind of fiction being written, but the lines generally move in the same direction, as we would expect. It is thus helpful to know the shaping factors of Fast's long and event-filled life, an exciting and very American life that tells us much about what it was like to be in the thick of things politically and socially in the mid- to late-twentieth century, the period of America's greatest power and influence.

This is not to say that the value of Fast's work lies in conscious or unconscious revelations about his own life. Biographical readings are

useful when we know enough about a writer's life to see what has been
done to turn reality into art; our emphasis should be on Fast's fiction,
on the patterns, themes, and characters that have intrigued and captivated several generations of readers who know nothing of the writer's
history. For that reason, the biographical material in this chapter should
be seen as a guide to what motivated Fast rather than as a key to un-
locking meaning.

The discussion is based mainly on Fast's excellent 1990 memoir, *Being
Red*. A second, less detailed source for the discussion is *The Naked God:
The Writer and the Communist Party*, published in 1957; this book began
as a magazine article about Fast's departure from the Communist party
and focuses almost entirely on his political life. Apart from incidental
facts culled from various standard references, the final source of material
for this chapter is Howard Fast himself, in the form of brief discussions
with me.

Fast's entrance on the American scene in November 1914 was une-
ventful enough, probably hardly noticed outside his own family, for he
was the son of working-class, first-generation immigrants, Barney Fastov,
the name shortened to "Fast" by immigration officials, and Ida Miller.
His parents were from the Ukraine and Lithuania, respectively. Barney
Fast seems to have been something of a romantic rebel before marriage
to Ida, apparently seriously planning to join a cavalry regiment invading
Cuba in 1898 during the Spanish-American War as a means of revenge
for the expulsion of the Jews from Spain in 1492. The military escapade
never materialized, however, and after five children were born, Howard
being the fourth, Ida Fast died in 1923, when the author-to-be was eight
and a half years old.

His mother's death left Howard's father with four children (Arthur,
the second child, died of diphtheria in 1912) and a limited means of
earning a living, as his original trade as a wrought-iron worker disappeared because of changing construction methods and his second live-
lihood as a gripper man on a cable car fell prey to new means of
transportation in New York. The elder Fast became a dress factory cutter,
a dead-end job never paying more than forty dollars a week. The eldest
child, Rena, left to marry soon after her mother's death, and the three
younger boys were thrown, according to *Being Red*, pretty much on their
own resources as their father slipped in and out of depression and employment, a distant parent who left at eight in the morning and returned
to their tenement as late as midnight. Jerome, known as Jerry, was one
year older than Howard, and the two took over the household. Fast says

their poverty, both financial and emotional, was unchanging. Significantly, what did change, the author says in *Being Red*, was his "ability to face and alter circumstances. I ceased to be wholly a victim" (31).

One need not be a Freudian analyst to see in this grim childhood history patterns later emphasized in Fast's work: the distant, somewhat unreliable father/authority figure, well meaning but ineffectual; the mother figure, absent and possibly idealized by childhood memory; the need to confront all problems actively; the power of brotherhood, as Jerry and Howard, almost the same age, confronted the hostile world of the ghetto and paid their own way with a constantly changing series of jobs, beginning at age ten for Howard. Throughout the Fast canon, we see protagonists in rebellion against authority, often an authority unaware of and uninvolved with the main characters, who soon learn to depend on themselves and on their own true "brothers," always a limited group against the world. Brotherhood abounds in Fast's books, both literal, as in *My Glorious Brothers*, about the rebellious Jewish brothers who become leaders of ancient Israel, or metaphorical, as in the union of mine workers in *Power*. And until a notable change in the 1960s when Fast turned to novels about women, the group is male, for women, though often well drawn, are subsidiary in the early works. Perhaps paralleling his mother's "desertion" of Fast and his brothers through her death and then his sister Rena's escape into marriage, the elegant, somewhat older female figure who is either distant or unreachable and sometimes leaves the protagonist is a familiar figure in the earlier works.

Fast's childhood also inculcated two formidable though contrasting shaping elements: the anti-Semitism of his rough immigrant neighborhoods and the uplifting power of the written word, the latter located most conveniently in the New York Public Library. After leaving the East Side Jewish ghetto, Fast's family moved to 159th Street, just west of Amsterdam Avenue, where Italian and Irish immigrants predominated. This was young Howard's introduction to racial and religious hatred, and although the Fasts had never kept a kosher household or felt any particular Jewish identity, the accusations of "Christ-killing" by the neighborhood children helped create a new unity among Howard and his brothers, a closed circle against hostile outsiders. Thus, in spite of his lack of early training in Judaism as religion or culture, Fast came, presumably beginning at this point, to entertain a lifelong interest in his heritage, even writing a novel, *The Outsider*, about a rabbi married to a nonpracticing Jew and struggling with his role in a Christian-majority society. Apart from *Moses, Prince of Egypt*, and *My Glorious Brothers*, both wholly on Jewish history, many Fast novels include Jewish characters, often in contexts such as the American Revolution or Reconstruction in which Judaism is usually given little or no credit for having a role. In *Citizen Tom Paine*, for example, it is a Jewish moneylender who finances one of Paine's revolutionary screeds, while in *Freedom Road*, Gideon Jackson's first mentor is Jewish. Doctor Gonzales, a Jewish physician, accompanies the main character of *Seven Days in June*. A Jewish family, the Levys, figures importantly in The Immigrants series. The struggles of Bernie Cohen, and later of his son Sam, over the proper place of a Jewish heritage in an "American" identity become important in the later novels of the family saga.

Apart from summer vacations in the Catskill Mountains when young Howard spent time with his aunt and uncle in Hunter, New York, childhood provided few pleasures. Even these escapes from big city poverty were tempered by family conflict with aunt and cousins, although Fast loved the mountains, forests, and wild animals, an appreciation of nature we see again throughout his work, even in the fictional descriptions of Mill Point Prison in West Virginia in *The Pledge*, where Fast in reality served time for contempt of Congress. We see a big city boy's love of open spaces in *Max*, whose hero, like Fast, moves from New York to California, and again in incidental descriptions of the American landscape, from *Freedom Road* to *Power* to more recent works like The Immigrants series, where the Napa Valley near San Francisco receives loving description. But New York did have one overwhelming formative influence: the availability of free books from the New York Public Library.

Fast reports reading everything and anything from the shelves of this wondrous collection of texts, and any serious reader of his novels believes him. Fast is complimentary enough about the public education he received, acknowledging that for all its rigidity and lack of imagination—he was forced to write with his right hand though he was born left handed—it might have been superior to more modern approaches that produce poor or few results. However, it is clear that his real education came through omnivorous reading—of the classics of American literature, of fiction that was mentioned or recommended, of whatever else took the fancy of the boy and the young man. We can imagine Fast's remembering himself when he wrote about Gideon Jackson, the semiliterate slave of *Freedom Road*, discovering books and the huge new world they offered, of Tom Paine's similar self-taught odyssey, and of myriad other scholars and readers who pull themselves up in his novels. Again and again the point is made that nonreaders are confined to the experiences of their own place and time. For the ambitious who are excluded from formal education, books are like wondrous time travel and space travel devices, machines that permit local experience to be compared to universal human practice. Education, always the key to the city on the hill for immigrants, came to Fast through a library card.

The evidence reveals varying experiences in Fast's early life—some very harsh, some, as in his relationship with his brothers, less so. His biography speaks of poverty and a fierce struggle for a decent life in a ghetto, of brutal street toughs and gangs that had to be fought for survival. Yet there must have been good times as well. A photograph of Howard at age three in *Being Red* shows a solemn straw-hatted and bespectacled toddler with toy spade and pail, on holiday in Hunter, New York, an image a bit at odds with the grim self-portrait in words of the same book. The photograph of his father, Barney Fast, shows a fairly well-dressed, even dapper man at ease, and the photos of brothers Jerome and Julius, as well as of Howard at twenty-one, show healthy and vigorous-looking young men of their time, looking out at the camera with adolescent confidence. The depression years were grim and New York street life violent, of course, and it would be churlish to question memories held so firmly, but it is at least clear that Fast's intellectual development as a child and youngster were completely out of character with the tenement housing, the street victimization, and the generally gritty physical environment he describes surrounding him. In this intellectual development, books from the New York Public Library played an important role in producing a writer, but Fast was also lucky in his teachers and in his literary models and influences. Even for poor boys from the ghetto, the times were rich with stimulants to the artistic and intellectual sensibility.

Fast's career as an author began with a number of different factors shaping his imagination. Jack London's prose was a recurring pleasure (now Fast finds it too flowery and mannered), and from London's *The Iron Heel*, Fast learned how the "wild word" *bolshevik* could be used to condemn a work of art even when the librarian in question had not read the book, a lesson of great importance later in his life when Communist party censors attacked his own works. An English teacher from Texas named Hallie Jamison is remembered fondly, a one-time friend of O. Henry who imbued Fast with a love of the lore of the American West and praised his gift for writing. She urged him to read Robert Louis Stevenson, George Bernard Shaw, and Shakespeare; Shaw's *The Intelli-*

gent Woman's Guide to Socialism and Capitalism was a Pandora's box, leading Fast to Thorstein Veblen's *The Theory of the Leisure Class*, Bellamy's *Looking Backward*, and Engel's *The Origin of the Family*. The movement away from the narrow world of poverty and provincialism had begun.

Captivated by these models of rigorous thought, Fast decided to become a writer at age fifteen, not so much by conscious decision but by default, for other avenues were closed to him due to his indifference to academic subjects other than literature and ideas. He describes himself as neither quiet nor contemplative as a child, but as "one of those irritating, impossible, doubting, questioning mavericks, full of anger and invention and wild notions, accepting nothing, driving . . . peers to bitter arguments and . . . elders to annoyance, rage, and despair" (*Being Red* 48). He says dryly that he probably had some good points as well, and then seriously and significantly claims that he and his brothers, in spite of their rough upbringing, had no hate of others different from themselves, hate being something picked up along the way, surely a key to understanding his later work. From this perspective, hatred is not part of the innocent young human but rather "picked up," learned or acquired from society as one grows older; human nature, he implies, is a blank tablet written on by experience, at least as far as this destructive emotion goes, with youthful decency poisoned by environment. The suggestion is of human perfectibility. Hatred, simply one of the characteristics of social organization, can be eliminated by reorganizing society, much as one could eliminate smoking or drinking by doing away with opportunities to learn about them. This question of the origin of hatred and prejudice is wrestled with throughout the canon.

The fledgling literary man was unenrollable in most colleges because of his spotty academic record, and at age seventeen he chose the National Academy, a prestigious New York City art school, to instruct him in how to illustrate his own writing. Each morning he would arise at 6:00 A.M. and write for two hours before art school. After learning two-fingered typing (which he still uses) and banging out a few dozen stories, he finally sold one, "Wrath of the Purple," to *Amazing Stories* magazine for thirty-seven dollars, a good deal of money in 1931. Now working for the public library, Fast was assigned to pick up overdue books checked out by prostitutes at a huge nearby brothel, an experience with temptation overcome by fear of syphilis that shows up in *Max*. In spite of such distractions, Fast still managed to write two novels, to try to read *Das Kapital*, to read *The Communist Manifesto* and John Reed's *Ten Days That Shook the World* with pleasure, to drop out of art studies at the National

Academy, to fall in and out of love with various young women his age, to resign from the public library job, to begin to meet other intellectuals and political folk interested in leftist ideas, and to work for a hat maker. None of these activities necessarily had any causal relation with the others, but he was learning that he was a writer and a thinker, not a student, that he enjoyed the company of women, and that his great interest was in the politics of the left. One young woman, Sarah Kunitz, was a member of the Communist party but discouraged the seventeen-year-old Fast from joining as well, and his designs on both Sarah and party membership gradually faded.

Next, in 1933, footloose and unencumbered by any formal obligations, Fast joined a friend on a hitchhiking tour of the South, catching rides down the eastern part of the country, through Richmond, Winston-Salem, Savannah, Tampa, and Fort Lauderdale all the way to Miami. These southern experiences gave him good background for *Freedom Road*, he says, and, one suspects, colored his attitudes toward that whole section of the country thereafter, since most of his contacts with southern officialdom and the general populace were negative—"jails and guns," he remembers—although a few individuals and the picturesque and romantic scenery are recalled fondly. On return to New York, the young Howard went to work as a shipping clerk and wrote six to eight hours a day, completing novels number four and five, both, like the first three, unpublishable. Then he wrote his sixth novel, *Two Valleys*, and found a publisher, Dial Press, in 1933. At nineteen he received the Bread Loaf Writers Conference Award. His next works were the novels *Strange Yesterday* (1934) and *Place in the City* (1937), but though he was being published, Sarah Kunitz, with whom Fast had stayed in contact, criticized his work, pointing out that his stories were "fairy tales" written by a legitimate working-class writer, while middle-class writers were writing about the depression and the life of the poor. In reaction, Fast tried a story about a street boy from his neighborhood, which he found so painful to write about that after publishing it as *The Children* he turned to research on the American Revolution, in part to "try to find out what had actually happened" and to avoid another "fairy tale" or the pain of writing about his own life (*Being Red* 65).

The scorn of Sarah Kunitz for his escapist tales was a watershed event, for Fast thereafter relied on research, to greater or lesser degrees to be sure, but for the most part avoiding "fairy tales" coming purely out of his own imagination until much later in his career. He was also temporarily lionized by the left and the John Reed Society for *The Children*,

whose politics agreed with their own. Fast, however, was put off by the
show trials and executions of old bolsheviks in Russia in 1936, and he
had no further contact with the Communist party until the end of World
War II. What he describes as the most important event of his young life
occurred at about this time: his meeting with Bette Cohen, a young
woman from New Jersey with whom Fast fell immediately in love and
who became his wife. Their life as a young married couple was one of
poverty, for Fast gave up factory work to write freelance for magazines
such as the *Saturday Evening Post* and the *Ladies Home Companion*. A jaunt
in an old jalopy to Valley Forge, then undergoing historical reconstruction, led to *Conceived in Liberty*, an interesting if harrowing book written
in the realistic style of Erich Maria Remarque's *All Quiet on the Western
Front*. The Revolutionary War had never been approached in this way,
and *Conceived in Liberty* was well received, including a very positive review in the *New York Times* by the American realist author James T.
Farrell.

A trip to the American West, including Oklahoma, Arizona, New Mexico, the Rockies, and Mexico, led to an enthusiasm for the history and
lore of the American Indian, and especially the Cheyenne. Fast, a quarter
of a century before it became fashionable, was interested in telling the
American Indian story from the Indian point of view. *The Last Frontier*
(1941) received particular praise as a taut and moving story of the abuse
and extermination of three hundred Cheyenne. The manuscript was ill
received precisely because of its innovative viewpoint, but after a lengthy
revision, it was published and praised by critics, including Alexander
Woollcott, Rex Stout, and the eminent Carl Van Doren.

The early 1940s were eventful years for Howard and Bette Fast. *The
Tall Hunter* came out in 1942, followed by *The Unvanquished*, in the same
year, about the lowest point for the Continental army, and *Time* magazine called it the "best book about World War Two," seeing in it a parallel to the current struggle. Also in 1942, at the suggestion of Louis
Untermeyer, Fast joined the Office of War Information (OWI) and
worked for the Voice of America. He began to write *Freedom Road* and
received, through a work colleague, an invitation to stay with an anti-
Semitic family of southern aristocrats in Charleston, South Carolina, to
do background research. Fast's visit shows up in *Freedom Road* in his
evocative descriptions of old Charleston mansions and the waterfront,
and especially in the descriptions of the dinner parties his central character Gideon Jackson attends, social gatherings equally notable for elegance and bigotry.

In this same period Fast and Bette were slowly drawn into the circle of New York communists. Fast is somewhat defensive about his ignorance of the true face of Stalin (he admits to being disturbed by the Non-Aggression Pact with Hitler), and he points out the stalwart Americanism of his Communist party compatriots, their decency and integrity. Fast asserts that the American Communist party led the struggle for the unemployed, the hungry, the homeless, and the oppressed, and he offers as evidence the known names of the best and the brightest who were party members, an honor roll of writers and thinkers of the time: W.E.B. Du Bois, Albert Maltz, John Howard Lawson, and Dalton Trumbo. (Much later, Trumbo would write the screenplay for the film version of Fast's novel *Spartacus*.) Many others were secret members of the party, and, of course, were trapped by their "premature anti-Fascism," in the euphemism of the McCarthy years, when U.S. policy shifted quickly from embracing the Soviet Union as an ally to defining itself against the U.S.S.R. as its mortal enemy.

These years leading to Fast's identification as a "card-carrying member of the Communist party," as the rhetoric of the time termed it, were clearly painful and difficult for him to deal with, even decades later. He was a successful writer, with both critics and the public, now financially secure and newly married. But with the war, all carefully laid plans for the future were disrupted. Bette Fast miscarried their first child, and there were apparently strains in the marriage over her depression and the prospect of Howard's possibly serving abroad; however, a job with the OWI offered a compromise in which Fast could help the war effort yet remain in New York. His work with the OWI turned out to be not just a temporary stopgap but rather another turning point; he would become ever more involved in politics, and his novels based on wartime and postwar experiences would eventually take him in new political and artistic directions.

Fast's OWI work was writing propaganda. Initially hired because he knew something about the American Revolution and might therefore produce patriotic pamphlets, he was recommended as a newswriter by the eminent theater producer John Houseman, who had read the proofs for *Citizen Tom Paine* and thought Fast could write good, clean political prose. The young novelist, still in his late twenties, became the wordsmith for the still-forming Voice of America, writing daily fifteen-minute scripts to be read by actors in English and a wide variety of European languages. The irony of the future communist's being chosen as mouthpiece of the U.S. government and the army is not lost on Fast's retrospective view of his work. Millions of Europeans of different nations enslaved by the Nazis heard Fast's words and formed their mental images of the United States on that basis. Generals, bureaucrats, representatives of shipbuilders and the State Department, of the U.S. Chamber of Commerce and the Merchant Marine: a full contingent of unlikely folk beat a path to Fast's office trying to get their story told on the Voice of America. The opening words to his news show, "Good morning, this is the Voice of America, and here is the situation today," still deeply affect Fast: "this is the voice of mankind's hope and salvation, the voice of my wonderful, beautiful country, which will put an end to fascism and remake the world" (*Being Red* 14). Fast's political beliefs brought him to many criticisms of American culture, yet the pure and idealistic patriotism expressed here is consistent throughout his long career as an author.

A measure of how innocent the future communist was about things Russian is captured in an amusing Voice of America story. One day the State Department told Fast that President Roosevelt wanted the entire broadcast for that evening—and it was already 6.00 P.M.—devoted to the virtues of a Russian soldier, an Ivan Ivanovich. Roosevelt assumed that Fast knew that "Ivan Ivanovich" was the nickname for the typical Russian infantryman, the counterpart to the American G.I. Joe, but Fast and his staff, in blithe ignorance, spent two hours calling around trying to find information about this particular Soviet before learning from the Russian news agency TASS that there was no such individual. Far more troubling was the necessity of watching battlefield film clips from the Allies and enemy forces in order to make the radio reports realistic; the films made war real and hateful to Fast in a way that prose could not, and he found his early antiwar sentiments reconfirmed. We might note also that throughout his seventy-odd novels, scenes of war are always realistic, engrossing, and horrifying; the wartime battle footage he viewed, unedited for the public, must have shaped his later descriptions.

Under Fast's direction, the Voice of America broadcasts became polished and successful, and during this period of fourteen months or so of broadcasting, *Citizen Tom Paine* came out and garnered rave reviews. Fast applied for the overseas VOA position in North Africa but was told that the State Department, on the advice of the Federal Bureau of Investigation, would not issue him a passport because of his communist sympathies and Communist party connections. Fast says that he had neither, only a fair-minded appreciation of the sufferings of the Soviet Union in its struggle against Nazism and a refusal to advance the anticommunist agenda. In January 1944 Fast resigned angrily, admitting much later to intemperance in his speech (a lifelong characteristic) but never in his actions, which were entirely loyal and proper.

At this time, Fast took his first trip to California to discuss a possible film of *Citizen Tom Paine*. (Images of California in this era abound in *Max*.) The deal fell through, as have most other arrangements to film Fast's works, but he met many movie people, including Paul Robeson, the African-American singer and actor. He discovered in the Hollywood community a number of communist sympathizers, and, when again in New York, he and Bette were asked to join the party. They did so that year, 1944, and he says that there were no party cards involved, simply a self-identification: we are with you.

Ironically, this was also the moment of Fast's greatest success as a novelist, for *Freedom Road* had won enthusiastic adherents, including Eleanor Roosevelt and W.E.B. Du Bois. A Soviet bibliography counted its publication abroad at eighty-two languages; another Soviet estimate called it the most widely printed and read book of the twentieth century. Fast was receiving requests for publication forty-six years after the original publication, and pirated editions were in the millions at least. One African scholar was inspired by the book to create a written language for his tribe, in which the first work printed was *Freedom Road*. During this period Fast received the Schomburg Race Relations Award (1944), the Newspaper Guild Award (1947), and the Jewish Book Council of America Award (1948). But irony abounded: as soon as word of Fast's communism began to spread, his literary reputation began to disintegrate, just as, over a decade later, his name was obliterated from Soviet literary journals and courses once he quit the party.

Fast's memories of the party in the postwar period are of a benign, almost mainstream group, one very much in the American socialist tradition dating back to the Levelers in colonial days, through the labor movement of the nineteenth century, the International Workers of the World (the Wobblies), and on into the Socialist party of Eugene V. Debs. Fast claims the party did believe in violent revolution in the nineteenth century but gave it up for labor and community organizing in the twentieth, a position in accord with party dogma but in dispute among historians. In fact, Fast's descriptions of his first party meeting, held in the New York brownstone of an upper-class aristocrat, make it sound like a discussion group sponsored by the Democratic party: how could the participants help reelect Franklin Delano Roosevelt? Fast insists that he never heard a single call for the overthrow of the government by violence. Of the sixty thousand or so party members in the United States at the time, Fast asserts that the vast majority were decent, honorable people of great talent and idealism. In fact, Fast met Harry Truman, then vice president, and later was invited with his reelection committee to the White House for lunch with the Roosevelts. Mrs. Roosevelt chatted with Fast about *Freedom Road*.

The next great adventure shaped a number of novels. Fast received an offer from *Coronet* magazine to go to the China-Burma-India theater as a war correspondent. In fact, the war was virtually over, and Fast was moved from one public relations office to another in places where the battles had been won long before. In Casablanca he was impressed by the easy, luxurious life led by officers and troops far from the front lines, the palatial quarters and picnics at the beach with champagne and caviar. In contrast, in Benghazi, he was taken into the desert to see miles of wrecked military vehicles—German, American, and British tanks, jeeps, and so on—piled together in testimony of the enormous waste of war. The experience, says Fast, made him a pacifist at that moment. (In fact, he has made this statement about a number of experiences.) In Cairo he saw human misery unparalleled even by that in Calcutta, which he was to see later. He flew over the Negev and Sinai, then over Iraq, Iran, Abadan, Bahrain Island, and Palestine, absorbing images of the "terrible mountains and desert" that would show up in *My Glorious Brothers*. In Saudi Arabia his huge C-46 cargo plane put down to pick up empty Coca Cola bottles in a desert airstrip where the thermometer read 157 degrees Fahrenheit. The plane lumbered back into the air but could not gain altitude in the desert heat because of its load of empty soft drink bottles. Fast yelled for the crew to dump cases out to save all their lives, but they refused, explaining that while military equipment might be sacrificed, they would be in deep trouble for "messing around with Coca Cola." The plane, flying just above the ground, landed on its belly at an emergency air field with no loss of life and no broken bottles, but was ruined. Both *Coronet* and *Esquire* refused to write the story, which eventually appeared in *The Howard Fast Reader*, where most readers took it as fiction.

In India, Fast encountered the British, a people who generally come off very negatively in all his writing, from *Citizen Tom Paine* to *The Pledge*, the fictional version of this trip. A severe critic of colonialism, Fast blames the British for their toleration and perhaps encouragement of Indian poverty under the raj, the rule by the British empire, and, even worse, their personal indifference to the humanity of their colonial subjects. Two events from this trip sum up this dehumanizing attitude, both of which show up as incidents in *The Pledge*, in slightly different form. First, Fast sees two British officers being dried after a shower, their Indian servants toweling off their private parts to the complete indifference of the officers, as if the servants were not human. A second story was told to Fast, that when the British high commissioner at New Delhi learned that poor people were using a lamppost as an open air night school to learn reading, the commissioner acted quickly to help this literacy effort: he had a larger light bulb installed!

Fast saw Gandhi from a distance at a train station, but the greatest influence on him, apart from the negative effect of the snobbish, class-conscious British officers and officialdom and the self-indulgence of the American military in essentially peacetime circumstances (the front-line fighting was far away), was the Indian communists and their seriousness about fighting poverty and misery among their people. The chief of the Delhi Communist party sent a message through Fast to his opposite number in the United States: four hundred million Indians have been learning to spit together, and they will wash the British into the sea. A journey from Delhi to Calcutta by train revealed all the wonders and horrors of India, including unknown tribes, a man dying of starvation, wild exoticism, and appalling poverty—topics too alien for the conventional *Coronet* magazine, which had sent Fast. Many of these impressions would end up in *The Pledge*, observed by his character Bruce Bacon, a stand-in for Fast. Barbara Lavette of The Immigrants series also serves as a correspondent in Calcutta, as depicted in *Second Generation*. *Being Red* and the two fictional works describe the huge numbers of the homeless—people living outdoors permanently, with streets set aside for sleeping and possibly for dying from starvation. Fast was told that six million people had died, at least in part because the British authorities had arranged with Muslim rice dealers to withhold food in order to weaken the will of Indians who might support the Japanese.

This story is central to the plot of *The Pledge*, and as in the fictional version, Fast gets second-hand confirmations but never enough direct evidence to break the scandal into the mainstream media. Again as in *The Pledge*, Fast met with Indian communists and dined at a Jewish restaurant founded in Calcutta two hundred years before the birth of Christ. He traveled by bicycle with a communist organizer into neighborhoods so poor that the organizer would read the one-page party newspaper to residents, who would pay, if they could, with a single grain of rice—scenes of poverty so wretched that Fast compares them to Dante's *Inferno*. This is one of the most affecting portions of *The Pledge* and makes understandable Fast's belief in the self-denial and commitment to the poor of the party. Fast was well aware that change was unlikely and that ordinary human common sense leads people the way of self-protection and self-interest. Yet the "saintliness" of Sind, the Communist party organizer, remains shimmering in the memory, his gestures toward reform perhaps absurd and futile, but clearly the only right thing to do.

Back in the United States, Fast delivered the message from the Delhi party secretary to Gene Dennis, head of the American party, and was very let down by the man's coldness and lack of interest in his Indian colleagues. As in *The Pledge*, no mainstream American paper would touch Fast's story on the British-caused famine, not even the leftist *New Masses*. In Fast's mind the allegations of British culpability constituted proof, and the issue ended there. The twice-told famine story (thrice told, if we count Barbara Lavette's version) is a window on Fast's strength, his ability to feel the suffering of others deeply and to render their misery in dramatic example and detail, but also on his weakness, a tendency to shoot from the hip that can deny moral complexity and varying shades of responsibility. To call the British action the moral equivalent of Hitler's Holocaust, a charge made by the Indian communists that Fast repeats without comment, was sure to provoke counterclaims and countercharges at a time when the British were firm U.S. allies. In a self-revealing anecdote in *Being Red*, Fast is talking with a sympathetic lawyer when a professional red baiter walks by. Fast calls the anticommunist a "sonofabitch," and the Philadelphia lawyer chides him, "Come on, Howard, you only hate him because he's their sonofabitch. If he were our sonofabitch, you'd cover him with roses" (28).

Fast's trip to India served him well as a writer, for it resulted in a powerful novel and a good repertoire of story material. As a reporter, however, Fast made a good advocate but not an objective investigator ferreting out evidence of the truth, an activity that was perhaps denied him by circumstances but that also seemed to interest him less. *Coronet* may well have been correct in rejecting some of his reports (some were later written up as effective stories). We should note, of course, that these versions of events, in *Being Red, The Pledge*, and *Second Generation*, were published long after the fact, when the distorting mirror of time and memory must have had some effect. Their consistency with each other, however, suggests that Fast is sure in his own mind about his experiences and has, with all his skill as a storyteller, shaped them for maximum effect. And this, of course, is his forte.

Fast met and got along well with Jean-Paul Sartre, then visiting New York, and found much in common with the French philosopher and party member. Both were ignorant of the atrocities of Stalin and the party in Russia. Fast notes the excesses and contradictions of the American Communist party in these postwar years but also its distinguished membership and good intentions. In a way, the U.S. government's increasing intolerance of the left in general and of communists in particular caused Fast to harden his position and to explain away the antidemocratic and arbitrary practices he saw in the party as simply responses to oppression.

And the left was increasingly being isolated and persecuted in the immediate postwar years. The House Un-American Activities Committee, known later as HUAC, and Senator Joseph McCarthy's Senate committee were particular goads and tormentors, with their listing of communists and leftists in various institutions and their requiring of loyalty oaths as a condition for membership or employment, as the Taft-Hartley Labor Act of 1947 had done for labor union leaders. Fast was called up before HUAC because of his support of the Spanish Refugee Appeal, an innocuous enough organization raising money for food and medical supplies for displaced persons in Spain. Nervous (the eminent Clark Clifford had abased himself before the committee for sending out fifty copies of *Citizen Tom Paine* to friends, claiming he did not know it was "communist propaganda") but convinced that Congress did not send people to jail for their beliefs, Fast testified along with other members of the Appeal executive committee and was called back alone to answer charges that the record shows were clearly trumped up. The record does show, however, that Fast was impolitic in the extreme, calling the committee members names and pointing out their stupidities to them.

Tolerance of any views outside the mainstream was shrinking. While living under the threat of a jail term, Fast wrote a play, *Thirty Pieces of Silver*, about a White House staff member who betrays a colleague; it was never produced in the United States but was successful in Europe and Australia. Another event indicated the changing climate in the postwar years. A friend's temporarily lost child stimulated a Fast story, "A Child Is Lost," scheduled to be published in *This Week*, a nationally distributed Sunday newspaper supplement, but Fast's literary agent asked that he publish under a pseudonym, since his own name would not be acceptable. A movie deal for this short story failed for the same reason, as the witch hunt for communists infected Hollywood, led in part by actor Ronald Reagan. A measure of the increasing attention from the government was that Fast's FBI file eventually reached eleven hundred pages, costing over $10 million to compile; he says that he is proud of every incident reported, none being immoral, illegal, or indecent but rather just the opposite. After a trial in 1947, Fast and other members of the board of the Joint Anti-Fascist Refugee Committee were found guilty of contempt of Congress for refusing to name the contributors to their cause. Appeals delayed the serving of Fast's three-month prison sentence until the spring of 1950.

In 1948, Fast became involved in the rebirth of the Progressive party, with Henry Wallace as presidential nominee. At pains to show the Progressive party as centrist, Fast traces its history back to Theodore Roosevelt through the Farmer-Labor party of 1924 led by Robert La Follette of Wisconsin. However, at the Philadelphia party convention, Fast was sought out by H. L. Mencken, who, after praising Fast's recent book about Altgeld, *The American*, asked Fast bluntly "what in hell" he was doing with the "gang" that formed the Progressive party (*Being Red* 192). Fast, a great admirer of the iconoclastic Baltimore journalist and scholar, mumbled in reply that he did not have a better place to be in the Republican or Democratic parties. Mencken answered that there was indeed a better place—"with yourself"—adding that he, Mencken, was a "party of one," an observer rather than a participant, and that Fast should be too. Fast should not join the party, for if he did, "these clowns will destroy you as surely as the sun rises and sets" (*Being Red* 193).

These were prophetic words, for the Progressive party failed, winning only 2 million votes nationwide in 1948, marking, as Fast points out with great accuracy, the end of the left-liberal-labor alliance that had been a major force in American politics since Eugene V. Debs before the turn of the nineteenth century. Labor distanced itself from the left in order to prove its patriotism and "Americanism"; liberal intellectuals were cowed and defensive, both groups defeated by the anticommunist fervor of Richard M. Nixon and J. Edgar Hoover, head of the FBI. The Communist party shrank steadily until by the end of the 1950s, it numbered only ten thousand or so members and had lost all its previous influence with movers and thinkers. Fast kept publishing, with *Clarkton* coming out in 1947, but his next book brought him trouble on two fronts. *My Glorious Brothers*, about the heroic Jewish Maccabee brothers in biblical times, appeared in 1948; it received the Jewish Book Council of America annual award, but Fast's name was removed from all subsequent lists of the award. Fast was banned from speaking at fifteen colleges and universities. In 1949, J. Edgar Hoover tried to remove *Citizen Tom Paine* from New York school and public libraries, as well as from libraries in other cities.

Fast blames almost all of these shameful happenings on the FBI, HUAC, and the generally conservative (and cowardly) times, but even his own testimony shows some culpability on the part of the party itself. As the U.S. government moved to censor ideas it disliked, so too did the party. For example, *My Glorious Brothers* was widely read in the just-formed state of Israel as a well-told historical parallel to Jewish aspirations for freedom but was panned by some party members as "Jewish nationalism." The party enforced political correctness thirty years before the term became current: Fast was criticized widely for using the word *wolfish* to describe a nonwhite, and for other linguistic offenses. Fast dutifully covered the trials of the party leadership for the *Daily Worker* but admits that many individuals were "arrogant" and "thick-headed"; he uses these words to describe his own "stupid" behavior in driving off his own nonparty friends because of the party's dictates, including the eminent Moss Hart.

Yet even forty years after the fact, Fast's testimony in *Being Red* reveals conflict about the true nature of the Communist party. He defends his assertion about the decent and principled nature of most party members he knew, listing a series of outstanding luminaries who participated in the Scientific and Cultural Conference for World Peace, a meeting rejected by the party leadership but promoted by Fast and others to support the ideas of the left. Participants included poet and critic Louis Untermeyer; poet Langston Hughes; writers John Lardner, Dalton Trumbo, Dashiell Hammett, and Thomas Mann; composer Leonard Bernstein; and other notables of the time (including writers Mary McCarthy and Norman Mailer as rump speakers). But while many of these figures surely had motives above reproach and while Fast states unequivocally that there was no Soviet money or influence on the conference, the role of the Russians in the American left in general remains murky, at least if recent information from KGB archives is to be trusted. The final chapter is yet to be written about these years.

At the International Peace Congress in Paris where he was embraced by everyone from taxi drivers to Chilean poet Pablo Neruda and Pablo Picasso (who kissed Fast full on the mouth, he notes), Fast secretly delivered a charge of anti-Semitism against the Communist Party of the Soviet Union, a charge made by the American Party. Alexander Fadeev, the head of the Soviet delegation, repeated over and over, even in the face of Fast's listing of facts and evidence, that there was no anti-Semitism in the Soviet Union. Fast found himself irritated and angry but even in the retelling tries to explain away Fadeev's stonewalling as honest ignorance. He never fully acknowledges the deep corruption that suffused the Soviet system—not just in the party leadership but also the winked-at anti-Semitism that was so much of the normal way of doing things, and the inherent dishonesty that it created in those who could see beyond the Potemkin village of ethnic, religious, and racial harmony. Like one of his own literary characters—Tom Paine, or Ely and Jacob in *Conceived in Liberty*, or the Maccabee brothers—Fast's compass points stubbornly in one direction only, and he refuses even forty years after the event to admit wholeheartedly that this commitment was wrong. (In some ways the angry denunciations of ideological betrayal in *The Naked God* are more revealing than the sometimes defensive autobiographical explanations four decades later.) Yet literary commitments to truth are easy; real-life relationships to organizations are shaded in all the grays of ambiguity. As always, Fast wrote the plots of his stories far more neatly than the sometimes messy scripts of his own life.

A watershed event occurred when Bette Fast took a trip to Europe, and Howard, with a newly hired nanny to replace the Japanese woman who had taken care of the children in the past, repaired to Mt. Airy in Croton, New York, for some weeks in the country. The singer Pete Seeger contacted him about a peace meeting near Peekskill in Westchester County, New York, including a concert by the great Paul Robeson. The event was a disaster, with rural hoodlums surrounding the entrance and yelling, "Kill a Commie for Christ" and "white niggers" at the concertgoers, then attacking them with fists, clubs, rocks, and even knives. Fast organized the forty-two men and boys among the peace contingent into a defense force, which held off repeated charges by hundreds of drunken tormentors. He reports that the experience was important to him, and it is easy to see the Peekskill defense as a metaphor for Fast's view of his relation to society: a band of diverse believers, bonded into brotherhood by an ideal, holding off superior forces and triumphing by enduring. *My Glorious Brothers* fits this pattern, but so do all the books about the American Revolutionary army, and a number of other works as well. Peekskill had all the elements that define the Fast hero, his immediate surroundings, and society at large. Shortly after retelling the Peekskill story, Fast even says that people in the Cultural Section of the Communist party felt, because of their persecution, an identity with the early Christians!

In June 1950, after all appeals had failed, Fast began to serve his prison sentence, an experience told vividly in fictional form in *The Pledge*. (Barbara Lavette also goes to jail for contempt of Congress, but on Terminal Island, not far from Los Angeles.) After being held briefly in a Washington jail, Fast was transferred to a federal prison in West Virginia, Mill Point Prison, a minimum security institution where he lived with moonshiners from the Kentucky mountains and blacks convicted of relatively minor crimes. This "prison without walls" was established by Franklin Roosevelt and run by Kenneth Thieman, a civilized and humane man, and while it would be a distortion to say that Fast talks of his time there with pleasure, he calls the prison the best-run institution he had ever seen, prison or otherwise, and views his three months there as less a punishment than an indignity. Fast gave reading lessons and provided Bible exegesis for the moonshiners, met novelist-screenwriter Albert Maltz and director Edward Dmytryk there, both victims of the purge of Hollywood by HUAC, taught himself to cast a concrete statue (of a little boy urinating), began to think about his plan for *Spartacus*, one of his best-known novels, and in general fared a lot better than he expected to.

Back in New York, friends had produced a Fast play called *The Hammer*, about a Jewish man with three sons. The Communist party Cultural Section leader had arranged for James Earl Jones, the physically imposing black actor with the booming voice, to play one of the sons. When Fast saw the father, played by a slight, pale, fair-haired man and the huge Jones playing his son on the same stage, he reacted in horror: the audience would be confused at best by this genetic unlikelihood and might even think it comic. The cultural commissar accused Fast of white chauvinism, an absurdity Fast thinks indicates precisely what was wrong with the party: its inability to deal with reality in place of its elaborate theory. Fast also criticized the party for its unwillingness to defend the Rosenbergs in the famous spy case, and he pushed party officials to take action.

Fast by this time had finished *Spartacus*, a controversial treatment of the great slave revolt of 71 B.C. as a metaphor for all oppressed people's struggle to throw off the shackles of their inhuman oppressors. Though it was well reviewed by Little, Brown Publishing, J. Edgar Hoover had given express directions to the president of the company not to publish any books by Fast. One by one other publishing houses rejected the book: Viking, Scribner's, Harper, Knopf, Simon and Schuster. Finally, Doubleday, though afraid to publish the novel, agreed to sell copies through its bookstore chain if Fast published it himself. This led him into the adventure of self-publishing, which began the slow process of making *Spartacus* a success; he sold 48,000 self-published copies and untold numbers abroad, both legal and pirated. By the end of the 1950s, hundreds of thousands of paperback copies were sold. *Spartacus* won Fast the Screenwriters Award in 1960. From 1952 to 1957, still unable to find a publisher, he founded the Blue Heron Press (a word play on a friend's suggestion that he call it the Red Herring Press) and published *The Passion of Sacco and Vanzetti, Silas Timberman,* and a collection of short stories. During this controversial period in the 1950s, Fast founded the World Peace Movement and served as a member of the World Peace Council. While denied the freedom to publish under his own name by the blacklist, he began to write under the pseudonym of Walter Ericson, first with a detective thriller, *The Fallen Angel*, which was later made into a film, *Mirage*, starring Gregory Peck as the amnesiac hero.

Ever since Mill Point Prison, Fast had experienced cluster headaches, an excruciating condition then untreatable. While vacationing at White Lake resort, owned by the Fur and Leather Workers Union, a friend suggested that the headaches resulted from frustration about his inability to strike back and that Fast should take drastic action to relieve this stress: he should run for Congress. Thus began Fast's quixotic run for office in the Twenty-third Congressional District on the American Labor party ticket, an experience reflected long after in *The Immigrant's Daughter*. Fast amusingly calls his affliction *candidatitus*: the conviction that one can win office against impossible odds. An incident with another symbolic candidate, a rich man's son, illustrates what Fast thinks of as an almost unbridgeable gap between wealth and poverty, a chasm of understanding that divides so completely that the rich can never think or understand life as the poor do. His fellow candidate invited him over for dinner and allowed a full gallon of ice cream to melt away while they talked, oblivious as the nervous Fast agitated over the waste of food. The incident appears in several Fast novels as a touchstone of the difference between rich and poor. In the election, Fast polled only two thousand votes, to over forty thousand for the Democratic candidate, but he clearly enjoyed the experience of running for office.

Fast's cluster headaches worsened, and he took oxygen for partial relief, and learned meditation that would eventually take him to the study of Zen Buddhism. He was awarded the Stalin International Peace Prize in 1953 (later renamed the Soviet International Peace Prize; he and Paul Robeson were the only Americans ever to receive it) and reports that the Russians frequently consulted him because of their ignorance of and bewilderment about the United States, *Pravda* reporters believing that, for example, in the American South any person disapproved of by the majority would be hanged. As with Fadeev, Fast seems to take straight these assertions of Soviet ingenuousness, but the reader can be forgiven some skepticism: why would Russian reporters with access to superb KGB sources of information go to a New York novelist for advice? Fast had always viewed the American South negatively, and one must wonder about the motives of journalists' asking tendentious questions. For all his growing frustrations with party discipline, Fast seemed to give too much credence to the purity of Soviet intentions, which were no doubt less than absolutely pure.

The Fasts spent two months in Cuernavaca, Mexico, as a temporary refuge from the red-baiting and harassment by FBI phone tap and surveillance that were becoming more and more oppressive. He met the famous artist Diego Rivera, who told him that artists *must* offend, a sentiment Fast definitely agreed with. Significantly, though Fast loved the sensual and beautiful landscape of Mexico, the Mexican people, and the American communist exiles from Hollywood and the rest of the United States, he quickly grew bored, unable to write or even to live fully without the opposition that had been so long a part of his daily life. Cutting short their intended three-month stay, the Fasts planned to return to the United States, only to face the newly passed Communist Control Act, a piece of legislation he claims turned America into a police state. As Fast points out with considerable self-understanding, creative artists (and others) living abroad, separated from their country and culture, lose all perspective. They begin to think like refugees and therefore frequently exaggerate their oppression to justify their new lives as refugees. The Soviet ambassador to Mexico offered refugee status in Russia, which Fast turned down, remarking later to Albert Maltz, his old colleague from Mill Point Prison who had exiled himself to Mexico, that they had no roots in the country and they did not have their native language: "Our lives are our language" (*Being Red* 342).

The Communist Control Act was never used or even much noticed. Back in America, the Fasts lived in the suburbs, in Teaneck, New Jersey, and Howard joined the *Daily Worker* as a permanent staff member. By 1956 the stories of life under Stalin had become undeniable, and a conflicted Fast struggled to maintain his ideological faith. When Nikita Khrushchev's secret speech detailing his predecessor's horrors became public, as John Gates, executive editor of the *Daily Worker*, notes in *The Story of an American Communist* (1958), Howard Fast, "the only literary figure of note left in the Communist Party," was one of those most shaken. Gates points out that Fast had gone to jail for his beliefs and had stuck his neck out more than most others, defending everything communist and attacking everything capitalist "in the most extravagant terms." He adds, "It was to be expected that he would react to the Khrushchev revelations in a highly emotional manner, and I know of no one who went through a greater moral anguish and torture" (*Being Red* 351–352). Gates goes on to describe party leaders leaping on Fast like a "pack of wolves" when he formally quit the party, though no leader bothered to discuss the problem with Fast when it might have done some good. He also went from being one of the foremost American writers read and taught in the Soviet Union to being a nonentity, his literary reputation ruined almost overnight by his change in politics.

Although *Being Red* was published in 1990, it ends with this leave-taking from the Communist party in 1957, when Fast was forty-two. He clearly feels that a major phase of his life ended here, though in the next thirty-odd years he published scores of books, pushing his total number of publications to somewhere around one hundred, most of them substantial. (Even Fast is not completely sure of the total number of publications; title changes and his own pseudonyms have confused the issue. Given the huge number of his books that have been translated and published abroad, many without benefit of legal permission, the total number of sales may be as high as 80 million copies.) In the midst of this phenomenal production, Fast also became a writer of detective stories and novels about strong women, completed a highly successful series of popular novels (The Immigrants series), moved to California and back to the East Coast, to Connecticut, traveled the country and the world, studied Zen Buddhism, and, as always, wrote. He has kept these decades out of the newspaper headlines and lived privately, enjoying a life free from government and media harassment. He gives occasional interviews but has generally stayed out of public notice. Writing under the pseudonym of Walter Ericson and later as E. V. Cunningham, under which name he produced twenty books, Fast reinvented himself as a writer of detective fiction, creating the character of the Japanese-American detective Masao Masuto and enjoying the writing of this form of popular fiction immensely. As he says in *Contemporary Authors Auto-*

biograpy Series, he underwent what he calls an "explosion" of creativity repressed until after he left the Communist party; and his bibliography shows he does not exaggerate. He has published almost sixty novels and major works since his departure. The Fasts moved to Los Angeles in 1974, where they lived until 1980; although only one of his screenplays from this period was ever produced, residence in California paid off in The Immigrants series, especially in the unforgettable portrayals of Los Angeles, San Francisco, and, in particular, the fictional Napa Valley winery called Higate.

Despite his comparative reticence about this period, his writing reveals much about his interests. In the 1960s, Fast built a series of novels around extraordinary women, some criminal, some instigators of crime, and others co-investigators with a male detective. This was a new emphasis; apart from *Agrippa's Daughter* (1964) and a handful of characters in other early works, Fast had focused on male protagonists. The potential had always existed, for female characters in even the earliest novels were consistently well drawn. These later books, however, constitute a near full turn in perspective: they are tributes to the intelligence, courage, resourcefulness, and wit of women and a reprimand to the husbands, lovers, and friends who underestimate their capabilities and pluck. Shirley (*Shirley* 1964) is a tough, wise-cracking Bronx diamond-in-the-rough, who exasperates the tough cops she deals with, while Sylvia (*Sylvia* 1960), once an abused child and then a teenage prostitute, has, through sheer guts and determination, read voraciously, taught herself several languages, and fought her way into polite society. Penelope (*Penelope* 1965), an independently wealthy socialite, bored by male pretensions and her banker husband's arrogant complacency, plays Robin Hood to the local parish and associated charities, stealing from rich acquaintances whose sentiments and values offend; even when the police commissioner and district attorney confront irrefutable evidence of her activities, their preconceptions prevent their accepting the truth of her wit and professionalism. The unflappable Margie (*Margie* 1966) is an innocent mistaken for a thief and then for an oil-rich countess, her whole adventures comic and resolvable despite serious negative possibilities. Other heroines from this set of novels face more sinister dangers and threats. For instance, Phyllis's mother is brutally beaten to death (*Phyllis* 1962), Lydia's father is forced into suicide (*Lydia* 1964), and Alice's child is kidnapped and terrorized (*Alice* 1963). Helen (*Helen* 1966) faces sexual sadists, as does Samantha (*Samantha* 1967), a would-be star, who is raped by a half-dozen young men on a Hollywood set and seeks bloody revenge, while Sally

(*Sally* 1967), thinking she is dying of an incurable disease, hires a professional gunman to end her pain quickly, only to learn the original
diagnosis was incorrect and to have to battle an assassin she herself is
paying. Some of Fast's usual villains show up in these works: German
ex-Nazis, still loyal to Hitler's memory, hypocritical military and political
leaders (a general and a senator heading a heroin smuggling operation),
and international terrorists. However, the main thrust of these novels,
whether comic or deadly serious, is a paean to women. Although their
characters move around a great deal in familiar Fast settings, a number
of these books have a California setting. Fast clearly became fascinated
by the state, the new goal for immigrants searching for the American
dream, and much of his best work in the 1970s and after has a California
setting or at least includes a few scenes in the West. The tension between
the new lifestyles and personal philosophies on the coast, summed up
by the competition between Los Angeles and San Francisco, was clearly
a deeply felt personal issue, and its working out in fiction, sometimes as
tragedy, sometimes as high comedy, constitutes much of the pleasure in
the works of this period.

In The Immigrants series, Los Angeles comes off comparatively badly,
a diffuse Johnny-come-lately town, offering opportunities and excitement
of a kind but also being a place populated by con men and vulgarians.
Fast's depiction of the movie industry is especially caustic: Martha Levy
commits suicide as a result of exploitation by a sleazy producer; Sally
Levy finds one honest man, her director and mentor, but no emotional
satisfaction from movie industry life; the filmscript of Barbara Lavette's
first novel is taken out of her hands though she has been hired as a
screenwriter. Portraits in other books, such as the Masao Masuto series
and *Max*, Fast's novel about the development of the movie industry,
depict Los Angeles more positively, or at least neutrally. But the contrast
remains: Los Angeles can be summed up by the powerful Devron family,
opportunists who trace themselves back to frontiersman Kit Carson. San
Francisco has the Lavettes, perhaps just as opportunistic, but driven by
nobler motives than the struggle for filthy lucre. The Devrons watch their
fiscal bottom line; the Lavettes know the value of a dollar but are also
capable of the grand gesture, such as when Dan supports Bernie Cohen's
quixotic trek to Israel or Jean gives a huge amount of money to Barbara
in support of a cause Jean has no part in. Los Angeles is driven by profit,
in other words, while San Francisco, for all its gold rush origins, has a
romance and a nobility of style that Fast regards with approval.

Even the contrasting climates show Fast's preference for the Bay Area.

For all the perfections of the southern California weather as described in *Second Generation, The Legacy*, and *The Immigrant's Daughter*, readers will almost certainly retain stronger impressions of San Francisco's bracing chills or of its fogs cut through with rays of bright sunshine. The tactile imagery—of color and light, smell and temperature, the texture of daily life—in The Immigrants series is the most pronounced and effective in Fast's extensive canon. Readers of these glowing portraits of San Francisco and the Napa Valley might assume that Fast lived in the Bay Area, for the descriptions seen through the eyes of Barbara and others suggest a longing for home, the nostalgic ache for the place that defines normality of climate, of sight, smell, and sound. In fact, the Fasts were simply visitors to the area, taking driving tours of Napa, with San Francisco as a temporary base for travel. Perhaps the six years Fast spent in Los Angeles account for his ambivalence about that city, and especially for his dislike of the hypocrisies of the movie industry. However, Fast insists that a writer's personal setting is irrelevant to his work; where he lived, he says, had little or no effect on his fiction. During the Los Angeles period Fast wrote screenplays for three films, only one of which was produced; he turned his novel *Citizen Tom Paine* into a theatrical play (produced in Williamstown, Massachusetts, and later at the Kennedy Center in Washington, D.C., in 1987, starring Richard Thomas), and he wrote a charming, intuitive play, *The Novelist*, which was based on the life of Jane Austen and was staged at Williamstown, at Theater West in Springfield, Massachusetts, in Mamaroneck, New York, and in New York City. *The Novelist* postulates a Ms. Bennett–Mr. Darcy style encounter between the British writer Jane Austen and a dashing, vigorous, but also highly intelligent navy captain, who has fallen in love with her through reading her books and who sees beneath the quick-witted and distancing repartee to find the strong but romantic woman behind the facade.

While much of Fast's work includes settings he has known intimately from residence in them, the Bay Area portraits, seemingly so personal and complex in their links of character and setting, give credence to his assertion: a good writer simply needs the appropriate mental imagery and an understanding of how people live in a place and what they feel about it in order to describe their lives credibly. Readers of The Immigrants series may be forgiven for identifying Fast and California, but his comparatively brief residence in Los Angeles and his brief excursions in the Bay Area are in fact typical of his other travels earlier in his career to the Middle East and India, travels that produced a whole series of books notable for their sense of place. Throughout his career, Fast has absorbed information through research and setting through travel, fusing both into convincing stages and backdrops for his characters.

The post–Communist party years were not simply characterized by a retreat from the newspaper headlines into private family and professional life for the Fasts. Although the California years were clearly enjoyable and stimulating at the time, Fast recently remarked that he has never missed the West Coast because the California he knew then is dead and gone; in fact, every time he has visited there since leaving, he has disliked it more, a result of overpopulation, pollution, and a rape of the natural beauty and purity that attracted people there in the first place. But one influence has remained with Fast, and it is related to his split with the party: the influence of Zen Buddhism.

After rejecting communism, Fast studied Zen formally for eight years. That philosophy, of course, is not necessarily related to a particular place, but the Masao Masuto books illustrate the connection of the discipline with California. Fast calls his study "very important" even now, living long after in the environs of New York City. Zen provides a context for the moral issues that have consumed Fast's attention all his life. Also, Zen stresses a form of unconventionality—the student of Zen is not allowed to give an expected or conventional answer to an assigned *koan*, or puzzle—that is an obvious Fast characteristic. But Fast stresses that after living much of his adult life with the socialist framework providing direction and answers to the puzzling questions of existence, one does not simply give it over and move on easily. Zen provided an "ability to focus, to center . . . [his] life" that was invaluable then, in the difficult years after the party, and now. Fast clearly still believes in the humanist principles that underlie a good deal of socialist thought, but the loss of party discipline and structure must have involved a true crisis for a writer fond of clarity and order. Zen provided such a focus, and we may not be reading too much into the Masao Masuto books if we think of both their hero (a lean, six-foot-tall Nisei attached to the Beverly Hills Police Department) and their author as outsiders, somewhat alienated by perspective from the majority culture in which they must operate, but finding their center through Zen meditation.

Masuto, like Fast, finds in the Zen meditative philosophy the calm, the self-assurance, and the introspective insights necessary to carry out his work, and, again like Fast, he empathizes with the common worker, despite the wealthy environment in which he works. Like Fast, Masuto cultivates the yin and the yang, loves roses and the exquisite calm of the tea ceremony, and has fond memories of the peaceful and productive farm life of the San Fernando of bygone years, the romantic agrarianism that runs through so many of Fast's books. Like his creator, Masuto has an American maverick streak beneath his surface Zen serenity: his independent thinking and contempt for overbearing authority. Reflecting his creator, Masuto says, "I try not to respond to fools" (*The Case of the Russian Diplomat* 65). Masuto speaks Spanish as well as Japanese (Fast does not), and he sometimes faces cruel taunts about his nisei heritage, but just as Fast survived similar attacks because of his Jewish background, he has learned to cope with the crass lifestyles and acid tongues of southern Californians.

Fast says that he enjoyed writing the Masuto detective novels because the use of a pseudonym (E. V. Cunningham, a name suggested by his agent, Paul Reynolds) gave him a sense of freedom that allowed him to toy with ideas for pleasure and to write in a style and with a focus quite different from what he had done before; he describes the experience as "captivating" and his results "half-serious." He could have his hero share his pet peeves (for instance, California funeral homes in *The Case of the Murdered Mackenzie*), battle his favorite villains (the S.S. in *The Case of the One-Penny Orange*, former Nazis in *The Case of the Russian Diplomat*, and the CIA, which fixes evidence and phony charges and condones double murder, in *The Case of the Murdered Mackenzie*), and reflect values dear to him, including a deep distrust of any group that tries to repress the individual, force the human into mechanical categories, or deny genuine emotion.

The detective hero Masuto combines Buddhist meditation with Holmesian ratiocination to make intuitive leaps of both reason and imagination that leave his colleagues and superiors puzzling over the assumptions that further investigation, physical evidence, and testimony confirm. The close observation that allows the Buddhist in Masuto to see beauty where others see ugliness also allows him to see the mundane, the corrupt, and the repulsive behind the beautiful facade of Beverly Hills. These stories look at the wealthy California scene from the perspective of an outsider, racially, culturally, and economically. Masuto can bring Asian perceptions to unraveling the mysteries of his adopted community and counters the mainstream disintegration of family values with his own deep-seated commitment to home and family. His son and daughter are quiet, obedient, and respectful, and his Japanese-American wife, Kati, though at times truly Californian (she participates in consciousness-raising sessions), observes traditional Japanese customs and rituals (providing hot baths, fine cuisine, and soothing solace) to help him recuperate from the conflicts of his job.

Fast's mystery plots, which occupied his thoughts throughout the late 1970s and early 1980s, are amusing puzzles, but they have political undercurrents. In *The Case of the One-Penny Orange*, for example, Masuto penetrates the link between seemingly unconnected events (a local burglary, a murdered stamp dealer, and a missing S.S. commander) with an 1847 Mauritius one-penny stamp worth half a million dollars and a revenge ritual that originated in the bitterness of the Holocaust, while in *The Case of the Russian Diplomat*, fascistic Arab and East German terrorists assassinate a Russian diplomat and plan to sabotage an airplane full of Soviet agronomists, all to undermine the Jewish Defense League. In *The Case of the Sliding Pool*, powerful financial and industrial speculators play games with people's lives, impede Masuto's investigation, and break rules with impunity, while *The Case of the Poisoned Eclairs* explores the uglier costs of wealth in marriage and divorce. Fast's Masuto believes that crime encapsulates the general illnesses of humanity and is an affront to human dignity and conscience. A Buddhist involved with humanity but faced with the materialism, corruption, and inhumanity of the Beverly Hills rich, he must constantly battle external political pressure to limit or even end his investigation and the internal hatred that discovering evil makes him feel. His family is vital to providing the moral and emotional foundation necessary for Masuto to carry on in a society and culture that attacks his values.

Fast's later life has not all been Zen meditative calm. When asked about his key interests in the mid-1970s, Fast cited, "my home, my family, the theater, the film, and the proper study of ancient history. And the follies of human kind" (*Something about the Author* 82). It is the "follies of human kind" that have dominated his journalism and writing in general. For instance, Fast calls *The Dinner Party* a "direct result" of his being unable to get over his "problem of indignation" (Rothstein 16). He brooded over the question of sanctuary, particularly as related to helping illegal Central American aliens enter the country, and the moral questions involved in sending a wired informer into a church to record conversations that could later be used to threaten priests, a minister, a nun, and others with five years of imprisonment. And he found himself posing questions about the responses of an honest man, particularly one who might have a certain amount of clout from a position of authority, like that of U.S. senator. *The Dinner Party* is an exploration of such questions of responsibility and duty, infused and driven by righteous indignation. Critics compared it to a well-made play. This is an appropriate comparison, for Fast's strengths as a writer often involve dramatic confrontations. His political essays written for the *New York Observer* include provocative attacks on drug dealers, political hacks, anti-Semites, racists, arms traffickers, women bashers, and presidents Reagan and Bush. In other words, he has used his political commentary to carry on the liberal politics that have consumed his interest all his adult life.

The Fasts moved back to the East Coast in 1980 and lived quietly, with Fast still producing on the average about one major work every year through the 1990s. He wrote a weekly column for the *New York Observer* from 1989 until his wife's illness in 1994 and collected a number of these essays in a book entitled *War and Peace*. The Fasts moved to Connecticut in the early 1990s. Bette Fast pursued sculpture and art until she died in 1994. Fast's tribute to Jane Austen in his play *The Novelist* is to a great degree also a tribute to the charm, intelligence, and talent of Bette Fast, with whom Fast fell in love at age twenty, with whom he had two children and three grandchildren, and to whom he was married for over fifty-six years.

Fast resides in Connecticut not far from his native New York, living the life of a writer, with *Seven Days in June* published in 1994. *Seven Days* represents five years of work, and though the novel was not marketed effectively, it marks a return to Fast's earliest successes, the Revolutionary War works. Fast says of his reasons for this reprise that "so much of our early history is pure invention, pure lies." The fire of the reformer still burns hot: Fast writes a column on politics for a local newspaper and takes vigorous daily walks, preferably in company that will stimulate lively conversation. Fast believes that books "open a thousand doors, they shape lives and answer questions, they widen horizons, they offer hope for the heart and food for the soul." Another novel, *The Bridge Builder's Story*, concerning the Holocaust, was published in 1995.

Modern criticism teaches that every biographer is also a creative artist, and Fast's memoir, *Being Red*, is a good example, for his autobiography sometimes reads like one of his own novels. His indisputably modest beginnings were the start of a very American life, with a child of recent immigrants fitting the mythic American model of pulling oneself up by one's bootstraps; he is a kind of bad boy Horatio Alger hero, an unsentimentalized rags-to-riches character and a member of the loyal (in the eyes of the House Un-American Activities Committee, *disloyal*) opposition. In this sense Fast was a generation or two ahead of his time, for his jaundiced but pro-American point of view would not become common until the last decades of the twentieth century. As with his pro- and anti-Americanism, contradictions abound: while he values working-class heroes, his own life has been lived as a creative writer and as an intellectual commentator, under varying but apparently comfortable material circumstances. The best model for Fast is the newsman in *Power*, a sympathetic observer of the labor movement rather than a constantly involved participant.

But his story is American in other ways, a conflict between the big city urbanism of his youth and the California mellowness of his later years, between the lure of success and wealth and the call of conscience, between writing what the public wants and saying what one feels must be said. Fast says of himself, "No matter what direction my writing took, I could never give up a social outlook and a position against hypocrisy and oppression. This has been a theme that runs through all of my writing" (*Contemporary Authors Autobiography Series* 184).

Literary Background:
American Gadfly

> The practice of creative writing is the practice of an art, an ancient
> and rich art, and regardless of the skill or lack of skill of the writer,
> he cannot escape his definition. . . . He is an artist and his only obli-
> gation is to the truth.
>
> —Howard Fast, *Counterpoint*

Howard Fast's *Citizen Tom Paine* is prefaced by a quotation from Dr.
Benjamin Rush, an influential physician and participant in the American
Revolutionary War who said, in 1787, that "there is nothing more common than to confound the terms of *American Revolution* with those of the
late American War. The American war is over, but this is far from being
the case with the American revolution. On the contrary, nothing but the
first act of the great drama is closed." This quotation is an apt introduction to one of Fast's best books, his compelling biography of Tom Paine,
the Anglo-American Revolutionary who devoted a long and cluttered
life to what he perceived as the forthcoming new world of the common
man. Paine's life alternated between elation and despair as he learned to
see revolution as a constant and possibly unresolvable struggle rather
than as a discrete historical event. Progress in civilization is agonizingly
slow in *Citizen Tom Paine*, with the real battle being against simplistic
expectations for a quick and clean victory over society's entrenched
forces. The real Revolutionary has a long view, not the dilettante impa-

tience of Paine's "summer soldier"; even a war of five or six years is simply a skirmish in a larger, more subtle battle for justice that will follow.

Rush's quotation, and Fast's affecting novel that follows it, is an excellent place to begin an exploration of Fast's canon, for Paine, the self-invented revolutionary of the late-eighteenth century, and Fast, the protean novelist of the mid-twentieth, have a great deal in common. Paine, the son of a staymaker (stays were stiffeners for women's corsets and men's vests), dragged himself out of a working-class background by sheer force of will, overcoming the degradation of his alcoholism in London's "Gin Lane" (a notorious slum) to educate himself and assume a career as an informal and self-appointed spokesman for the radical wing of the American revolutionaries. Absorbing the intellectual atmosphere around him and reading constantly, Paine articulated the theories of natural reason and natural rights, and from these ideas he developed the concepts of political equality, civil liberties, tolerance, and human dignity in language comprehensible to colonial farmers and unlettered workmen. He refused compromise and the seductions of a formal position, preferring to write as a freelancer. Uninterested in profit, he took no royalties for the original editions of *Common Sense*, which sold in the hundreds of thousands of copies. Before the term existed, Paine thought of himself as a writer for the working class; he was a rough, shabby, unkempt commoner, a working man who read his political tracts aloud to ordinary soldiers on bivouac. When the Revolution ended, the middle-aged Paine could easily have retired to the farm given to him by the grateful new nation, yet he moved first to England to try to provoke a working-class revolution and then to France, where he became a citizen and a representative to the revolutionary National Convention. Refusing to be intimidated by the increasingly radical Jacobins, Paine wrote the first part of his book, *The Age of Reason*, about the place of God and religion in the revolutionary new world. He was imprisoned during the Reign of Terror but survived the guillotine and returned to America, where many of his old comrades rejected him.

One can understand why Fast sees so much of Paine's life in his own career. Like the English immigrant/revolutionary, Fast, though born in the United States, came of new American stock, his parents having immigrated from Eastern Europe, and he escaped oppression as onerous as that of Paine's eighteenth century. He too dragged himself out of slums and rough neighborhoods—not those of London but of New York's East Side. Like Paine, Fast taught himself; he graduated from high school and attended college but gives credit to the New York Public Library for much of his education. The great social forces that shaped Fast were the Great Depression and World War II, and it is clear that his early talent for historical research was matched only by his sympathies for the ordinary man and woman, drawing him to his fine series of novels on the American Revolutionary War and to Paine himself in *Citizen Tom Paine.* Like his biographical subject, Fast in the World War II years and after exhibited streaks of stubbornness and a willful independence, following his political and social compass at a time when many other writers saw discretion as the only way to save their careers. By embracing left-wing politics and then communism, Fast gave up the very real prospect of great wealth as a successful novelist and screenwriter, instead at times publishing his own books and selling them out of his own residence. Like Paine, Fast eventually found himself at odds with his radical compatriots, and after breaking with the Communist party, he turned to the spiritual and psychological aspects of personal liberation.

Happily, Fast's later life has been in sharp contrast to the poverty and decline that afflicted the old American Revolutionary War hero, but his success as a writer in the last decades of the twentieth century has in no way tempered the old passion and fire. Fast's books still cleave to the idea expressed by Rush in the preface to *Citizen Tom Paine*: the war is far from over, the backsliders are everywhere, the old enemies simply have new faces. On this point, Fast and his American Revolutionary forebears are in complete accord, and the typical Fast political hero remains astonishingly consistent despite enormous changes in setting and geography, in time period, in culture. The Fast hero of the political novels is a kind of Tom Paine in action, a manifestation of his spirit in varying costumes, languages, and folkways: the essential revolutionary.

The quintessence of revolt for Fast lies less in single acts of anger or reaction to injustice and much more in character, in personality, in attitude toward authority and power. In 1944 *Citizen Tom Paine* presented its eponymous hero as the first professional revolutionary, but character studies of rebellious figures from much earlier times run like a red thread through Fast's canon. *Moses, Prince of Egypt* (1958) traces the ancient lawgiver as a man of his people, a stirring of the egalitarian principle long before most would place it in history. *My Glorious Brothers* (1948) tells the story of Judas Maccabee, the longest lived of the Maccabees who led the Jewish uprising against Hellenistic Syria; in the modern Chanukah (Feast of Lights) celebration, the story is called the revolt of the "weak over the strong, the few over the many, and those who fear Thy Name over those who desecrate it." *Spartacus* (1951) gave currency to a previously obscure slave revolt against Roman oppression. *Freedom Road* (1944) showed the human face of slavery in modern times by focusing on the struggles of African Americans in South Carolina to cope with the Reconstruction period after the American Civil War.

Clearly Fast's works show him locating the revolutionary impulse not in a particular ideology and certainly not in any particular time or place but rather in, primarily, characteristics of human psychology and, to a lesser degree, in elements of cultural heritage. The formative elements of revolution so familiar to nineteenth- and twentieth-century popular tradition—dialectical materialism and Marxism, charismatic leaders, rabid nationalism and cultural chauvinism, anticolonial fervor and identification as victims of oppression—fade to the background as contributory causes rather than as necessary ones. Again, *Citizen Tom Paine* provides a good example. The American Revolution would have taken place without this immigrant rabble-rouser's pamphlets, for British oppression and the desire for freedom would have provoked the revolt in one way or another. Paine's role was to ride the aroused revolutionary beast, steering it when he could, spurring it on when it flagged, perhaps ensuring its triumph but never confusing himself with the will of the people or the event itself.

A descriptive catalog of the characteristics of Fast's political heroes would fit all those named above, with minor exceptions because of time, setting, and culture, and would also fit many other protagonists in less political books. Most of Fast's heroes originate from humble backgrounds, or if privileged, turn their backs on wealth and comfort in pursuit of ideals of justice and self-realization. Most struggle to educate themselves, if not formally, then in the new challenges they face as leaders or spokespersons for a stirring rebellion. The Fast revolutionary hero is often rough and unpolished in the social sense; he (for all are male) may suffer bouts of depression and black despair, and may be inarticulate and moody to the extreme. He tends to be alienated from women and family members, having close relations with at most a few other male compatriots. Most suffer what might now be called a midlife crisis when, after initial goals have been met with great success, there is a dawning realization that the real struggle has just begun. Whatever the judgment of history, most Fast political heroes are at best ambivalent about their effectiveness and may be misunderstood by contemporaries who see only the superficial manifestations of temporary victory.

What keeps these men going in the face of such unpromising circumstances? Fast's answer is difficult to pin down, for motivations are described with a vagueness that has cost the novelist points with both ideologues and with critics seeking simple formulas. Though at times the texts are wordy to the extreme about the hero's inner thoughts, no single dominating passion emerges to link Moses and Judas Maccabee and Spartacus, Tom Paine, and Gideon Jackson. *Freedom* is a key word and an understandable ideal, but the essential question is left somewhat hazy: what makes some people willing to put aside wealth, honor, respect, comfort, even love, for the sake of an idea whose exact nature may not even be clear to them? How is this admirable idiosyncrasy different from true abnormality, perhaps even the pathological? Paine, for example, was accused (correctly on occasion) of drunkenness and (incorrectly in retrospect) of lunacy and perversion. How do we distinguish the true revolutionary from a paranoid babbling persuasively about myriad plots against "freedom"? These are hard questions, and Fast, perhaps with admirable honesty, provides no simple answer. Hindsight tells us, of course, that Paine was "right" and Edmund Burke was "wrong," but the interior monologues and dramatic dialogues of the political heroes do give us some insight into the definition of true political heroism.

First, the hero's perspective on his struggle is an informed one, enlarged by books or a rebellious tradition that widens his viewpoint beyond the personal. Tom Paine and Gideon Jackson read omnivorously, absorbing the truths of other generations and cultures, finding their own place in the confusing present through secondary knowledge of the landmarks of other times. If books are not available, then a cultural tradition is relied on to provide guidance and direction, as with Judas Maccabee's incantation about the Jews, "Once we were slaves in Egypt": the brief mantra, an incomprehensible reference to ancient history for the Roman emissary who hears it, is a controlling verbal formula to Judas, a compass pointing his true north.

A second shaping element of political heroism is culture itself. For Fast, certain cultures seem, because of peculiarities of their history, to produce the kind of stiff-necked, resistant citizen who has the fortitude to resist tyranny. Oppression creates its own equal and opposite reaction; like an invisible hand in history arranging figures on opposing sides of a chess board, slave masters are eventually opposed by their opposites, and since groups like the Jews in Egypt were defined by their status as slaves, a tough, stubborn, freedom-seeking population results. Slavery in the old South of the United States gives rise to a Gideon Jackson, whose physical force is matched by the psychological strength that allowed him to endure the beatings and humiliations of slavery. A third element seems to be a spartan life, imposed at first by circumstance perhaps, but later embraced willingly for its own simplicity and purity. The ancient Jews and Roman slaves, the farmers of the Revolutionary War, the African Americans living in shacks clustered around plantations: all live simply in comparison to the decadence and self-indulgence of their masters. Their life is characterized by a simple, healthy diet of country food, homespun clothing, minimal shelter, and an existence uncomplicated by ambition for high position and status. This element seems to be an idealized rural life of elemental simplicity, but one also governed by religious belief, especially a fundamental and personal one.

To a large degree this revolutionary vision, whatever its cultural setting, is a very American one, an irony lost on the House Un-American Activities Committee members who took Fast to task for his fellow traveling and communism. In fact, Fast's works fit with the progressive liberalism that was the central influence on most intellectuals and artists in the period of Fast's youth and early manhood, the liberalism institutionalized by Franklin Delano Roosevelt and the more leftist wings of the Democratic party well into the 1950s. The elements of this philosophy are very familiar: a sympathy for the working class but an essentially middle- to lower-middle-class ethic in most questions of behavior and mores; democracy, but a distrust of mob rule by the "many-headed multitude"; a tolerance for individuality, radical individuality included, even as the rhetoric of solidarity is indulged; approval of small business and entrepreneurship, along with a suspicion of big industry and large, intrusive government; a striving for personal status along with a commitment to meritocracy as a primary engine of change, a means of entrance into the society by immigrant newcomers, and a weapon against established wealth and inherited social status. Thus Fast's political philosophy looks quite moderate over the long haul, as opposed to the perspective of inflamed passions of the 1940s and 1950s. In some ways, as we shall see, he defies simple categorization by combining ideas: those of the institutional left of the 1930s, of nineteenth-century American populism, and of the libertarian attitudes of the American West.

The chapters that follow refer to Fast's "protest" novels and "exposés" as if these were clearly defined categories, but in fact these terms are inadequate to define their fairly eclectic forms. Fast's approach owes much to Theodore Dreiser and Sinclair Lewis and his characters to the heroic protagonists in some proletarian fiction. He is most at home in the carefully researched historical novel, whose focus on a central figure shaped by environment is part of the naturalist tradition. Yet Fast is always notoriously individualistic, as the cultural commissars of the Communist party kept discovering; he refused to hew to any party line, and particular works reflect multiple influences, including the biographical and contemporary. Fast is fond of a quotation from Rosa Luxemburg, the nineteenth-century German socialist:

> Freedom for the supporters of the government only, for the members of one party only—no matter how big its membership may be—is no freedom at all. Freedom is always freedom for the man who thinks differently. This contention does not spring from a fanatical love of abstract justice, but from the fact that everything which is enlightening, healthy, and purifying in political freedom derives from its independent character, and from the fact that freedom loses all its virtue when it becomes a privilege. (Rosa Luxemburg, quoted in *Being Red* 27)

This quotation sums up Fast's political philosophy and shows why he sooner or later had to part with the Communist party. Luxemburg's statement is Fast's artistic credo as well. Never in his long and phenomenally productive career has he adopted a literary form except to change it into his own, to twist it to his own purposes. He has always taken pride in being the "man who thinks differently."

Fast is justifiably famous for his political works, but it would be inaccurate to limit him to the political arena. Although his best early works are the political novels, such as *Citizen Tom Paine*, *April Morning*, and *Freedom Road*, and although his notoriety—his public endorsement of communism, his testimony before the House Un-American Activities Committee, his jail term, the Stalin Peace Prize in 1953—has defined him sharply, the real canon and professional career that lie behind the reviews and headlines are so varied and complex that they cannot be reduced to simple slogans. Most writers would be satisfied with a book list as extensive as that of Fast's nonfiction works, a list of at least a dozen books about topics literally all over the map, as their titles indicate: *Haym Salomon, Son of Liberty*; *Lord Baden-Powell of the Boy Scouts*; *Goethals and the Panama Canal*; *The Picture-Book History of the Jews* (with Bette Fast); *The Incredible Tito*; *The Passion of Sacco and Vanzetti*; *Intellectuals in the Fight for Peace*. What common interests link *Literature and Reality*, *Tito and His People*, *Peekskill, U.S.A.: A Personal Experience*, *Spain and Peace*,

The Art of Zen Meditation, The Novelist: A Romantic Portrait of Jane Austen, War and Peace: Observations on Our Times? Similarly, Fast's enormous output of nonpolitical fiction defies easy categorization, for although his views are easily discernible, they shift smoothly from left to liberal depending on the subject, and much of the canon is best described as social criticism or social commentary couched in the mode of American realism. Like Theodore Dreiser, whose fiction Fast edited early in his career in *The Best Short Stories of Theodore Dreiser*, Fast describes in cinematic detail, sometimes allowing readers to reach conclusions on their own, sometimes shaping reactions with authorial voice. *Power*, for example, a fictional biography of a John L. Lewis–type mine workers' union president, follows the career of its protagonist through the sometimes skeptical eyes of a former newspaperman and the union president's somewhat alienated wife, with a resulting distance on the militant labor politics involved that gives an understanding of the human costs of political success. However sympathetic to his subject, Fast is no cheerleading ideologue; his vision is unblinkered and fair. Other novels, such as *The Outsider* and *The Dinner Party*, though peopled with characters who are politicians or act in politics, are in fact, like *Power*, also concerned with human values, family relationships, and, especially, how changing social environments affect human character and action. With a book like *The Confession of Joe Cullen*, Fast, perhaps allowing personal outrage about U.S. actions in Central America to motivate his writing, comments directly and pointedly on a particular foreign policy, but the majority of the works of social criticism are more like *Max*, with its portraits of immigrant poverty in late nineteenth-century New York that are eloquent indictments without being overtly propagandistic. The highly popular five-novel series beginning with *The Immigrants* (followed by *Second Generation, The Establishment, The Legacy,* and *The Immigrant's Daughter*) also touches frequently on political issues and questions. Social criticism here is in the form of a family saga, one set in San Francisco at the end of the settling of the American West, but also at the beginning of the period of American international power. The series allows Fast to explore in a popular form serious questions of assimilation, ambition, greed, ethnic conflict, business ethics, and so on during the formative years of California down to the present.

These works would constitute a major achievement for most writers, but Fast, in a most unlikely metamorphosis, also became a writer of detective stories and mysteries as well. As E. V. Cunningham, the pseudonym necessitated by the blacklist of the 1950s, he created the Harvey

Krim series of mysteries, again illuminating his stories with a social conscience and an appreciation for a simple life free of the corruptions of
wealth and power. Long before it was fashionable, Fast focused on what
would now be termed a feminist issue: the absence of fully realized female characters in the detective fiction genre. His dozen works with
women's names—*Sylvia, Phyllis, Alice, Shirley, Lydia, Penelope, Helen, Margie, Sally, Samantha, Cynthia,* and *Millie*—explode stereotype with their
strong, independent, and capable female characters, women who may
be treated horribly in a world run by men but who nevertheless endure
and usually prevail.

Fast's nisei detective, Masao Masuto, a Zen Buddhist who works for
the Beverly Hills Police Department, preceded the current fashion for
multicultural detectives. Reflecting the new influence of religious meditation in Fast's own life, Masuto attempts to combine the lessons of his
Eastern philosophy with the strength of the West: the rational and orderly thinking of Sherlock Holmes. This attempt at reconciling East and
West in the New World is a time-honored American theme, given its
most articulate form by nineteenth-century writers such as Thoreau, Emerson, and Whitman, and we again see Fast working in the heart of the
American literary and intellectual tradition. The hard-boiled detective
story itself is a standard American form, and though it might seem a
peculiar form for a writer who cut his teeth on historical fiction and
political works, the crime format is a perfect opportunity to write realistic
and effective social commentary: the underside of society shows its flaws,
and the American detective story has a long history of exploring the less
obvious skirmishes of the unending class war. Fast wrote a half dozen
"The Case of the . . ." books, beginning with *The Case of the One-Penny
Orange* and continuing with the *Russian Diplomat, Poisoned Eclairs, Sliding
Pool, Kidnapped Angel,* and *Murdered Mackenzie.* This is Erle Stanley Gard-
ner territory, but Fast is quite at home and in fact uses this new genre
to make familiar social criticisms, now in the home-grown form of the
detective novel, a form quite receptive to serious looks at poverty and
violence. Thus, Fast may seem to reinvent himself as a writer with his
California-based works and settings, but in fact we can regard this
change as a logical one for a writer whose overall work is prototypically
American.

Apart from his historical and political fiction, the nonfiction biographies, his social criticism, his family saga series, and the detective and
mystery works, Fast somehow found time for a number of other projects.
He wrote two works for children, *The Romance of a People* and *Tony and*

the Wonderful Door (*April Morning* is sometimes listed as a book for young readers but probably belongs with his Revolutionary War fiction). He also wrote some poetry, several television plays, a screenplay for *The Hessian*, film adaptations for *Rachel, Spartacus, The Winston Affair* (called *Man in the Middle*), *The Immigrants, Freedom Road*, and *April Morning*. He edited the Modern Library edition of *The Selected Work of Tom Paine*. He has had a long love of the theater and is especially fond of his play *The Hammer*, probably the best among the eight or nine plays adapted from his fiction for production. He has four collections of short stories, a collection of essays (*War and Peace*), an anthology of his own shorter writing, an autobiography (*Being Red: A Memoir*), and another autobiography of his political life (*The Naked God: The Writer and the Communist Party*). To use an adjective like *phenomenal* about this level of production seems quite justified, simply at the level of putting down words. The achievement of so much ink on so much paper would alone be worthy of a record book; Fast's *oeuvre*, however, is distinguished by a high level of quality—sometimes reaching the level of excellence (*Citizen Tom Paine, April Morning*), more often simply achieving great competence in storytelling and style. This consistent quality accounts for Fast's long-term popularity in spite of the political attacks against him and the varying fortunes of his reputation. Such a powerful relationship between writer and readers over such a long period, in spite of politics and critical neglect, is a phenomenon worthy of exploration.

Part of Fast's appeal is his accessibility, created out of several consistent qualities: his sure sense of what readers will find interesting and dramatic, his ability to embody complex historical issues and background in quickly sketched characters, and his clean, lean prose style. The drama initially came from the subjects chosen: the American Revolutionary War, Reconstruction, the American frontier, the Jews in biblical times. These are all inherently interesting topics in their own right, and meticulous historical research allowed detail and setting to heighten their effect. In his later works, Fast moves his setting to modern America with great success, focusing on social and political cruxes that will intrigue the reader. Fast's central characters also sum up the problems and contradictions of their periods: Tom Paine, like his American Revolutionary compatriots, is rough, simple, and direct but honest and dedicated to his cause; Moses and Judas Maccabee epitomize the way of life of their different biblical periods; Gideon Jackson is a perfect representative of a slave elevated by Reconstruction to statesman. Each inhabits a clear place in the memory, efficiently summarizing the complex social and political environment of the setting.

Finally, Fast's prose has many of the virtues of the early New England settlers he admires. His language is clear, unadorned, direct; it delivers its message without calling undue attention to itself. Unlike some writers favored by academic critics, Fast limits his experiments with prose, choosing the functional over the self-consciously artistic, and he obviously aspires to a "transparent" language, which allows us to see directly to the subject. This is a modest and conservative way of writing; it is also the style advised by every writing teacher and scholar familiar with American prose. One could compare Fast's writing to one of the Protestant churches of a strict colonial sect, perhaps to the one described in *The Outsider*: spare to the point of self-denial but also elegant, pure, and uncluttered by useless detail.

Howard Fast's works have never been studied in their entirety. His fascinating career, a very American one, has been largely ignored in spite of his phenomenal popular success in a wide variety of forms over a very long period. This neglect of a writer of undeniable importance is partly due to his politics and his having been blacklisted, but also to the American ambivalence about popular culture. A country with strong egalitarian values has come to honor its most widely read authors less and less and to celebrate obscure academic writers with little appeal to the general reading public. Popularity is no guarantee of quality, of course, but it is not an automatic sign of mediocrity or worse. Rather, the pleasure of millions of readers over extended periods of time is probably the best final test of literary quality, for "literature" can be defined as the works that enough people care about reading and urging on others to read (or to imposing on others!) to ensure survival into future generations. The judgments of critics and academics should not be ignored, but neither should the academic establishment ignore the experiences of committed readers.

The sheer size of Fast's canon provides numerous problems of classification and grouping; evaluating the contributions of this plethora of novels of so many kinds and types is a daunting task. Also, this abundance of works necessarily means some were written with less care than others, and critics have often complained that Fast substitutes quantity for quality, resorting to sentimentality or melodrama rather than the carefully crafted work of which he is clearly capable. Certainly the best novels set a standard impossible to maintain over scores and scores of works, and any writer creating so much will descend into valleys as well as climb peaks. Some successes will be described in the chapters that follow, and a few failures identified, as well as the reasons for these judgments.

The goal of this book is to provide a fair and objective evaluation of Fast's work and contribution to American literature and culture. This chapter has delineated the major events in his life that affected his work, and has discussed some patterns revealed in different groups of works in his canon. Next, we will examine single representative novels, beginning with *Citizen Tom Paine*, probably the best known of the Revolutionary War books; *Freedom Road*, one of the earliest works to focus sympathetically on the African American experience; *Spartacus*, a sharply drawn portrait of ancient Rome that challenges modern attitudes toward empire; *April Morning*, a charmingly homespun yet convincing retelling of the battles of Lexington and Concord; The Immigrants, an extremely popular family saga that spins out its California tale over five novels; *Seven Days in June*, Fast's latest Revolutionary War book, a powerful balanced view of the Battle of Bunker Hill; and *The Bridge Builder's Story*, an exploration of the long-term psychic damage wrought by Nazism.

Fast's best work will survive the generations of critics who reviled his politics, his occasional forays into sentimentality or melodrama, or his popularity. His works give a picture of America that is often unsettling and sometimes uplifting, but whatever the emotion evoked it is always an interesting picture. He is always, to return to Rosa Luxemburg's words, "the man who thinks differently."

3

Citizen Tom Paine
(1944)

> The current of American history as expressed by the mass of American people is revolutionary. Emerson and Thoreau, who were the great intellects of their time, believed in John Brown and the righteousness of his cause. Today, Hollywood turns out pictures showing John Brown as a fool, a swine, and a murderer. I am going to try a one-man reformation of the historical novel in America.
>
> —Howard Fast in *Current Biography*

The works I am calling "novels of the Revolution" constituted a deep reservoir of material for Fast and an emotional fountainhead as well. *Conceived in Liberty: A Novel of Valley Forge*, a passionate and empathetic portrait of the Continental army at its lowest point, was published in 1939, when Fast was only twenty-five; Fast was still publishing Revolutionary War novels in 1984, with *Seven Days in June*, when he was eighty. (*Two Valleys*, Fast's sixth novel but his first published work is not technically about the Revolution, since it is largely set on the frontier, with the fighting spilling over to involve the characters; it is still fine reading and a well-written book, but copies are difficult to find.) After *Conceived in Liberty*, the next Revolutionary War novel was *The Unvanquished* (1942), a vastly sympathetic account of George Washington's military losses and retreats from the Battle of Long Island to his first crossing of the Delaware River in 1776, told mostly from Washington's own point of view. A year later came *Citizen Tom Paine*.

FAST'S REVOLUTIONARY GADFLY

Among Fast's best novels, *Citizen Tom Paine* is a startlingly original portrait of the great rabble-rouser and revolutionary who energized the Revolution with his pamphlets. *Tom Paine*, published when the author was only twenty-nine, has a central position in Fast's canon. Taught to generations of high school students for its dramatic evocation of colonial history, it is often the best remembered and perhaps the most respected of all the varied works produced by this prolific author. It has shaped several generations of Americans' view of the American Revolution, the intellectual fervor and passionately independent and democratic spirit of the period, and the role of the common man. Certainly *Tom Paine* was regarded as a serious book simply because of the political and social importance of its central character. Although Paine's role in the Revolution had long been recognized, there had been few biographies of the stay-maker-turned-revolutionary, and none that captured the popular imagination. The conventional heroes of the Revolution—Washington, Jefferson, Franklin, and Revere—had been written about again and again, in both popular and scholarly venues; here was a new and interesting figure, somewhat disreputable but certainly central in importance, whose life was dramatized as few of the lives of the other central players in the birth of the nation had been.

Tom Paine also probably profited from the time in which it came out, a time ripe for a hero depicted as a common man. The terrible years of the Great Depression were over, replaced by a life-and-death struggle for the survival of democracy, of the cultures in which ordinary folk had primacy. European fascism heaped contempt on nations that celebrated the alleged mediocrity of the common man, the "decadent" democratic countries that were satisfied with mass culture and the "lowest common denominator." In 1944, even American aristocrats saw the wisdom of embracing working-class values, for it was the industrial might of that class that would be the key to defeating Hitler and fascism. As a statement of the philosophy of that working class, *Tom Paine* was a book for its time. Fast's timing was impeccable.

If we look for something of the contemporaneous war in *Tom Paine* (it was written while Fast was working for the War Information Office and the Voice of America), we will see little in colonial Philadelphia or even in the struggles of Washington's army that serve as direct parallels. In Tom Paine himself, however, there is much that captures the personality and spirit of a still-youthful America, a country that, like Paine, continually seemed to lose its ideals in the midst of messy indulgences, a country rough, inelegant, sometimes confused, but ultimately far more solid and reliable than any of its European progenitors. As Fast's biography shows, he saw his own rough-and-tumble upbringing as a strength as much as a liability, and the equation between Fast, Paine, and colonial America holds firm in a number of ways: rude (in the older sense of unpolished, but sometimes in the modern sense as well), pointed toward some ever-evolving ideals, full of promise.

PLOT DEVELOPMENT

Part One of *Citizen Tom Paine* is titled "America," but the book in fact begins in England in 1774, in the study of Dr. Benjamin Franklin, the greatest American of his time and on his way toward being, in Fast's words, the most famous man in the world. Franklin's work is interrupted by a threadbare, dirty Tom Paine, a failed stay maker, a fallen Quaker, and generally an unimpressive man. Paine wants to go to America, and Franklin, after talking to him, agrees to write him a letter of introduction. Paine catches a fever on the nine-week crossing to Philadelphia and is saved from death by a physician anxious for new patients, who takes him in. Paine, down and out, does some tutoring, and some drinking and talking in taverns. That Philadelphia is indeed the promised land is clear from the fact that the bedraggled Paine can meet Robert Aitken, a dour Scots printer, and be hired to edit and write for the new *Pennsylvania Magazine*.

The next chapter is a flashback to Paine's boyhood in England, showing the roots of his disreputable behavior in Philadelphia. He is whipped for trespassing by the local squire's son, Harry, he rebels against his father's docility in the face of class oppression, and he runs away—first to serve as a cabin boy aboard a privateer, then, after jumping ship, to live as a hobo on Gin Row in London, drinking and scrounging for food. Apprenticed for a while to a stay maker, he witnesses his friend Stivvens's hanging for petty theft and in despair becomes a Gin Row drunk again. Then he apprentices himself to a cobbler before leaving for America.

The scene shifts back to Philadelphia, where Paine has become a familiar coffee-house figure, a journalist who is becoming more and more American. The Continental Congress has met in Philadelphia, and Paine finds himself in a period of political ferment. On April 19, 1775, the battles of Lexington and Concord trigger the start of the Revolution; we get a summary version of events, the same story that Fast would tell thirty years later through the eyes of Adam Cooper in *April Morning*. The scene in the next chapter shifts back to Paine in Philadelphia and then flashes back to England to tell the story of the younger Paine and Mary Lambert, his wife, a former servant of limited ambitions who dies while pregnant because the desperate Paine cannot afford food and medicine. Back in Philadelphia, we see Paine marveling at the armed populace of America, a phenomenon impossible in England; he squabbles with his printer, Robert Aitken, about his own increasing radicalism and meets Franklin again. The Second Continental Congress convenes in Philadelphia, and Paine meets George Washington, Thomas Jefferson, the Adams cousins (Sam and John), and John Hancock. The stay-maker-turned-writer-and-revolutionary drinks and eats with the intellectual and political elite of the colonies, absorbing their ideas and promoting his own.

Leaving Aitken, Paine strikes out on his own as a freelance writer, and after discussions with Jefferson and others he begins to write down what he thinks the justifications for revolution are. On a walking tour outside Philadelphia he meets the Rumpels, Jacob and Hester, a prosperous farm family richer in possessions than some English squires yet very different in their closeness to the land. There is a mutual attraction between Paine and the elder Rumpel daughter, Sarah, but Paine cannot choose domestic happiness. He tells Sarah about Mary Lambert, and about another, earlier wife (the widow of a benefactor of Paine whom Paine had married to protect from scandal, yet who left Paine when his small business failed). Clearly Sarah has come too late; Paine is a psychological disaster, consumed with guilt about his past failures. He gives up the Rumpels for Philadelphia and his writing, neglecting food and personal hygiene. The result is a book read around the world, *Common Sense*.

George Aitken will not print *Common Sense*, but Robert Bell, another Scot, will, and it comes out on January 10, 1776. Paine refuses all royalties, considering the work an obligation, not a project for profit. In Chapter 7, titled after the book, Fast gives page-long glimpses of *Common Sense*'s travels up and down the narrow strip of civilized territory that was then the colonies, as it is passed from hand to hand, supplanting Defoe, Fielding, Voltaire, and even the Bible as reading matter and the stuff of conversation. The scenes make clear how diverse the colonists are in background and motivation, and how different the geographic regions. The book inspires the Continental army with reasons for their rebellion and inspires the British General Howe to order Paine hanged.

Paine is not caught and in fact joins Washington's army. He has become totally identified with his book, but lionization by the distinguished leadership of the Revolution leaves him uncomfortable, for he has always felt his place is with the common man. He still drinks to excess, wears dirty clothes, and refuses to be politic and diplomatic. Though a favorite of Washington, he refuses an officer's commission, traveling with the retreating army in an ambiguous status we might now call political cadre: neither common soldier nor regular officer, but a political-spiritual adviser and uplifter for the troops. Paine shares Washington's long series of retreats from Manhattan Island to north of New York and on into New Jersey. After the first crossing of the Delaware, Paine returns to Philadelphia, where he prints *The Crisis*, a manifesto explaining the dire difficulties that face the fledgling nation but offering hope and rage as responses. Its opening line, "These are the times that try men's souls," becomes a rallying cry. A second installment of *The Crisis* follows.

Paine is again tempted by domestic bliss in the person of Irene, the daughter of General Roberdeau, especially after her father arranges a comfortable position for the now middle-aged Paine as secretary to the Committee for Foreign Affairs. She, however, recognizes Paine as "damned," and he eventually returns to the army. Nonetheless, he visits father and daughter off and on until Valley Forge. He continues his *Crisis* series, even in the face of attempts on his life. As secretary, Paine becomes aware of the frequent double-dealing in financial and military supply matters, and he shuttles back and forth from Congress to army to try to support the common soldier. The Revolution comes to an end, and Paine, though ecstatic, is at loose ends.

Part Two, "Europe," follows the revolutionary's failed enterprises in England and France. Saying confidently that given seven years he would write a *Common Sense* for every nation in Europe, he produces *The Rights of Man*, but the conservative British try to bring him to trial for treason, and at the urging of poet and painter William Blake, Paine escapes to France, where he has been named to the French Assembly as a representative from Calais. Paine, however, can speak little French, and his understanding of the French political situation is always somewhat shaky. His dream of a united Europe comes to nothing, and his publication of *The Age of Reason*, intended to unify opposing parties as had *Common Sense*, instead brings him immediate condemnation in both the United States and Europe. The book, a treatise on natural religion written from a deistic point of view, advocates a tolerance of religion but its separation from government power; however, its attack on many traditional religious practices as superstitious offends many readers. Since he is out of political favor in France, he is consigned to Luxembourg Prison for ten months. Barely escaping the guillotine, Paine, now sick and aging, is released and meets the young Napoleon Bonaparte, but his influence is waning rapidly. He returns to America, where he has been depicted as a devil with horns because of his supposed attack on religion in *The Age of Reason*. He finds himself alienated from most of his old acquaintances, and many of his Revolutionary War comrades are dead. He dies in 1809 and is buried on the farm in New Rochelle, New York, given to him by the government, but his body is removed to England ten years later.

STRUCTURE

Common Sense's two parts, "America" and "Europe," might as easily be relabeled "Paine's Rise" and "Paine's Fall." America was very good to Paine, at least during the Revolution, just as Paine was very good for America. The European experiences, except for the production of his writing, were disastrous. As a result, Fast devotes ten chapters to Part One and only five to Part Two, with chapter 15 actually about Paine's last years back in America.

The movement of the narrative is indicated in part by the chapter titles, which set up the main idea, although some chapters include contrasting or complementing material. For example, chapter 1, "My Name Is Paine," accurately sums up the aggressive fashion in which Paine approaches Benjamin Franklin, but chapter 2, "America Is the Promised Land," is both literally true and ironic, for though it includes Paine's being offered the editorship of *Pennsylvania Magazine* by Robert Aitken and portraits of Philadelphia as a wealthy town full of entrepreneurs of diverse ethnic backgrounds, it opens with a doctor rescuing Paine from the fever in the hope of landing a large fee and shows Paine attending a brutal slave auction.

Chapter 3, "The Rat Trap," is a flashback in time and space to Paine's youth in England, which establishes the reasons for his bitterness, insecurity, and dislike of aristocratic privilege. Chapter 4, "The Nineteenth of April and 'Seventy-Five," cuts from scenes of the Revolution, especially the battles of Lexington and Concord, to scenes of Paine working in Philadelphia, becoming Americanized, and absorbing the spirit of the Revolution. Appropriately enough, chapter 5 is titled "The Making of a Revolutionist"; Paine is now ready to throw himself into the American political turmoil. This chapter includes a second long flashback to England and the poverty that caused his first wife, Mary Lambert, to die while pregnant; Paine's guilt and anger enter into his decision to "stir the devil's broth of rebellion," as Aitken calls it.

Chapters 6 and 7, "How Tom Paine Wrote a Small Book," and "Common Sense," come almost at the center of the novel, and of course Paine's "small book" was his greatest achievement. The episode of the Rumpels' farm comes in the middle of chapter 6, probably to show the kind of nearly utopian society Paine wished to create and also to depict Paine's resisting the temptation of retreating into domestic life; Fast's Revolutionary soldiers always reluctantly turn their backs on their peaceable homes, and Paine is a soldier sacrificing himself for the Revolution. Chapter 7 cuts between scenes of different colonials being affected by *Common Sense* in a prose version of a common filmic technique; it is one of the best-wrought chapters of the novel, combining historical-demographic research and vivid depiction of period.

The final three chapters of Part One, chapters 8 through 10, telescope the war years into three units: "The Times That Tried Men's Souls," the years when Paine wrote his *Crisis* series; "The Long War," which is self-explanatory; and "Revolutionist at Large," about Paine in his less effective role of politician and his feelings of being at loose ends once the war was won.

Part Two has only four chapters about the Continent: "Give Me Seven Years," a reference to Paine's boast about a *Common Sense* for every nation of Europe; "The Republic of France," covering his life in Paris; "Reason in God and Man," the period of decline and *The Age of Reason*; and "Napoleon Bonaparte," when Paine met the dictator. "But No Man Knoweth of his Sepulchre," chapter 15, covers Paine's return to America and the sad consequences of change: no one needs the old revolutionary any longer, and he did not know either his literal and figurative sepulchre, for his physical remains were taken to England, and his literary "remains" went in and out of fashion, having results he could never have predicted.

The narrative, then, moves from highly detailed and specific scenes in the early chapters, which cover the years immediately before and during the early part of the war in some depth, to the publication of *Common Sense*, and then covers the later war years more summarily. The fifteen or so years in Europe receive the briefest treatment. The chronological development is interrupted by two extended flashbacks that develop Paine's motivation for becoming a revolutionary.

GENERIC CONVENTIONS

The dominant genre of *Citizen Tom Paine* is historical biography, and the book delivers a wonderfully evocative and affecting portrait of its subject. The historical research is sound, the characters clearly delineated, and just enough period detail is included to allow readers to create a mental backdrop against which the characters can play their parts. Fast's achievement here is not in describing a great deal but in knowing just how much detail to provide, and no more. Writing blocks of descriptive prose is no great task for a professional writer who does his research homework; the trick is to integrate this description into the plot so that it remains backdrop and never moves to center stage. The settings are worked admirably well into the narrative; for example, when Paine brings his manuscript of *Common Sense* to Bobby Bell, a printer friend of Robert Aitken, we sense a setting rather than actually seeing it through Fast's words. The details are few but telling: Bell is "hatchet-faced" with "ink-grimed hands," and he leans on his counter while reading silently. Paine drops into a chair and dozes, waking from time to time to watch the Scots printer read, with no expression on his face to reveal his reaction to Paine's book. When Bell puts the manuscript down on the counter, Paine says, "You don't want it" (*Citizen Tom Paine* 99). The passage is typical of Fast's descriptive approach, with its focus on character rather than physical setting and its seemingly minor detail that accumulates into a mental image. For example, Bell folds the manuscript and secures it with a paperweight, something no modern person would do. Similar details suggest rather than depict, leaving Bell and Paine firmly in view. The technique is deceptively simple, and very difficult to duplicate.

To a lesser degree than in its identity as a historical biography, *Citizen Tom Paine* is a protest novel or exposé, revealing to the reader a historical figure who has been slighted and perhaps intentionally denigrated. Tom Paine was always an embarrassment to gentlemanly Philadelphians, and the people he communicated with so effectively through *Common Sense* and his other writings have been fairly well excluded from standard histories, if only because they were not in the political leadership and were so diverse as to be impossible to generalize about easily. Fast's point is that the war was fought and won by the suffering of ordinary folk, farmers, benchworkers, laborers, new immigrants—in general, the dispossessed and alienated. Even the military leadership was essentially amateurish and sometimes hardly competent, and Fast is at pains to show the few professionals as having minimal influence. The popular imagery of the Revolution is of bewigged aristocrats in elegant eighteenth-century rooms, not of half-drunken scribblers arguing in taverns. Fast's "exposé" is meant to change our view to his more raffish, and certainly more historical, view of what the Revolutionaries looked like.

Finally, Fast is fond of coming-of-age stories—the convention of tales about young people finding themselves through some important event. Paine did not arrive in America until he was thirty-eight years old, so he hardly fits the model of a youth maturing, yet the novel does in fact focus on Paine's finding himself. In Fast's view, he is the first professional revolutionary, and it took the New World to provide a context in which he could exist.

KEY CHARACTERS

As is necessitated by the convention of historical biography, the subject is the central character. Although many other characters play parts in the novel, they come and go as the focus stays firmly on the protagonist. As we have seen, Fast is unflinching in his description of Paine, who is described as neither handsome nor prepossessing. He is between thirty and forty years old, with a sharp hooked nose that makes him seem older: "His chin was sharp, his mouth full, his oddly twisted eyes tight with bitterness and resentment; virtue or evil in that face, but no joy for a long time and no hope either" (4). Paine is disheveled, with week-old whiskers, and is unwashed. He is neither tall nor short but of medium height, "with the powerful, sloping shoulders of a workman who has put in long hours at a bench, and his hands were from the bench, meaty and broad" (4). He wears a cheap coat, split under the arms, breeches worn paper-thin, and his toes poke out of the end of shoes that were cheap to begin with. As the description implies, Paine had nothing going for him except, as we learn later, his amazingly resilient revolutionary spirit. Bred a Quaker, Paine left much of his heritage behind, and like

the American nation he adopted, he was self-creating, a new invention
forged out of ragtag elements of the European background by the unique
circumstances of the New World.

Paine's wife, Mary, died before he left for America, and his anger over
her unnecessary death from malnutrition helps fuel his life-long resentment over injustice. Paine, thinks Fast, had some quality deep inside him
that allowed him to see and know justice and injustice and, unlike others,
to "feel in his own soul the whip laid on the backs of millions" (66). In
America, Paine became a professional revolutionary, perhaps the first in
history, rejecting officer status in the Continental army but serving willingly as a kind of political cadre, unpaid, unranked, spoken to familiarly
by Washington yet able to share the dawning of a new age of "small
men" after five thousand years of such men being treated as slaves (144).
Mary Paine, though she plays a tiny part in the actual narrative, is present as a representative of the constricted life from which Tom Paine
escapes.

The characters around Paine can be divided into the real/historical
and the fictional. The real characters include Benjamin Franklin, who
helps Paine get to America and to whom Paine turns for advice and
conversation several times in the book. He is depicted as wise and wily,
the best representative of the kind of new person America can produce.
Another unlikely friendship is with George Washington, perhaps the
richest man in America, who nevertheless develops a liking for this odd
journalist. Like Franklin, he comes and goes in the book in a series of
brief cameos. Paine also shared meals with Thomas Jefferson (Jefferson
is thought to have gotten the name the "United States of America" from
him), an interesting contrast since Jefferson had dreamed enough about
democracy for it to seem real to him but could never quite "grasp the
concept of revolution. For Paine it was the other way around" (95). Their
relationship continues even when Paine is in France and Jefferson comes
to visit. A dozen other historical figures people the novel: politicians,
military leaders, well-known colonials. (As Barbara Lavette says in *The
Legacy* about her novel *The President's Wife*, some "real people . . . anchor
[the story] in history"[153].)

But it is the "little people," Fast's fictional American colonials, who
are Paine's real supporting cast as he shuttles back and forth between
the intellectual-political leadership and those led. Paine identified with
the common man—the cobbler, the weaver, the exciseman, the stay
maker—because he had been all of these himself. He was able to com-
municate with farmers and workers not just because his vision of life

was essentially egalitarian but because he had painfully mastered an idiom that could speak to them directly. As Fast points out, *Common Sense* was biblical in style—that of a "backwoods preacher" in Jefferson's judgment—hammering out a message in easily remembered aphorisms: "These are the times that try men's souls. The summer soldier and the sunshine patriot will, in this crisis, shrink from the service of their country" (145). Through the common run of Americans depicted in the book, we come back to the enormity of Paine's achievement, of his capacity to convey complex new political ideas in the idiom of the ordinary person.

The fictional characters we see in the novel are the representatives of many others. The little book with the modest title had possibly 1 million readers, or one out of three colonials, and quite possibly all who could read. (Since Paine virtually gave the book to printers, no royalty records indicate readership; Paine himself had no idea, and pirated editions were legion.) It was read out loud over campfires and around hearths, its stylistic nuggets of revolutionary propaganda easily remembered by illiterate backwoodsmen for whom eighteenth-century intellectual eloquence was a foreign language.

Yet for all his friends and acquaintances, whether high achievers or ordinary folk, the novel most often shows Paine alone. When he is in the company of others, he is even then separate and isolated by his social class or by his perception of his difference. His abuse of alcohol and his carelessness about personal appearance do little to help his social reputation, and he rejects women as impediments to his revolutionary vocation. At the end of the book he is isolated by age and the change in his reputation, and he dies as he lived, a man set apart.

THEMATIC ISSUES

Social Class and Opportunity in America

The wonderfully conceived introduction to Paine (quoted at the beginning of the section on key characters) goes far to define what is good about America. Franklin's servant immediately identifies Paine as "no gentleman" and none too clean either, and rudely keeps him waiting; in contrast, Franklin's good-natured courtesy, his automatic granting of the title "Mr." to Paine, and his willingness to write this strange, unknown man a letter of introduction define the best of the new America far better than any words of praise could. We quickly understand the prevailing theme: social class, though never totally absent, is far less a barrier in this narrow little fringe of land, as Fast calls it, where no one has been long established and where talent and originality can be valued. This key concept, of the valuing of people for whom and what they are, not for their family or background, runs throughout the book. Tied to the theme of fluidity of social class is the concept of equality of opportunity, with the New World offering possibilities undreamed of in Europe. Paine faces a choice that is a thematic thread throughout Fast's work: the option between a rural near-utopia and involvement in the turbulent world of urban political conflict. A final and related theme is Paine, paralleling his creator Fast, as a spokesman for the common man. For the first time in human history, the ordinary citizen had someone who could express his wishes and hopes in language accessible to people without extensive formal education.

Diversity and Opportunity

One reason for the open-mindedness about background is the sheer diversity of the colonists—diversity of origin, religion, race, and opinion. This diversity, Fast suggests, has been lost in the properly correct school versions of the revolt, just as its radicalism was defused and turned into pious dogma. Fast's description of Philadelphia in 1775, the year of Paine's arrival, emphasizes the multiplicity of cultures and influences rubbing shoulders with each other: the proper merchants of the coffee-houses and warehouses, importing and sometimes creating a high culture to rival the European; Scots Calvinists and Jews, important in the community but also alienated; red Indians and backwoods whites, equally wild and uncouth; slaves of all colors, including white indentured servants; Europeans—the Dutch, the Swedes, the Germans, the Irish—practicing versions of their original cultures but also, sometimes uncertainly, becoming Americans.

A sharply drawn picture of a slave auction reminds us of a subtheme, the great moral divide that would split the country in two almost a century later, but Fast's main emphasis is positive, on the new land of opportunity that made even a Tom Paine welcome. It is an original portrait, one we would now call multicultural, for while lip-service has always been paid to the amalgam of races and cultures that formed the new America, attention usually focused on the white European English-

men at the center of the political debate. The great masterpieces of art-
work that have hung in museums for two centuries have inevitably
created the mental imagery that peoples our vision of the Revolution, of
pale Washington and bewigged Continental Congress lookalikes; in
Fast's description, the streets outside looked more like a bazaar. We
should note that Fast's imagery no doubt reflects the streets of New York
that shaped his childhood, a picture of immigrants that more actually
describes the rank and file of Philadelphia and the Revolution than the
paintings of Emanuel Leutze (the very familiar *Washington Crossing the
Delaware*), William Mercer, John Trumbull, or Currier and Ives.

To say that Tom Paine fit in to this turbulent gumbo is to misappre-
hend the situation; rather, Philadelphia practiced rough toleration of
multiple points of view since no one element could easily prevail except
under strictly local circumstances. As Paine perceives,

> Here was a land of no one people, of no one prejudice, of no
> one thought, a country so big that all England could be tucked
> away in a corner and forgotten, a country so youthful that
> half the people one met were foreigners or the first generation
> of foreigners . . . and the promise . . . was freedom . . . no more
> and no less. (*Citizen Tom Paine*, 41)

In contrast was Paine's English wife, Mary, a former servant who "was
[only] what she was." Paine knew and understood that she was unable
to imagine herself in any other way. However, this knowledge only
made him feel worse. Mary was "beaten into shape by her tiny world,
a tribal creature laid over . . . with a thousand taboos" (64). *Tribal* captures the closed world of the English working class; their vision was
limited to their village or London neighborhood and the dead-end oc-
cupations open to people with little education and fewer prospects.

Agrarian Peace versus Revolutionary Turmoil

Paine's enormous success as the Revolution's rabble-rouser and gad-
fly—he was a "campfollower of Revolution, a scribbler, a pamphleteer"
(167)—came at a large ultimate cost to himself. Jefferson wondered if
Paine understood what devils were being loosed on the quiet eighteenth-
century world, and the question has to be answered in the negative. Fast

gives Paine one hope of personal happiness and contentment in the book, an idyllic vision of family life that recurs in Fast's books from *Moses, Prince of Egypt* to The Immigrants series. Paine stumbles across the Rumpels, a farming family on the outskirts of Philadelphia, and is fascinated by the attractive daughter. Fast notes that nothing like them existed in England or in the rest of the world—people rich in property and quality of life yet humble socially, allowing the hired man to sit at table as an equal. All family members work with their hands, even the children at chores, and do most of their own labor, yet the paterfamilias reads Voltaire, Defoe, and Benjamin Franklin. The family is serious, forthright, and self-sufficient. They hate slavery, respect the independence and rights of others, and are willing to fight for self-determination and to defend freedom with guns. The image of a rural-agrarian utopia, wealthy yet egalitarian, working class yet intellectually lively, is common in Fast's novels. The Rumpels are something new under the sun, neither peasants nor English-style yeomen, and certainly not aristocrats.

In a pattern we will see repeated in other works, circumstances and personal choices lead Paine away from an idyllic rural life as the Rumpels' son-in-law, and he returns to the turmoil of urban society. His lifelong work must be to make real the image of society as a gentle brotherhood, a world where divisions of class would mean nothing and everyone would, like the Rumpel farm family, sit at the same table to eat, just as Paine sat with Jefferson. Manual labor and intellectual effort would not be divided into competing spheres, and a deism divorced from sectarian dogma would provide decent values and a spiritual dimension to life.

Natural religion would provide humane values; a return to a communal economic relationship would make moot all the urban problems that Marxism sees in the divorce of labor from the fruits of its effort. Wealth as direct investment in productive capacity to be used by the Rumpel family does not seem to trouble Fast; this is small business as it should be: direct ownership directly serving the consumers of its production. Fast is not so utopian as to depict the Rumpels as completely self-sufficient, but they are free from the dependency that destroys any hope of change in Europe, as we see in the pathetic case of Paine's English family and friends. Such economic self-sufficiency leads to social equality, a basic egalitarianism: the hired man sits down to eat with the family, who shares his toil.

Spokesman for the Common Man

Another theme throughout this novel is Paine as spokesman for the common man. This is emphasized through a Fast-Paine parallel. Fast, too, was seen and saw himself as the spokesman for the common man, as a "proletarian writer," and he sold millions of books, often with little control over or worry about pirated editions abroad. Like Paine, Fast wrote out of passion and commitment, earning just enough to move on to the next work. And just as Paine mastered a straight-forward, workmanlike English, so Fast prides himself, rightly, on his ability to write clean, clear prose, with a minimum of stylistic or intellectual artifice. Paine absorbed the biblical rhetoric familiar to farmers and laborers; Fast has researched eighteenth-century colonial English, not just the elegant prose of the familiar documents but also the common speech of the time. (As noted in chapter 1, his historical accuracy about speech almost got him ejected from the Communist party.) This parallel between author and biographical subject should not suggest identification or egotism but rather the complex way in which writers choose their topics and shape their philosophies to reflect both personal interests and what they see as moral imperatives.

ALTERNATIVE READING: A FREUDIAN/ PSYCHOANALYTICAL INTERPRETATION

Citizen Tom Paine lends itself readily to Freudian analysis. Sigmund Freud, the nineteenth-century theoretician and father of psychoanalysis, was the first to explore the unconscious mind using case studies to ensure scientific validity. Freud's investigative methods of introspection, empathy, and dream analysis focused on discovering hidden motivations and repressed thoughts and memories. Although his theories have been modified continually since their nineteenth-century genesis, his underlying premise that early childhood experiences determine later behavior remains the cornerstone of modern Freudian psychoanalytical approaches. His emphasis was on the effects of traumas in early childhood on adult behavior, the way unresolved conflicts could continue to shape motives and subconscious actions. Of particular significance to Freud were conflicts with parental authority and, especially in the male child, conflicts with authorities or father figures.

A Freudian critic, finding explanations for human behavior in early childhood and in relations with parents, would see Paine as a case of adolescent conflict with authority never resolved by adulthood. Paine's revolts, against his strict Quaker father, against the squire's rules about trespass, and against the series of masters to whom he was apprenticed, would be seen as clear evidence of an inability to negotiate a reasonable accommodation with the authority figures that we all face. Paine's ultimate revolt is against George III, king of England, first through Paine's revolutionary activities in America and then again when he returns to England. The king would be seen as a displaced father, a figure of authority as a target of conflict over unresolved questions of adolescent freedom.

Further evidence of Paine's immaturity in such a psychological interpretation would be his inability to create an adult relationship with a woman. Mary Lambert, his second wife (the woman he marries in a gesture of thanks to her dead husband, his mentor), Sarah Rumpel, Irene Roberdeau: all would be seen as evidence of Paine's inability to leave behind his past difficulties with his father's controlling authority and to move on to create a new family of his own. Instead, Paine repeatedly turned to writing, and his journalism, pamphleteering, and book production would be seen as sublimation, the channeling of sexual energy into socially acceptable patterns.

Paine's inability to "retire," to enjoy the fruits of his labors as a writer and a revolutionary, would be final evidence of his essential immaturity. Resisting the passage of time and the normal developmental stages of life, Paine tries to find his youth in the French Revolution, which finally rejects him as passé. He would thus be seen as a classic case of arrested development.

Such an interpretation essentially destroys Paine's achievement by reducing it to the product of warped behavior, no matter how admired the product might be. For this reason the Communist party and other groups interested in promoting change in society have been wary of psychological explanations of behavior. (We shall see this phenomenon in the Communist party's attacks on *Spartacus*.) Psychologists often seem to such groups more interested in changing individuals to fit the needs of society than in changing society to fit the needs of individuals. This venerable debate need not concern us here except to mark where Fast stands, how forcefully he promotes Paine as a valid force for change and with what skill Paine's admitted personal failures are presented as shaping influences on his personality, not just as weaknesses (though Fast is quite direct about Paine's many faults).

Americans, who are presumably committed to the principles that formed their nation, should thus consider their position on Tom Paine carefully, for he constitutes a Rorschach ink-blot test measuring attitudes toward egalitarian/democratic political change. Those who accept a negative psychological portrait of Paine as an unhappy rabble-rouser, an ultimately failed revolutionary beset by personal problems, are accepting the older view of the Revolution as a staid and rational process led by aristocratic eighteenth-century gentlemen. Those who see Paine, as Fast does, as the manifestation of a living force for freedom, often denied but never totally forgotten, are more in line with the revolutionary heritage of the United States.

Freedom Road
(1944)

The book I wrote which has sold best—in fact, its sales exceed that of all other works of fiction in modern times—is *Freedom Road*. Internationally, this book has sold over twenty-five million copies [of its translations into eighty-two languages].

—Howard Fast, *Counterpoint*

Fast's interest in radical politics over the years caused him to ponder questions about resistance to literal and metaphorical slavery, and this led at different times to the Revolutionary War books and a number of other works about servitude, including, most notably, *My Glorious Brothers* (1948), about ancient Israel, and *Spartacus* (1951) about a slave uprising in ancient Rome. It is not surprising that the American writer should have turned his attention to slavery in the American South with *Freedom Road*. He had traveled through parts of the region as a youth and had visited Charleston, South Carolina, walking the streets, enjoying the beauties of a lush, moderate climate, but also encountering the hard inner core of racism and prejudice so evident in the South of the 1930s. The huge nationwide push for equal rights for African Americans began with World War II, with new roles for black soldiers and the eventual postwar integration of the military services; with improved communications that allowed a mass movement to exist; with the new American consciousness of the nation as having special responsibilities created by

the war. With the end of the depression of the 1930s, the excuses for
denying black equality because of poverty and economic limitations no
longer applied; the pie was growing larger, and the black community
clearly deserved its place at the table after so many decades of denial
after the Civil War. It was clearly a time for a book explaining the African
American experience with slavery and freedom after the war, just as *My
Glorious Brothers* came out in time to catch the wave of Israeli nationalism.

THE HARD PATH TO LIBERATION

Yet what sets *Freedom Road* apart is not its subject matter but its time
period, the immediate post–Civil War years of Reconstruction, rather
than the long prewar period of slavery or the four years of the war itself.
Fast by this time had researched and written several of his Revolutionary
War novels, including *Citizen Tom Paine*, which has an affecting and
vivid scene of a Philadelphia slave auction; the author might well have
recycled some of this material into an exploration of the issue of slavery
during the forming of the new nation, the huge moral blind spot in the
otherwise remarkable movement toward freedom and equality. Or, a
writer in his late twenties still trying to establish his reputation could be
forgiven for being swept up in the romance and passion of the great
American agony, the Civil War itself. Thousands of books and hundreds
of novels have been written about the war, and its connection to slavery
is so tightly bound as to make it difficult not to discuss the two in tan-
dem. Yet Fast resisted the siren call of the obvious to focus on a generally
ignored period, Reconstruction, a period unromantic and ultimately
shameful, when many of the high hopes and aspirations of the war years
were sacrificed in an effort to reinstitute prewar "normalcy." While there
have been a number of fictional treatments of Reconstruction, almost all
have been from the victors' point of view, that is, of the southern white
establishment's perspective on its postwar struggle for economic, social,
and political primacy. A regular Fast theme is that revolutions consume
their practitioners. Here we see that phenomenon at work: after the revolt against slavery had been won, the newly freed slaves and the poor
whites who shared some of their oppression ended up as losers. For
once, we see the story told from their point of view.

PLOT DEVELOPMENT

Gideon Jackson, a slave who had fought for the Union army in the Civil War, returns to Carwell Plantation in South Carolina, the only home he knows. Federal troops still occupy the South, and a new, free system of government is planned. His family still lives in the old slave quarters, and Gideon, a huge and powerful figure who is well respected by his neighbors, is elected to be a delegate to the Constitutional Convention in Charleston that will set the new course for the government of South Carolina. Although Gideon, his wife, and his fellow former slaves have little initial understanding of what voting involves or what the convention will do for them, Gideon sets off on foot for the state capitol wearing borrowed and mended clothes. He passes the farm of Abner Lait, a white racist who is astonished, as is Gideon himself, that a black man is free to take part in the convention. Halfway to Charleston Gideon spends the night at the house of James Allenby and his blind adopted daughter; he is a wise old man, an African American mentor who provides Gideon with a perspective of his duties as a delegate and of the role of the African Americans in the South.

In Charleston Gideon works briefly on the docks to raise money and finds shelter at Jacob Carter's rooming house, where he struggles to read the newspaper; he is barely literate. After presenting his credentials at the convention, Gideon is befriended by Francis L. Cardozo, a light-complexioned black man of Jewish heritage. Cardozo has always lived as a free man, and he invites Gideon to dinner to meet some middle-class black delegates, among whom Gideon feels ignorant and inadequate. Cardozo lends Gideon a speller, a grammar book, and a copy of Shakespeare's *Othello*.

The loan starts Gideon on the road to true literacy and intellectual development. At thirty-six, Gideon has almost no book learning, and he begins the arduous task of transforming himself, working harder than he had ever worked as a farmhand. His struggles with formal English bear fruit in the meetings of the convention, where after a great deal of initial hesitation, Gideon becomes a participant and then eventually a leader in the discussion. He starts studying his way through a fifty-thousand-word dictionary and buys himself a decent suit. At another dinner with Cardozo he meets Stephan Holms, a white "scalawag," or former slave owner, who is cooperating with the Union authorities and freed slaves.

The convention is beginning to further alliances between former black slaves and poor whites, and Gideon innocently accepts Holms's invitation to dinner. The occasion is a trap, an opportunity for unreconstructed white aristocrats, including Dudley Carwell, Gideon's former owner, to get a look at the potential threat posed by the developing opposition. Holms, it turns out, is preparing to unleash the Ku Klux Klan to destroy the new mixed-race leadership of the South.

Back home after the convention, Gideon discovers that his recent education in politics and books has distanced him from his wife, Rachel, but he perceives that his new learning is the only route to change. James Allenby has set up a school at Carwell at Gideon's suggestion, and Gideon's son Jeff falls in love with the blind girl, Ellen. Gideon forms a contract labor work force to cut timber in a swamp, earning pay for the first time; he then spearheads a movement to pool the resources of the former slaves and their poor white neighbors, including a hill country white man named Anderson Clay, and to buy up the former plantation. Denied a loan by a local banker, Gideon at Cardozo's suggestion travels to Boston to ask help from Isaac Went, an old abolitionist intimate of John Osawatomie Brown and Frederick Douglass. Given the necessary funds, Gideon marvels at how he is treated as an equal for the first time, and Dr. Norman Emery even arranges for Gideon's son Jeff to study medicine in Boston and eventually in Glasgow. Back home in South Carolina, Gideon learns the Klan has been riding at night, destroying farms and killing the now-integrated poor farmers. He forms a self-defense group and the Klan is temporarily stopped. Gideon has promised Cardozo he will run for the state legislature, a position he later wins.

The plot then jumps forward to Gideon, now age forty-five and a U.S. senator from South Carolina, trying to convince outgoing President Ulysses S. Grant that he must keep troops in the South to protect the fragile democracy created by Gideon and others. He fails, since a deal has been struck to return home rule to the South, with the effect of returning plantation owners to power. Gideon also has a debate with Holms, now also a U.S. senator, with Holms arguing for oligarchy and even offering Gideon power if he will lead his black and white coalition in the direction Holms wishes. Gideon refuses, and with son Jeff, now returned from Scotland, he returns to Carwell.

The final scenes of the novel trace the winding down of Reconstruction, with Gideon's community under increasing pressure from Klan attacks. Gideon leads a last stand in the old plantation house, which comes under artillery fire by a virtual army of Klansmen. Overcoming fierce resistance, the Klan wipes out the former slaves and poor whites and eradicates the brief experiment in egalitarian democracy.

STRUCTURE

Appropriately enough, the structure of *Freedom Road* is built around a series of journeys, both literal and metaphorical. Gideon is in constant movement, slow at first, and then with increasing speed and determination. He returns to Carwell from fighting for the Union army, his first "freedom road." Then he travels to town for "the voting," and we see his family greeting him as he comes back to Carwell to prepare for his service as a delegate to the Constitutional Convention. The trip to Charleston for the convention is the physical journey described in the most detail, as Gideon meets Abner Lait, a racist he will eventually bring into his fold, and James Allenby, the wise old man who will become teacher to Gideon's flock.

After the convention, the physical journeys begin again, with Gideon returning to Carwell, but then traveling to Charleston, and then by train to Washington, D.C., New York, and finally to Boston to arrange funding for the purchase of Carwell Plantation and an education for his son Jeff. Finally, Gideon and Jeff travel by train from Washington, where Gideon has been serving as U.S. senator, to Carwell for their final resistance.

The metaphorical journeys take Gideon an even further distance. He is almost illiterate at the beginning, able to pick out words and print his name laboriously, but is as unlettered as a child in the early grades of school: words such as " 'Constitutional Convention' might have been Sanskrit" (11). The speller and book on proper usage begin his journey to literacy, and although he makes very little sense of Shakespeare's *Othello*, he is on his way to an education. The dictionary he buys, the newspapers he puzzles over, the books he borrows and purchases: all open up a new world he never suspected existed. Gideon discovers the Constitution, and each new text leads to another, as Fast shows us just how limited the bucolic life could be without the magic of literacy, the force that allows readers to transcend time and space to know the thoughts and feelings of people long dead or very far away. By the end of the novel, Gideon is addressing Congress in measured, eloquent terms; although he is losing the political fight, clearly he is triumphing over the language and his own original ignorance.

Gideon makes a long social journey as well. In the early chapters we see him with his fellows, hardly speaking except in short sentences or even single words or phrases. He is ill at ease with strangers and feels clumsy and inarticulate at Cardozo's first party. We share Gideon's social agony at the bizarre dinner party given by Stephan Holms, when Gideon, the only African American except for servants, meets his former owner. Yet by the time he travels to Boston, he is able to hold his own with Isaac Went and Dr. Emery, and in his final conversation with President Grant he is at ease and in control.

Apart from the literal and metaphorical journeys, the formal structure of *Freedom Road* has a straightforward division into two parts, "Part One: The Voting" and "Part Two: The Fighting." A brief prologue sets the time and the scene before Part One, and then the parts are subdivided by chapters or sections, each described by a heading beginning with "How Gideon Jackson . . .": for example, "1. How Gideon Jackson Came Home from the Voting"; "4. How Gideon Jackson Labored with Both His Hands and His Head." There are seven sections in Part One, reflecting Gideon's slow rise upward, and only three in Part Two, a measure of his precipitous decline. The verbs used in these chapter headings signal the stops and starts on Gideon's journeys: How Gideon Jackson *Came*; *Talked*; *Went* to Charleston; *Labored*; *Was* a Guest; *Went* Home; *Journeyed* Far Afield; *Went* to See; *Came* Once More to Carwell; *Fought* the Good Fight.

Readers come to expect rigor and logic in the structure of Fast's books—he is an orderly thinker—but for all the neatness of the patterns described above, the continuity of the narrative flow is as unbroken as one of Gideon's South Carolina dirt roads, stretching out ahead with lots of interesting things along the way to look at. We are aware of the chronology, the ten years from 1867 to 1877, but except for the division between the two parts, the narrative is perceived as seamless and unified.

GENERIC CONVENTIONS

Freedom Road is a protest novel, like so many of Fast's other works about servitude and oppression. It is also a historical novel, and at times this uneasy marriage between the two genres may have damaged its credibility, however unfairly. The protest novel asks us to root for Gideon and his clan, a request we are likely to cooperate with because of his and their appeal as characters: their innocence, their vulnerability, their basic decency. It would be inhuman not to feel for these victims of two hundred years of slavery—people, as the book tells us, bought and sold like cattle. Yet Gideon and his Carwell neighbors are so continuously highminded, so lacking in human vice, that they do not always engage our full belief. At the same time, Stephan Holms and his plantation aristocrats, backed by the night riders of the Ku Klux Klan, act as villains, and their behavior is so repulsive that we begin to perceive a morality play structure, with noble heroes opposed by Simon Legree-like antagonists.

Unless we are predisposed to view history as a morality play—and, on the evidence of his best works, Fast does not see it this way—we may begin to doubt the historical veracity of the events depicted. Such doubt is a shame, for the historical underpinnings of *Freedom Road* are easily confirmed, and Fast is correct in his short afterword, where he states that the memory of black-white cooperation was expunged as unhelpful to some powers that be. (We might compare the invisibility of black soldiers in every war since the American Revolution or the lack of any dark-faced cowboys in the myths of the Old West; only recently have these historical omissions been partly corrected.) Unfortunately, the protest novel conventions of emotionally satisfying heroes and villains give little credibility to the more neutrally depicted version of the past given in good historical novels.

Freedom Road is also, oddly enough, a coming-of-age novel. Gideon is thirty-six at the start of the book, far too old for a youthful adolescent discovering the complexity, wonder, and finally the deceit of the larger world, yet that is exactly what happens. Slavery enforced a childlike existence, robbing adults of their human right of choice. Gideon's movement from innocent acceptance of the social world of Charleston to his cynical, worldly wise doubts about President Grant's motives is the conventional change we expect in the maturation novel.

KEY CHARACTERS

In a sense, *Freedom Road* is Gideon's story and Gideon's alone. As with *Citizen Tom Paine* and many of Fast's other historical novels, the focus is on a central character who remains on the main stage as minor characters pass on and off; here, however, unlike Paine, the central character is fictional in a real or historical setting, like Adam in *April Morning* or Dan in *The Immigrants*. The fictional Gideon may well represent thousands of former slaves all over the South who pulled themselves upward when the opportunity presented itself, but in this novel he is the center of all action, and his presence overwhelms most of the other characters. He is a large man, "built like a bull, heavy in the shoulders, narrow in the waist, lean in the legs"; yet he is not like a bull in his actions, never using his size or his muscles to gain his way. Gideon has little time for sayings or proverbs or other received notions. He is distinctly his own man, and as a result the people around him turn to him for advice and guidance. He might move slowly, in both his physical movements and his thinking, but he can also move quickly when he is sure of what he is doing: "When he had an idea, he turned it over and over, but when he had it at last, it was his" (*Freedom Road*, pp. 7–8).

Gideon is far more than physical presence and powerful will; in style he is like Frederick Douglass, a leader whose works he reads in the book. He is grave, dignified, serious. If a movie version had ever come to be, James Earl Jones would have been a perfect Gideon. (No film deal ever materialized; a television miniseries was made but received poor reviews, apparently deservedly.) Gideon's capacity for leadership, the quality seen in him almost immediately by Cardozo, involves his patience, his ability to see clearly and completely, and his capacity for change. This last characteristic is painful, for he loses the emotional depth of his relationship to his wife and finds that being a leader is a lonely business.

Gideon is set off against Stephan Holms, a far less satisfactory character. Fast works to give him depth, providing him with a mother who is far more of a racist than he is, and allowing Holms to argue for pure Realpolitik, the pursuit of cynical self-and-class interest, as opposed to the idealism Gideon espouses. Holms can even be charming in a reptilian way, admitting with barefaced honesty the most evil machinations against Gideon and his people. At the end, expressing a kind of *übermensch*/superman philosophy, he in effect offers Gideon a job leading his followers in the directions favored by the plantation owners. Accepting Gideon as an equal, he is no racist, only a southern fascist.

Other characters are also set off against Gideon. His wife, Rachel, remains at Carwell, representing the static life Gideon rejects. His son Marcus also stays at home, while his other son Jeff, a courageous spirit like Gideon, becomes a medical doctor in Glasgow, one of the few people of color in Scotland. Abner Lait is the white racist neighbor who comes into Gideon's orbit and joins the mixed race community. Anderson Clay's hill country roots strike a sharp contrast to Gideon's African American culture, enforcing Fast's point that a multiethnic coalition had been formed around shared economic interests. Francis Cardozo of Charleston and Isaac Went of Boston are interesting portraits of enlightened men of influence. Cardozo is half Jewish, a free man of color who is cautious and moderate yet deeply committed to both change and Gideon, whom he perceives as a true leader. In contrast, Went is a wealthy banker of abolitionist stock who knew the poet Emerson and John Brown before Harper's Ferry. He too comes to support Gideon.

Yet it is perhaps just this attractiveness as a character that is Gideon's weak point. At the end of the book Hannibal Washington in the midst of praising him tells Gideon he has his faults, "God knows," but we as readers never see any. A Gideon alienated from his wife, contemplating an affair with a northern woman who understands him; a Gideon tempted however briefly by money or power; a Gideon moody and angry at his followers, sulking like Achilles in his tent: any of these Gideons would have helped to humanize the character by giving him recognizable weakness. Stephan Holms could have used a touch of Gideon, and Gideon would have profited by a small measure of Holms's bitterness.

THEMATIC ISSUES

The Importance of Literacy

Fast's courage in *Freedom Road*—and surely the word is justified for such an original choice of protagonist—lay in putting himself in the shoes of a freed slave rather than in the more familiar boots of a soldier, an ideologue, a politician, all of whom Fast had treated in previous work. Gideon Jackson was a courageous imaginative leap for Fast, for although it is a writer's business to see the world through the mind's eye of very different characters from himself, a suddenly freed slave in the rural South in the previous century is a daunting point of view to assume. Though the story is told in the third person rather than the first, it is an omniscient third person; we see through Gideon's eyes, and hear his thoughts and doubts. And what a view that is! As Father Walter Ong, the psychologist and expert on literacy, has pointed out, there may be no divide greater than than between literate and nonliterate people, humans living the freedom of the imaginative and symbolic life provided by books and print, and those tied to the here and now by their inability to decode the ciphers of written language. And while Gideon is literate— barely, for he can only laboriously work his way through simple prose at the beginning of the book—he has virtually no abstract vocabulary and no experience weighing and comparing and evaluating one piece of writing against another, the scandal-mongering hate sheets put out by the white establishment having the same claim to authority for him as that of more respectable newspapers and printed works. It is not only Gideon's near illiteracy that holds him back, of course, but also his limited experience, having spent nearly his entire life as a peasant in the immediate confines of Carwell Plantation. This limited world is constricted even further by the intentional ignorance fostered by the white aristocrats, for slaves unaware of the outside world are slaves unaffected by movements for reform and freedom.

Human Perfectibility

In spite of the difficulty of creating a mental landscape for Gideon Jackson, one credibly simple and innocent yet also complex enough to give him dignity and the reader interest in his fate, it is easy to see why Fast might be intrigued by the problem he set himself. At this point in his life he was becoming increasingly interested in socialist thought, and at the beginning of the book Gideon is a test case for human perfectibility, an ideal subject for an experiment in the controlled-laboratory environment of fiction: can Gideon learn enough and credibly transform himself into a statesman? Can the almost blank tablet of the mind, the tabula rasa philosophers believe is written upon by experience, become a rich and complex text?

The issue is not simply an academic one, for the failure of Reconstruction has, in the popular mythology of the white South, often been blamed on the failure of the former slaves to rise to the heights needed for self-government, and, in fact, the whole socialist ideal requires the transformation of the ordinary man and woman, whether factory laborer or peasant, into a self-controlling, self-abnegating individual.

The Role of Environment

This is the transformation Gideon makes. From a farm worker valued simply for his muscle, a large, silent man living with wife and children in a primitive shack who is highly unsure of what voting means, he becomes a man of thought, applying his knowledge to practical and theoretical situations. He is only "two summers away from slavery," but he is no longer a prisoner of ignorance:

> They might have argued the question [of how to remove the stumps] half the day, had not Gideon seized upon an inspiration and suggested that they have a vote. Even as he said it, he was not sure it would work, not certain of the application of so miraculous a principle to a work-a-day occupation like cutting wood. But the idea caught hold [and even though] the mechanics . . . [were] new and revolutionary . . . in the end, the principle was applied and it worked. (21)

Such scenes are touching and affecting, especially since not all the former slaves can make the transition with ease. Fast makes us feels the constricting nature of a rural community untouched by the literary or the urban world. Gideon's son Jeff at fifteen is "chafing" and struggling to be free of the limits imposed by his environment.

> In this little community, where no one could read or write with any facility, where there was never a newspaper, time became the elastic, primitive thing it had been many thousands of years before. Not even a clock; the sun swung overhead, a big orange timepiece, and the slow parade of the seasons made an easy calendar. Jeff's memory of the time before the war was blurred and uncertain. The constant talk about the difference between freedom and slavery made little impression upon him; . . . all his young boyhood had been chaos. (23)

Human memory is short without texts, and new generations constantly push aside the verities of their elders. Gideon, though he has come out of the "Carolina back country, out of slavery, out of darkness" (56–57), begins his way along the literal and figurative "freedom road" to the city. Cardozo even envies the freed slave, for he sees him, correctly, as the hope of the South.

It is not only Gideon who changes. At the convention, poor whites, long the victims of the aristocratic landowners in the South, find common cause with freed slaves, and, ironically, together they make progress because they are naive and unaware of what is possible and permitted. They are starting from scratch, and the fictional convention, like the real one after the war, abolishes dueling, does away with imprisonment for debt, and almost gives the vote to women. (The delegates back away nervously when they realize the radical nature of this proposal; they do, however, institute divorce and protection of women's property rights.) The great experiment is beginning to pay off, as new alliances of poor blacks and whites form. Gideon almost memorizes the U.S. Constitution, and other delegates find new commitments to education and literacy.

Revolutions Consuming Their Practitioners

If the theme of human perfectibility is inspiring and hopeful, the novel's other major theme is not. Revolutions consume their makers, and the "revolt" against slavery in the South is no different. Isaac Went's nostalgia for the Revolutionary War puts Gideon's situation in historical perspective:

> And we did great things . . . in our meeting houses, democracy became a thing that lived and breathed. The old prophets walked with us, and in the Revolution our farmers and fishermen fought with a living, just God peering over their shoulders. That's all forgotten now, isn't it? (141)

The Civil War, like the new mixed-race society of the oppressed in the South, was also a brief coalition of citizen-soldiers that lit a conflagration illuminating the world but that could not be sustained: this rapid demise of revolutionary fervor is Fast's repeated theme throughout his protest novels. Curiously, Fast has relatively little to say about the Civil War itself. However, *Freedom Road* looks on the Reconstruction period in South Carolina as a brief flare-up of freedom, inspired by the American Revolution, the Civil War, and the Constitution, but burning itself out quickly as the planter class, maneuvering for a quick pull-out of northern troops, uses the Ku Klux Klan to push the black population back into another kind of slavery. Gideon tells Went that three forces can stop a return to the past: continued voting rights, education of the poor blacks and whites, and land reform. These three forces could combine to form the literate, informed citizen-farmers so dear to Fast's thinking, farmers who will no more stand for oppression by landed gentry than did their predecessors at Lexington and Concord. Went provides Gideon with money to help buy Carwell and divide it up among its former slaves, but the attempt will prove too little, too late.

Gideon and his people vow to fight on, however, and in the apocalyptic ending, with Carwell under attack by Klan artillery, we see how Gideon fits into Fast's pantheon of heroes. Gideon's wife whispers to him that he is a good man. He answers that he is a "makeshift," that it is the strength of the people who could take a former slave and teach him to transform himself, to become a leader. Some day there will be people who will know what to do about such things as Klan attacks, and who will be able to teach people to work together, to build, and to keep what is built from being burned down. Gideon is a figure like Spartacus, a man arising out of the people, serving them without thought of personal profit, and staving off the forces of darkness as long as is possible. People are not perfectible, but individuals can surpass their backgrounds and transform themselves in service to their fellows. Gideon becomes a true statesman, a leader in every sense of the word.

ALTERNATIVE READING: A DECONSTRUCTIONIST INTERPRETATION

Freedom Road lends itself readily to a deconstructionist interpretation. Deconstruction began with the work of linguist Ferdinand de Saussure and theoretician/critic Jacques Derrida, who postulated that it is the distinction or difference between words that gives them meaning. Polar opposites, especially those basic to Western thought, create verbal distinctions between conceptual categories—for example, being-nonbeing, hot-cold, truth-lie, light-dark, male-female. These linguistic ways of categorizing the world may be useful in stimulating an awareness of opposing forces, but they also inevitably value one pole over another, for example, *male* over *female*, as feminists point out.

Deconstruction challenges the assumption that a particular text or literary work has the final word since the process of construction-deconstruction of meaning is essentially endless. The critic first finds the point or moment when the oppositions or interior contradictions in a text become apparent. As Steven Lynn suggests, the deconstructionist must "locate an opposition, determine which member is privileged, then reverse and undermine the hierarchy," that is, the pole valued over the other ("A Passage into Critical Theory" 263) Since meanings are created by oppositions, both ends of the binary opposites require the other pole, and valuing one over the other is simply arbitrary. Examining texts in this manner allows the "deconstruction" of the original opposition.

It is not difficult to find the oppositions in *Freedom Road*, for the novel sets the freed black slaves of South Carolina and their white allies against the old establishment of planters and slave owners. The former slaves are clearly the valued pole in this opposition, but so much so that the people who oppose them, the white aristocracy, lose much credibility and dramatic force. In a sense, *Freedom Road* deconstructs itself by finding no fault in the side it values and by depicting the antagonists as monstrous to the point of inhumanity—not in the normal sense of the word (slave owners were clearly inhumane), but in the sense of not human and therefore not believable, a bipolar opposite. The reader who perceives this opposition might find the novel peopled with two very different kinds of characters, so different that they seem to belong in different worlds. What is fascinating about this perception is that it seems to have changed with time, for, a few reviewers aside, contemporary readers apparently read the novel without this sense of difference.

Freedom Road was extravagantly praised when it came out. Mainstream newspapers and news magazines such as the *New York Herald Tribune* and *Newsweek* used terms like "stirring . . . passionate" and "moving . . . terrifying . . . timely" (quoted in *Being Red* 84–85.) Regarding the book from the perspective of 1944, *Newsweek* was particularly effusive: "No other novel about race relations carries the strength of characterization, historical setting, and moving honesty of *Freedom Road*. Howard Fast has written a terrifying book, as timely as headlines describing our latter-day battle for freedom." Leading black newspapers liked it, as did W. E. B. Du Bois, the renowned African American leader. The *San Francisco Chronicle* called it "powerful . . . persuasive . . . nobly wrathful" (*Being Red* 84). Eleanor Roosevelt even devoted a column to it. Yet commentators since then have raised the objection that Gideon and his freed slaves are simply too heroic, while Holms and the aristocrats are too evil for full belief.

As Fast says, with admirable insight and honesty about the critical reaction, "Perhaps it was . . . the time" (*Being Red* 84). Published in 1944, in the waning years of America's great patriotic war, the novel, dedicated to "the men and women, black and white, yellow and brown, who have laid down their lives in the struggle against fascism," was clearly read then as an analogue to the world war described in every newspaper and radio news show, in every movie newsreel and news magazine. Fast shapes Stephan Holms not as a racist but as a Nietzschean superman, a Nazi-like fascist who offers to rule with Gideon over the weakly democratic and egalitarian. The equation of plantation aristocrats with fascists has not survived the time, and we now wish for a more humanly frail Gideon and a more humanized Holms.

Ironically, the sensitivity of modern readers to tendentious spins on history may well derive from the acknowledged success of Goebbels, Hitler's propaganda minister, in convincing a large, well-educated, and sophisticated population that the unspeakable evil of the Hitler years was in fact normal. The modern sensibility looks askance at human nature, expecting to find in our literary figures the same faults we see in our neighbors, and perhaps even in ourselves. *Freedom Road* deconstructed thus elucidates a paradigm shift—a complete change in philosophical framework—in how people conceive human nature. We no longer value morality play–like opposition between good and evil, and *Freedom Road* has suffered from this shift.

Yet the fact that each age reads through its own particular spectacles in no way invalidates *Freedom Road* as a highly successful book, and it can be read not simply as a 1930s-or 1940s-style protest novel but rather as an exposé in the best American tradition of Sinclair Lewis. As such, it also shares much with the revisionist movement of the last decades of the twentieth century, a movement whose own urge to deconstruct accepted views has so affected the modern sensibility. Fast points out that we have ignored the viewpoint of the successful black legislators and statesmen of the Reconstruction period, just as we have ignored so many other contributions by black Americans. What is remarkable is that he wrote this book in the 1940s, long before such a message was acceptable, let alone fashionable. Whether we agree the enemy is fascism or something else, the novel's analysis of history remains relevant for modern readers, just as the capacity of Gideon Jackson for self-education and self-transformation should make us examine our assumptions about human nature.

Spartacus
(1951)

> Each generation relives the moral dilemma and agony of a man who
> dies for other men.
>
> —Howard Fast, *Counterpoint*

Spartacus is the only one of Fast's novels to have been made into a major
film, a blockbuster, and appropriately enough for an important novel,
the film was a successful one. (It is still widely available on video, distributed by MCA Home Video.) The winner of four Academy Awards,
the film, released in 1960, was directed by the distinguished Stanley Kubrick and starred Kirk Douglas as Spartacus, Jean Simmons as Varinia,
Laurence Olivier as Crassus, and Peter Ustinov as Batiatus. Dalton
Trumbo wrote the screenplay, though Fast worked on it without a film
credit. Fast remembers the production as troubled, with power struggles
taking place between Douglas and Kubrick. Fast found both Kubrick and
Ustinov fellow sufferers at the hands of the imperious Kirk Douglas, who
at one point threatened to leave the picture if Kubrick were not fired.
Fast says he let Douglas think that he, Fast, very much wanted Kubrick
fired, and since Douglas hated Fast even more than Kubrick and would
go to any lengths to oppose the writer, this protected Kubrick's directing
job from the egotistical star's ultimatum. In spite of such gamesmanship,

the film, though a pale version of the book, managed to capture some of the spirit of its original and is well worth seeing.

The troubles on the film set were only the last of continual controversies surrounding the book. Fast had come across Spartacus while he was in prison in West Virginia, wondering why Rosa Luxemburg had named her socialist organization the Spartacists. Later, he read up on the historical figure in a history of ancient working people entitled *The Ancient Lowly*. A frenetic study of Latin and exhaustive research followed, and in 1951 the manuscript was finally finished, only to be rejected by Little, Brown even though the reader's report called it "a fine novel." Eventually, Fast, still blacklisted and unable to find a publisher, published it himself.

Overcoming enormous difficulties, Fast learned, as had Mark Twain before him, that self-publication is a hazardous enterprise, but the book came out and Fast printed 48,000 within three months. Although reviews were often hostile, with even the *New York Times* reviewer calling it "dreary," the book was a commercial success. It has remained, with *Citizen Tom Paine* and *Freedom Road*, among Fast's best-known works. Kubrick's film no doubt brought many readers back to the novel, but its greatest lasting appeal lies in the fascination of the slave revolt and in Fast's excellent portrait of Roman culture and mores.

PLOT DEVELOPMENT: SLAVE REVOLT

The novel begins with a journey by Caius Crassus, a young and decadent nobleman, along the Appian Way from Rome to Capua in 71 B.C. He is accompanied by Helena, his sister, and her friend Claudia. The road is lined with 6,472 crucified slaves, a punishment for the slave rebellion led by Spartacus. They stop at the Villa Salaria, a huge factory farm, or latifundium run on slave labor, owned by Antonius Caius, a distant relative. Also staying at the farm are Lentelus Gracchus, a successful Roman politician from the working classes, Licinius Crassus, an aristocratic general who had defeated Spartacus in the third of the Servile Wars (slave uprisings), and the famous Roman orator Marcus Tullius Cicero.

The thousands of crucifixions occasion some discussion among the guests at the latifundium, with Cicero quoted as arguing that the slaves are only "mute instruments" of their betters, incapable of feeling or higher thought. The conversation keeps returning to Spartacus and slavery, with Crassus, the victorious general, admitting to curiosity about the real nature of his defeated opponent, and the other guests revealing a profound, if only semiarticulated, unease at living in a society so dependent on forced labor.

Caius, the young traveler, admits to having seen Spartacus fight at a school for gladiators in Capua, and Crassus, the general, tells him of interviewing the owner of the school, Lentulus Batiatus, when Crassus was trying to defeat the mysterious revolutionary slave by collecting all possible information about him. At a roadside military encampment, he learns from Batiatus that Spartacus was from Thrace, one of the Greek city-states, and had been sold as a slave in Athens to work in an Egyptian gold mine. Batiatus had bought Spartacus from the mine because of his toughness, his refusal to die. At the gladiatorial school in Capua, he gives Spartacus a German serving woman, Varinia, as a joke, calling her Spartacus's wife.

In a flashback, Caius remembers his earlier trip to Capua, when he saw Spartacus fight at Batiatus's gladiatorial school. The narrative switches to Varinia and Spartacus, and we learn of their love. In a contrasting scene, we see Caius and his decadent Roman lover and a married couple preparing to see two pairs of gladiators fight to the death for their private amusement; the woman asks that they fight nude. David, a Jew, is matched against a Thracian in the first pair; he kills the Thracian but with insufficient brutality to suit the four Roman spectators. Spartacus is matched by Batiatus against an Ethiopian in the second pair, but the African refuses to fight his comrade; he attacks the Romans but is killed by guards.

The flashback ends and the action moves four years later to the Villa Salaria, where Cicero sleeps with Helena, and they discuss the Servile Wars, Spartacus, and Roman dependence on and obsession with slaves. Then the action shifts back again to Spartacus and Varinia at Batiatus's gladiatorial school in Capua; he has been so moved by the sacrifice of his Ethiopian colleague that he vows never to fight another gladiator. This necessitates a revolt, for he would be executed for refusing to fight. The other gladiators follow him willingly, and they overwhelm their guards and then the garrison of Roman soldiers stationed nearby as a precaution. The gladiators develop the fighting strategy that they use throughout the Servile Wars: they stay just out of reach of the heavily armed Roman forces, darting in and out, in what today would be called guerrilla attacks. While the Romans enjoy the best spears and defensive armor in the world, they are weighted down and relatively helpless if not challenged with a frontal attack; the slaves make use of their agility and cunning, fighting with passion against the mechanical style of the legions. Spartacus vows to destroy Rome, if necessary, and continues his march through the countryside near Pompeii and Mount Vesuvius, picking up escaped slaves as he moves on.

The scene moves forward in time to the group at the Villa Salaria, with the focus now on Gracchus, the politician. We learn that he is the Roman equivalent of a ward heeler, or local politician, a working-class politico who has moved up to the Roman Senate through cunning, a mastery of political patronage, and, in his younger days, survival learned in rough-and-tumble street fighting between competing gangs. Gracchus is enormously fat and is looked down on by the smug aristocrats who surround him, but he is also cynically wise and free of self-deception; we learn he had opposed sending the City Cohort, the dapper soldiers who defend the city, against Spartacus's slave army, and indeed the Thracian smashes the pride of Rome. Through Gracchus's reminiscences about the Servile Wars, we learn of the many battles won by the slaves over supposedly superior Roman legions. When Gracchus and Crassus engage in conversation, we find out about the final battle in which the general defeated Spartacus, about the Thracian's death, and about Varinia's having been sold as a slave in Rome.

In the next section, Crassus and Caius, still accompanied by his sister Helena and her friend Claudia, move on toward Capua. Crassus is treated as a hero there for ending the Servile Wars, which had started in the city with Spartacus's escape, and he makes love to Helena in Batiatus's gladiatorial school, now abandoned. But Crassus is really far more interested in a crucified slave outside the city gates: the Jew, David, who is still barely alive, the last of the rebellious slaves to die. Crassus is struck by the irony of this discovery but feels no sense of justice or revenge. The point of view now shifts to the dying David, and we learn of the visions and feelings of the crucified gladiator, as well as of his memories of his beloved Spartacus, whom he has always protected.

The scene shifts back to Cicero and Gracchus, leaving the Villa Salaria on their way back to Rome (the time is supposed to be the same as when Crassus and Caius's party left on their way to Capua). They discuss their competing visions of Rome. Gracchus meets his old friend Flavius Marcus, a failed ward heeler very like an unsuccessful version of Gracchus himself. Flavius shows up at Gracchus's Roman house, and Gracchus sets him the task of finding Varinia and buying her, no matter the price. Days later Flavius returns with the news that Crassus has bought Varinia and her infant son, Spartacus's child, and is trying to make her his willing mistress: he is in love with her, and conquering her resistance would represent a final victory over his now dead enemy. Gracchus meets Crassus in the Roman baths and tries to buy Varinia directly but is rejected. Spending a large part of his fortune, Gracchus arranges for Flavius to kidnap Varinia, saying he loves her. She is brought to his house with her child and she sits up with Gracchus through the night, after which Flavius returns with a chariot and he and Varinia depart for the north. Gracchus frees his slaves and commits suicide by falling on his sword. The novel ends with Flavius and Varinia leaving Roman territory and her finding refuge in a Gaulish woodland village in sight of the Alps. Varinia's son eventually becomes a guerrilla fighter against Roman tax collectors, repeating to his own children the tales and legends of his father, whose name would be remembered "so long as men labored, and other men took and used the fruit of those who labored" (*Spartacus* 363). Rome would one day be torn down, by slaves and peasants and free barbarians.

STRUCTURE

As the plot summary indicates, the narrative structure of *Spartacus* is complex and sophisticated, perhaps the most difficult of the Fast novels. It is also highly cinematic, with quick cutting between scenes, extensive use of flashbacks, heavy reliance on dialogue, and minutely described settings. The one element that is not cinematic is the shifting point of view; we see events through the eyes of at least a half-dozen major characters and a number of minor ones. The result is complicated to describe, especially given the large number of characters, but easy to follow when read, for the point-of-view shifts and scene cuts are clearly signaled and logically arranged.

The book is divided into eight parts, each subdivided into sections or scenes. Almost all the parts begin on the Appian Way, the road between Rome and Capua that has been lined with crucified rebel slaves. The travelers who make up the key characters have all collected at the Villa Salaria, an enormous latifundium owned by a rich Roman, either on their way to Capua, the resort town where the slave revolt began four years earlier, or back to Rome.

If, in the old Roman saying, all roads lead to Rome, here all the narrative paths lead back to the initial meeting at the latifundium, for even when Crassus and the youths leave for Capua and Gracchus and Cicero return to Rome, conversations help us recall characters met earlier. Appropriately, the last section, Part Eight, breaks the pattern, for in it Varinia, Spartacus's wife, leaves Rome forever on a northern route, taking increasingly less-well-made roads until she is literally off the beaten track and is safe from the influence of Rome. The Roman cultural ways (their folkways) and literal highways thus become potent double symbols, whether of the gross cruelty of the crucifixions along the Appian Way or of the brutal efficiency that bound the world together into a huge mechanism; however, in creating this interlocking mechanism Rome denied the human values that initially motivated its attempt to unify the world. The primary theme throughout the novel, and the focus of the characters' discussions, is what "way" Rome should take about slavery. Ironically, these discussions take place as characters are carried on litters by slaves, are served food by slaves at roadside taverns, see slave labor at work on plantations, and, most significantly, pass slaves crucified along the edge of the road.

A sense of the narrative complexity can be seen by listing how each part begins:

Part	Characters and Focus	Number of Scenes
One	Caius with Helena and Claudia	13
	Location: Appian Way	
Two	Crassus and Batiatus, flashbacks	5
	Location: Villa Salaria	
Three	Caius's first visit to Capua, gladiators, flashbacks	10
	Location: Villa Salaria	
Four	Cicero with Helena, Servile Wars	11
	Location: Villa Salaria	
Five	Gracchus with others, flashbacks	7
	Location: Villa Salaria	
Six	Crassus and Caius to Capua, crucifixion of David	10
	Location: Appian Way, Capua	
Seven	Cicero and Gracchus to Rome	11
	Location: Appian Way	

| Eight | Varinia's escape to Gaul | 2 |

Location: roads north of Rome

The sixty-nine scenes include half a dozen main characters and at least a dozen others who figure in the action. Keeping them all clearly identified for the reader—as Fast does—is a major accomplishment.

In sum, the structure of *Spartacus* follows the movement of characters back and forth on the main highway between Rome and Capua after the crucifixion of the almost sixty-five hundred slaves following a failed revolt. The close description of the characters' behavior and the sights and cultural practices along the Appian Way thus become a commentary on Roman cruelty, Roman degradation of humanity, and Roman corruption and decadence.

GENERIC CONVENTIONS

Spartacus is familiar territory for Fast, an amalgam of the protest novel he found so congenial to his political and emotional outlook and the historical novel that had given him such success as a young writer. Obviously, the two genres do not always coexist easily, since the powerful emotions associated with the protest novel lead toward reader-character identification for full effect and often toward an allegorical working out of ideas if solutions are proposed. The emotional technique of identification and the intellectual one of allegory, with characters standing for clearly limited ideas, may jibe poorly with the raw events of history, which may be meaningless as recorded or may only accidentally form themselves into a neatly moral plot.

The link between protest and history in *Spartacus*, presumably the element that attracted Fast to the somewhat obscure Servile Wars in the first place (Spartacus and the wars get only summary treatment in most encyclopedias and histories), is exposé: the facts of the revolts have been buried and pushed to the background in favor of more benign views of Rome because of intellectual and social biases in our own time. In other words, revolutionaries get little real respect from the academic historians; revolt history poses potential challenges to present interests and the status quo. (Fast makes much the same argument in his Revolutionary War book *The Proud and the Free* and in *Freedom Road*.) In this way the exposé becomes the revisionist novel, which leads smoothly into a protest against the established view.

The history in *Spartacus* effectively exposes the unsightly underside of Rome. Most modern readers are vaguely familiar with popular culture versions of gladiatorial combat, but such depictions are usually sanitized. (In *The Legacy*, Barbara Lavette, visiting Pompeii, quotes George Bernard Shaw's statement that the gladiators did not kill each other and is pointedly corrected by her Italian travel companion [79].) Here, we see a different picture: "The Thracian was hamstrung, cut across face, hands, body and legs, and bleeding his life into the soggy spreading blot of the sand beneath his feet" (*Spartacus* 121). Whereas most fictional battle scenes end with death, Fast's frequently continue to show us what happens to the bodies, an obvious question but one frequently passed over: "the soldiers whipped the donkey . . . so that he cantered around the arena at a sharp trot, dragging the bloody, brain-dripping corpse after him" (122). "Finally, the bloodbirds come, *avis sanguinaria*, the dainty little birds of spotted yellow who pecked so voraciously at the stained sand, filling their gullets" (126). As is always true in Fast's work, the descriptions of bloody work are unsparing and unflinching, never allowing the reader to gloss over the real effects of violence. *This* is what Romans watched for entertainment, it says, not the romanticized and sanitized Hollywood chariot races.

Crucifixion is another example of the Roman fascination with suffering and cruelty. For all its symbolic value in Christianity, descriptions of Christ's passion seldom go beyond words like *agony* and *torment*. In *Spartacus*, the reader becomes a connoisseur of crucifixion, as we see David die throughout sixty pages of text (the crucified could linger for up to four days), hear the testimony of a crucified slave brought back from death by a last-minute pardon, and learn of the theory and practice of this curious method of execution. It is difficult to imagine a sensitive reader regarding Rome in quite the same way after reading *Spartacus*.

If the measure of a historical novel is the quantity of its research, *Spartacus* almost overwhelms at times. How were perfumes manufactured at Capua in 71 B.C., by whom, and under what conditions? We find out in detail. What was the motion and feel of a litter moving along the Appian Way in the spring sunshine, and how many miles were the litter bearers good for? Where did the bearers go when the travel party stopped? We are told. As always, there is Fast's fascination with military uniform and procedure, and we learn what a legionnaire wore and how the Rome City cohort, the elite dress-soldiers who put down riots in the Eternal

City but did little real marching and fighting, affected stylish greaves, or leg armor, that wore holes in their legs when they actually had to move across country. Nor are these details simple window dressing; some of these privileged soldiers had over a dozen female slaves installed in their Rome tenement apartments and sold the children they produced with these women on the slave market at age six or so. What detail could be more telling about the casual brutality of the Roman system, the Roman "way"? The details of clothing and food as well (there are elaborate descriptions of food) build the moral case against the slave system. (Slaves eat barley porridge laced with pieces of pork fat, and are lucky to get it.)

Fast admits in *Being Red* that his self-education included no Latin, so he had to badger a high school Latin teacher acquaintance for quick lessons and even had poet Louis Untermeyer instruct him in the proper meter to be used for the lullaby Varinia sings to her baby. Studying Latin "furiously," Fast pushed through classical encyclopedias and other reference works to absorb the taste and feel of ancient Rome, but as a communist he was denied a passport to visit Italy, seeing his settings only long after the book was printed. (A middle-aged Barbara Lavette prowls Pompeii in *The Legacy*, with feelings of sadness and nostalgia.) Just as the evocation of Roman cruelty changes the reader's perception of Rome, so Fast's historical research instructs and clarifies: the novel will long be read by students of the period simply for its creation of a detailed and credible milieu.

KEY CHARACTERS

Fast's daring narrative method allows us to meet and cope with a large cast of very different characters, but implicit in it is a problem that weakens some of the impact of the book. Critics ridiculed the comic book characterizations of *Spartacus*, but the criticism is unfair, for the players, and especially Gracchus and Crassus, are sharply drawn and convincing, with quirks and unpredictable actions that are the antithesis of the simplistic comic book style. What does load the book down is the sheer number of characters, with the effect, for example, of leaving Spartacus and Varinia somewhat generalized. The slave and his wife are supposed to be simple people, and the book is supposed to be about the effect of slavery on Roman slave owners rather than just on slaves themselves, but the number of players on stage and the amount of action necessary allow little time for the complications and contradictions that would give the main characters continuous life, and in fact we do need to see them more. Apart from three good battle scenes, the four-year Servile War remains abstract and distant, an offstage action reported by others.

Other examples of this crowded arena are the three young Romans at the latifundium: Caius, Helena, his sister, and Claudia, her friend. Each is drawn sharply and well, and their placement at the opening of the book suggests that they will serve a significant narrative purpose, but in fact they only become bedmates for other characters, and Claudia, who seems to be based on a famous prostitute, simply disappears. Caius, who is the most fully realized character in this group, is spoiled and sulky, and his clear promiscuity defines the sexual morality of upper-class Rome. He goes to bed with Crassus, but this one-night stand goes nowhere in terms of plot. Claudia too sleeps with Crassus but has no apparent effect on his behavior as a character.

Another example of a character who is well drawn but drops out of the plot is Batiatus. The slave-school owner is important for reasons of exposition but has little impact on the struggle between the combatants once the background story of Spartacus has been told. Cicero is interesting and important for historical reasons and is a lively conversationalist in the book but takes no part in the final resolution. Antonius Caius and his wife, Julia, own the Villa Salaria but are otherwise irrelevant in terms of plot. We sense the spirit of Rome from these characters, of course, but they take little part in the main action, only filling out the crowd and conveying the unease that Fast wants us to perceive among aristocratic Romans. Another example, on the opposite side of the conflict, is the Jewish gladiator David, who is in the book to show loyalty to Spartacus and to allow us to see a crucifixion through the eyes of someone we have had sympathy for, since Spartacus, the most logical candidate for this death, has died in battle.

Spartacus presents splendid tableaux, in other words, but like any overly ambitious epic film, it sometimes gives us too many characters to deal with. The key characters are in fact few: Gracchus, Crassus, Spartacus, and Varinia. Their battle for primacy—for the soul of Rome, really—can be reduced to a simple change in relationships: during the Servile War, Gracchus and Crassus versus Spartacus, and at the end of the book, Gracchus and Varinia versus Crassus. The shift in relationships occurs because Gracchus, whom we have seen almost exclusively among patrician Romans, remembers his roots.

Gracchus is a fascinating portrait of a type familiar in every large city, the ward heeler. He is a self-made man risen from street fighting in gangs to political sparring with words, ideas, and theatrics. Through cunning and endurance, he has risen to the height of Roman society, to the Senate, where his correct reading of the danger posed by Spartacus gives him clout and respect. Though he has enriched himself in his movement upward, he retains a measure of integrity and honor. He cooperates with Crassus to destroy Spartacus, providing the means to create a force strong enough to smash the rebel, just as he lends his intelligence to the powers that be of his beloved Rome. His motivation is the protection of his city, but he has confused his own personal advancement with the well-being of Rome and the interests of the common folk with those of the patricians. His meditations lead him to understand that Spartacus is "all that they [the patricians] were not" (233) and that the Roman masters had turned over to the slaves all that they held sacred: the old virtues of industry, discipline, frugality, and mercy. With Spartacus dead, Gracchus develops an intellectual love of Varinia and a regained self-respect when he manages her escape, frees his slaves, and dies in the ancient, honorable way, by falling on his sword.

Gracchus is treated with a measure of contempt by the patricians he serves, for he is still a lower-class vulgarian. Crassus, who is lean and handsome in contrast to Gracchus's grossness, defines all the other opposite characteristics as well: patrician reserve, arrogant confidence, a sense of entitlement. Crassus is not particularly intelligent but is sure of who he is and what is owed to him, enjoying, as is typical in Fast's portrait of upper-class characters, the unassailable advantage of a privileged upbringing. He overcomes Spartacus's army by sheer force rather than cunning. Crassus has few real passions but rather a cruel decadence, pawing the female masseuse in front of Caius without shame and almost raping Helena in the abandoned gladiatorial school in Capua. Crassus's motivation is a patrician identification of Roman interests as identical to his own, but his victory over Spartacus is incomplete without Varinia's voluntary obeisance. It is not enough to triumph through force: her willing capitulation to his desires will be proof of his absolute correctness. He is thus left frustrated, his triumph spoiled.

The other important characters are, of course, Spartacus and Varinia. Spartacus is a pure example of slavery since he is the son and grandson of slaves. A well-written description of Spartacus's life in the mines in the middle of the desert is a classic Fast set piece, a chilling evocation of brutality and endurance under conditions hard to conceive (the slave miners must subsist on half the ration of water required for survival;

they slowly waste away, with only the strongest adapting to the desert conditions). Spartacus's scenes in the gladiatorial school are also specific and well drawn, as Fast gives us the tastes, smells, and sounds of life in an institution devoted to quick and violent death. Unfortunately, the depiction of this life is mainly from an exterior perspective, with little dialogue justified or possible. If anything, we learn more about this cruel life from the reactions of the Roman spectators than from the gladiators themselves, and Spartacus himself is taciturn and somewhat mysterious. Varinia is womanly and loyal, but we see little of her interior life.

Thus though attractive and traced back to his origins, Spartacus remains somewhat abstract and generalized, as does Varinia. Perhaps goodness is harder to delineate than evil, or perhaps simplicity is less interesting dramatically than complexity; at any rate, the two lovers are never quite as interesting psychologically as Gracchus and Crassus. Dr. Johnson said of John Milton that England's greatest poet was of the devil's party but did not know it when he made Satan such a fascinating character in *Paradise Lost* and left God and his angels relatively uncompelling; the clever observation is applicable to any number of only partially successful attempts to delineate goodness. Here, Spartacus is a man of few words but strong feelings, so we perceive a virtually mystical bond among him, Varinia, and his followers, but we also gain little insight into what makes him so effective where so many others have failed.

THEMATIC ISSUES

Roman Decadence

As Gracchus comes to see, Spartacus was all that the patricians were not, the Roman masters having turned over to the slaves all that they held sacred. Rome had been founded on the old agrarian virtues of *industria, disciplina, frugalitas,* and *clementia* (mercy or forgiveness)—virtues, as shown in *Citizen Tom Paine* and *April Morning,* that Fast considers the foundation of a decent society, one close to the land, simple, pure, uncontaminated by the corruption of labor and capital produced first by landed aristocracies and then by the industrial revolution. By the time of Spartacus, Rome has become a very large and complex society undergoing a sea change from traditional to modern.

Inevitably, analogies between Rome and the post–World War II United

States arise: both moving from nation-state republics to worldwide empires dominating other nations and multitudes of people; both enforcing a worldwide peace; both forcing small landholders off privately held family farms into factory farms (the latifundia of Rome, specializing in a few crops tended by slaves; the huge corporate farms of California's San Fernando Valley, where labor was provided by the dispossessed, like John Steinbeck's Joad family in *The Grapes of Wrath* or Mexican migrant labor); both societies supporting a growing number of layabouts permanently on the dole, interested only in bread and circuses. It is hazardous to push such analogies too hard, but it is after all slavery that is Fast's main interest in *Spartacus*, and it is wage slavery that constituted the Communist party's main charge against American society of the 1950s. U.S. workers lived one or two paychecks away from disaster, and while they were distracted by consumer goods, just as the Roman poor were entertained by public spectacles and gladiatorial contests, they had lost any real control over their own lives when they were forced from their farms and entered the factory system. In the Communist party's view, democracy was just an elaborate sham to create the illusion of power, which remained firmly in the hands of the aristocratic class, the large landholders, and the controllers of capital and industry. Most telling from the Fastian viewpoint is the disappearance of the old virtues of industry, discipline, frugality, and mercy. These simple characteristics define a good society, whether in Rome, in Revolutionary or post–Civil War America, in Judea, or elsewhere that Fast has written about. When they are denied and replaced by forced labor (which includes grossly overtaxed labor), the answer is the most famous set of words in the Marxist lexicon: "Workers, unite! You have nothing to lose but your chains!"

The Effects of Slavery

Spartacus is the literal slave (as opposed to the modern wage slave) in a society increasingly based on slavery. Slavery causes a society to become deeply corrupt, not only for the obvious reasons but also because decreasingly few Romans are competent at managing even simple tasks, let alone at feeling any elementary human emotion. We see in the behavior of the young people, Caius, Helena, and Claudia, and their elders a sexual and ethical decadence involving adultery, homosexuality, promiscuity, cruelty, and indifference to human suffering. All are consumed with the search for pleasure, but it is clear that none will find satisfaction. Even Crassus, the "richest man in Rome" and a successful general, cares little for the old patriotic virtues and can find little satisfaction in the pleasures of the flesh.

Rome is thus a nightmare society for Fast, and its analogues to U.S. society of the late 1940s and early 1950s made its relevance urgent. Americans too were losing their old verities in the sudden rush to empire after World War II and in the explosion of consumer wealth in that period. Fewer and fewer Americans lived on farms, industrial and farm factory work was increasing, and the working-class perspective and values that the Communist party represented were increasingly under attack. This historical context of the novel explains why the slave war was not simply a particularized revolt but rather Fast's contemporary cry for freedom and for the destruction of rigidity.

Agrarian Freedom

Spartacus and his followers live a free life, fighting continually, of course, but also existing untrammeled by possessions and property. They make their own law, which is simple: "whatever we take, we hold in common, and no man shall own anything but his weapons and his clothes" (166). They practice monogamy and respect women's rights. There is a conscious attempt to define themselves against Roman law and custom. Their future, though precarious, is based on honorable values: "It will be the way it was in the old times" (166).

This return to a past golden age of agrarian simplicity is Fast's consistent answer to the problems of modernity, capitalism, labor, and over-sophistication. However we categorize the politics of this answer, we can see why it might have disturbed his party line colleagues in the Communist party, for radical agrarian innocence fit uncomfortably in the matrix of socialism as it was practiced in the Soviet Union; the Russian collectivist factory farm had disturbing parallels to the Roman latifundia, as well as to the large plantations of the San Joaquin Valley. No matter the ideological line, Fast sees independence and self-control in small communal groups like those of the escaped slaves, not in capitalism or in the massive state that was Rome at the time of Spartacus.

ALTERNATIVE READING: A DECONSTRUCTIONIST INTERPRETATION

Deconstruction attempts to show the internal contradictions in a text, the way language and thought inevitably make the reader think of counter ideas that undercut the professed position of the work. (See chapter 4 for a full explanation.) Given Fast's involvement in Communist party politics at the time of the writing of *Spartacus* and his later acknowledgment of ambivalence about the party line, it is well worth asking if such counterforces are evident.

As it turns out, much of the work of deconstructing *Spartacus* was done by party ideologues themselves. Fast describes an amusing alternat ve reading of the novel in *Being Red*, one provided by a review in the *Daily Worker*, the Communist party newspaper for which Fast himself was a sometime columnist. The *Worker* objected to Gracchus's freeing of Varinia:

> What is intended here? Is this Goethe's idealistic vision of the Eternal Woman, leading us all, oppressor and oppressed, upward and on? . . . Can we imagine a Nazi pleading for the love of a Russian woman? . . . We get something very close to sexual reconciliation of the classes. . . . The incursion is felt here of the destructive influence of Freudian mystifications concerning the erotic as against the social basis of character. (quoted in *Being Red* 300)

Although he says that this attack at the end of two thousand words of praise "chilled his blood" with its insistence on ideological correctness, Fast himself seems somewhat bemused: should novelists clear happy endings with party cultural commissars? John Howard Lawson, the film worker and West Coast party chief, thought so, and he attacked *Spartacus* for its gladiatorial combat scenes, which supposedly demonstrated "an anti-human lust for brutality" (*Being Red* 300). Fast also reports in *The Naked God* that "the commissars" felt *Spartacus* was a study of "brutalism and sadism," contained "psychoanalytical words" such as *inner struggle*, and hated Gracchus, even though, for all his wealth and power, he never cuts himself off from the ordinary people of Rome and his own working-class heritage (*Being Red* 148, 152).

Putting aside the inflated prose of the *Daily Worker* review and tolerating for the moment the silliness of terming "inner struggle" as "psy-choanalytic," it may be useful to search for a kernel of insight among the chaff of Marxist rhetoric. Was Fast, consciously or unconsciously, truly balancing the individualistic values of the Western creative artist against the supposed collectivist theme of the novel? Giving the devil his due, the simultaneous infatuation of two Roman millionaires, Crassus and Gracchus, with a German slave woman they have never seen is an admitted stretch of credibility, however neatly it resolves their compe-tition. The thematic burden of the novel has been the reduction of hu-mans, and especially women, to utilitarian, less-than-human status. As noted earlier, privileged soldiers had a dozen female slaves installed in their Rome tenement apartments and sold the children they produced with these women. For Crassus and Gracchus to switch from this sort of casual treatment of people as cattle to regarding Varinia as romantic love object may not be "Goethe's idealistic vision of the Eternal Woman, lead-ing us all . . . upward," but it certainly justifies the term *idealism,* an ide-alism unprepared for in these two characters.

Too, Fast's descriptions of gladiatorial battle and war evoke sensations of exquisite cruelty, and it may be tempting to find a fascination with pain in a writer whose works consistently deplore human suffering. The Marxist critics, however, rather than truly deconstructing *Spartacus,* seem to be simply blaming the messenger for what historians acknowledge to be a Roman sensibility. Fast's battle scenes are always bloodily realistic and unromantically portrayed; here, the pornography of pain and suf-fering belongs to Fast's subject matter, not to the writer's approach. It seems that the cultural commissars took Fast to task for being too ro-mantic about Varinia's influence but not romantic enough about the glo-ries of battle and the nobility of a working-class politician like Gracchus.

A deconstructionist reading more in line with Fast's canon, then, is to see *Spartacus* as a romantic protest novel set against a grimly realistic historical account of Roman decadence and depravity. In straightforward narrative terms, the historical tableaux, though remembered with plea-sure, do not always fit together, and here Fast's party critics may have a point. One problem lies in the working out of the agenda of ideas, which may be too neat in an intellectual sense to give the satisfaction of seeing characters resolve issues in their own skin. Here, deconstruction must take second place to a recapitulation of character and concept.

The musings and experiences of Gracchus and Crassus at the latifun-dium and after lead each to desire closure about Spartacus. Naturally, they wish to put the Thracian gladiator out of their minds: he was a mortal enemy of the slave system that the Roman politician and general profit from but that they feel an uneasy, unacknowledged guilt about (in very different ways, of course: Gracchus organized the political effort to raise the army while Crassus led the actual fighting). The resolution of this Roman guilt is necessary for a moral conclusion to the book: Spartacus has been killed and the revolt put down, just as in Roman history, but if his uprising is to have literary meaning, then the Romans responsible, Gracchus and Crassus, must be moved emotionally and philosophically. Fast's solution is to have both men desire Varinia, each capturing her and trying to persuade her to love him as the winner in the battle against Spartacus. Might must be seen to make right, in other words, and only Varinia's free capitulation to her suitor would provide the validation of Roman ways that each man, in his imperial egotism, desires. Yet as Varinia accurately points out, she is a slave and is therefore not free to make any decision. This logic completely frustrates the rigid Crassus, but Gracchus, still in touch with the common man and the old Roman virtues, sets Varinia free and thereby achieves her gratitude and respect and the self-respect he desires.

These symbols work together as satisfactorily as an algebraic formula, but in the flesh and blood of Gracchus (and the less fleshy Crassus), they raise nagging questions and the suspicion of an ideological final resolution: would one, let alone two, millionaire Romans, each the holder of incredible power, desire the wife of a rebel slave they have defeated, a woman neither has seen before, herself a slave? The answer has to be no, not without a huge suspension of disbelief. In deconstructionist terms, the identification of oppositions that subvert each other makes perfect sense here: the raw, historical data (Roman brutality, the reduction of humans to livestock) are countered by the idealism inherent in the romantic/protest novel plot (Gracchus's and Crassus's love for Varinia, her escape, the struggle against Rome of her son by Spartacus). Linked in Fast's sensibility but in the text self-cancelling poles, they give weight to the complaints of the Marxist critics, although certainly not to their rhetorical flourishes.

In the 1960s Soviet film version of *Hamlet*, Hamlet is melancholy in part because socialism has not been invented yet (not for another 250 years), and here too we may be seeing in *Spartacus*'s ending an unsettling anachronism, a looking forward fondly to when times will be better: Spartacus's life will have meaning when Rome is gone and revolts against slavery have more chance of success. (The theme of premature revolt is common in Fast's political novels.) This is not to denigrate the ending, which with Varinia's escape reads better than the motivations for it would lead us to expect, a compliment to Fast's skill as a storyteller. However, the Marxist critics' readings do pinpoint a conflict common in Fast's earlier novels: a conflict between the protest novel's need to inspire hope and emotional uplift, and the historical novel's recounting of grim fact.

April Morning
(1961)

April Morning is as good a book as I have ever written, as nearly
perfect a book as I could hope to write. And I doubt whether I will
again equal the balance, the mood, of *April Morning*, and personally
I like it better than most of my work.

Howard Fast, Counterpoint

April Morning, first published in 1961, has gone through almost fifty editions in hardcover and has sold millions of paperback copies. Fast lists
it in his bibliography as a "book for young readers," and it is most
certainly a fine story for middle-school students—it is read in almost all
of the fifty state school systems—yet it is a tale for adults as well, a very
sophisticated portrait of the first day of the American Revolution and
the varying reactions to violence and the start of a new era. Of it Fast
says that generations of children "have taken from it a deep feeling of
what America is and how it came into being" (*Contemporary Authors
Autobiography Series* 185). *April Morning* partakes of many of the techniques and themes found in Fast's earlier books, but, possibly because it
came after the turmoil of his Communist party years, it has a quieter,
sweeter, almost nostalgic tone quite different from the earlier Revolutionary War books. Perhaps this is because *April Morning*'s narrator,
Adam Cooper, is only fifteen years old, but *Conceived in Liberty: A Novel
of Valley Forge* (1939) and *The Proud and the Free* (1950) both include young

men, initially in their teens, as central characters, and both indulge harsh, bitter sentiments about the war and their fates.

April Morning, in contrast, is characterized by moderation and balance. There is a virtually perfect relationship between literary character and research, with the sights and sounds of April 19, 1775, effectively integrated into the narrative. What Adam eats, drinks, wears, uses, says, thinks, and so on ring completely true, and become a touchstone for the character of Adam himself: we see that he *is* what his surroundings have made him, and we construct for ourselves mental images that duplicate his world.

Characteristic Fast messages about the Revolutionary War are present but moderated. The war, like all other wars, was messy, nasty, and brutish, fought by the young (sometimes the very young), the poor, and the old, not just the fit and hearty. The American forces were characterized by a nearly total lack of elementary discipline and order but made up for this lack of professionalism with their spirit, their sometimes wild improvisation, and their capacity to retreat—the British would say to run away—to fight another day. Most of all, the Americans were defending their own land and were thus true citizen-soldiers inspired by the ideal of liberty, in contrast to the conscripts and mercenaries of the British, who formed the best-disciplined armies in the world but were inferior as individuals.

Our vision of the complex series of events that made up the opening of the Revolution, the shot heard round the world, comes through the innocent eyes of Adam, and the great achievement of the book is that neither Fast's underlying message nor Adam as a character suffers. Just as in the earlier books, we see here that war is bloody, terrifying, and disgusting, yet we understand that the colonists had little choice and that some wars are more justified—or are at least more inevitable—than others. We learn this complex paradox through Adam, yet the limits of his fifteen-year-old understanding are never transcended. Among a distinguished set of novels about the conflict, *April Morning* is probably Fast's best Revolutionary War book.

PLOT DEVELOPMENT: COMING OF AGE WITH THE REVOLUTION

The plot is carried along by Adam's voice, as he tells us of his life and surroundings. He is criticized by his father for laziness and disrespect, and then he argues with Levi, his eleven-year-old brother, about Adam's saying a spell to remove a curse from the well water. Adam goes into his house and talks to his mother and then his grandmother. The family sits around the dinner table, and Adam's father again dresses down his son; we begin to see him as a man of strong opinions, firmly expressed. Joseph Simmons, a relative, stops by. He has been chosen to write a statement on the rights of man by the committee, the men of the village acting to define their positions on their hopes for liberty from Britain. Adam at fifteen is a year too young to participate in the committee meeting that night—he has gone to visit his girlfriend Ruth Simmons—but he recounts his father's version of events. We find that his village, Lexington, is in emotional and intellectual turmoil about the exciting events of the incipient revolution.

Lexington is awakened in the middle of the night by a lone rider with the news that the British army has left Boston and is marching on the village. Adam slips out to join his father and the reverend, who are discussing with the committeemen what their response should be if a thousand or more British troops march in to be opposed by the seventy-nine-man local militia. Adam, carrying his weapon, a fowling piece, signs up with the militia and joins his father on the village common.

The British army marches in just before dawn. There is a brief standoff; a shot is fired, redcoat soldiers shoot dead Adam's father and several others, and there is chaos on the village green. Adam and the militia scramble to escape, and the youth hides out for the night in a smokehouse. Almost caught the next morning by a British patrol, he escapes into the countryside, where he meets an older man, Solomon Chandler. They walk together toward where the British army has disappeared, up the road to Concord. They meet Adam's cousin, who learns of Adam's father's death. As they move toward Concord, they are joined by more and more men.

The men gather along a stone wall lining the road to Concord, and a rider announces the British army is retreating. As the redcoats march past, they are shot at by Adam and the other colonials, who retreat into the fields and then move ahead of the retreating army. Adam experiences terror, exhilaration, confusion. A wounded redcoat shot from his horse turns out to be a boy not much older than Adam. The men, about 150 of them, move on to Lexington, where houses are burning. They cut over to the Menotomy Road to catch the British in their retreat from Lexington. From a windfall of trees, Adam shoots at the British until he passes out from exhaustion. He straggles back to his home.

Adam bathes and then goes to mourn for his father. He and Ruth declare their love. Cousin Simmons points out that all the men will have to decide whether to join what will become the Continental army, now forming to attack the British in Boston. Adam returns home to his grandmother and mother; now he is a man facing enormous decisions.

STRUCTURE

April Morning covers the events of a little over one full day, April 19, 1775, in and around Lexington, Massachusetts, and on the Concord and Menotomy roads. As is frequently the case with other Fast works, the chronology and the geographic locations are carefully integrated, so that time and place serve to structure the narrative. The book is divided into eight titled chapters or sections, each constituting a stage or point in Adam's experience:

Chapter Title	Situation/Events
"The Afternoon"	Adam with father, brother on farm; Adam whipped for saying a spell over the well, showing disrespect. Adam boyish, family centered.
"The Evening"	Adam with family, Cousin Simmons at dinner. Adam still boyish, too young for committee meeting.
"The Night"	The British are coming. Adam joins men in militia on commons, signs roster. His father chides Adam about being unready for attack.
"The Morning"	The British come. Adam's father is killed. Adam and others run.
"The Forenoon"	Adam hides in smokehouse, talks to brother Levi. Escapes to countryside, joins Chandler on way to confront British.
"The Midday"	First battle on Concord Road. Adam fights, retreats, confronts enemy again. Talks with Cousin Simmons.
"The Afternoon"	Second battle, on Menotomy Road. Adam fights, sleeps, returns home to Lexington.
"The Evening"	Adam back at home. Confronts mourning for father, professes love for Ruth, discusses future with Cousin Simmons, accepts responsibility for future decisions. Adam has reached manhood.

Adam's movement from boyishness to incipient manhood takes place in under thirty hours, yet his rapid maturation is perfectly credible given the momentous events of that long day.. There is a neat parallel between Adam's coming of age and the colonial Revolutionaries facing up to the seriousness of their endeavor. We have been witnesses to Adam's complaints about being put upon by his father and to his near-whines about not being considered an adult. As we listen to Adam, we also hear what the adult colonials are discussing: their complaints about the oppression of the British. As cousin Simmons's final talk with Adam makes clear, the events of the day will force all the colonials to face signing the muster books and joining the army to drive the British from Boston: they can no longer simply complain and argue. Adam's story and that of his soon-to-be country come together: both have moved from adolescence to manhood, symbolized in the acceptance of responsibility.

GENERIC CONVENTIONS

April Morning has frequently been compared to Stephen Crane's *The Red Badge of Courage* (1895), and for understandable reasons. Both books focus on an adolescent boy's rapidly becoming a man as the result of brutal testing in combat. Both books show the young person as acting out the role of adult without a real understanding of what is involved, and both have the boy run and hide in terror at first, then later stand and fight like a man. Both focus on final acceptance by the community of men and on the acceptance of responsibility by the newly mature young person. As maturation novels combined with historical novels, they share the same genre.

The differences between *The Red Badge of Courage* and *April Morning* are, however, very instructive, for they show how opposite the intentions of Crane and Fast are. Fast is writing an antiwar novel, showing the enormous costs of even a "good" war like the American Revolutionary one, and Adam's loss of his father, his destroyed childhood innocence, and quite possibly his own future life and the well-being of his family are a huge bill to pay. War is not a game or a maturation therapy; there are no "red badges" in *April Morning*. For all the virtues of Crane's portrait of a young Union soldier coming of age, his story is in no way integrated into the larger social conflict, for Crane's interest is in the test of manhood, not in the interconnections of society and character.

Rather than comparing *April Morning* with *The Red Badge of Courage*, it might be more helpful to hold up as a model a novel like *The Catcher in the Rye* (1951), odd though that might seem at first. While all three novels are coming-of-age stories with an adolescent as their central character, and all three provide youthful perspectives, Holden Caulfield and Adam Cooper share tonal similarities in their complaints about the injustices and hypocrisies of the adult world. Both young protagonists test those around them with mildly rebellious behavior, and both move uneasily from childlike to adult reflections on their environments. Both capture the bitter-sweet ache of the teenage years, and both are memorable for their decency and purity.

The major creative contribution of *April Morning* is the wonderfully convincing voice of Adam, a first-person voice that not only commands our attention and affection but also reflects the surrounding community and time period very credibly. Whether J. D. Salinger's seminal novel about an adolescent male's losing his innocence paved the way for Adam is an interesting question of literary influence, but such a formulation of the question allows us to see *April Morning* in a quite different perspective. Certainly it is a book about a young person learning to fit into a sometimes uncomfortable, sometimes hostile, environment. Adam's physical awkwardness parallels his inability to come to terms with his father, as he tentatively struggles to discover his own beliefs. Adam, like a young person putting on outrageous clothes to test his parents, advances doubts about the existence of God, about the righteousness of community leader Isaiah Peterkin, about unexamined belief itself. He is his argumentative, contentious father's son and as such must find his own separate identity. As a result of this easily recognizable pattern, his story has a universality missing from the more limited dimensions of *Red Badge* and similar maturation stories.

Fast's forte, as we have seen, is the amalgam of the protest novel and the historical novel. As a protest novel *April Morning* is muted, apart from the very real antiwar elements. At this point in his career Fast seems content to allow descriptions and situations to carry the burden of the message, and there are no overt protest novel elements. The history is not so much downplayed as integrated into plot and situation, and in a way that is entirely appropriate to the limited domestic world of a fifteen year old who has not traveled widely. What did Boston-area colonials eat in 1775? We hear about the evening meal of soup, meat cakes, potatoes, parsnips, and boiled pudding, including a discussion about the Dutch influence on the pudding termed "donkers." What armaments did the Lexington and Concord farmers employ against the British army?

Muskets (lethal up to a hundred paces) and rifles (lethal up to four hundred paces), each dictating a very different set of tactics. What was on the minds of the colonials before the first shots? The conversation at the Cooper dinner table could supply a colonial history class topics for a seminar.

April Morning is thus a very well-integrated novel, perhaps Fast's best. Although nominally a book for young readers, the sophisticated topics it raises are equally valid fare for adults. Like young Adam himself, the book is moderate and sensible, one looked back on with a mental smile of pleasure.

KEY CHARACTERS

The key character is Adam, who has all the charm and frustrating qualities of a bright young person questioning his environment. Just as his father cannot say grace without giving the Lord a piece of his mind, so Adam, a chip off the old block, argues with Ruth and Granny about Isaiah Peterkin's well-known religious hypocrisy, about the free-thinkers he has heard hold forth in Boston, and about his rights to manhood: he is only nine months away from his sixteenth birthday. But Adam is sweet-natured and docile, and his main concern is his brother Levi's betrayal of him when he reports the spell Adam said over the well water, a superstition his father cannot abide. Adam provides the reader with an idealized version of growing up in a village, uncorrupted by big city values.

Adam has several sets of characters who guide him toward maturity in the short space of about twenty hours. Appropriately, these characters represent increasing distance from the family environment in which we first encounter him. Adam is clearly a favorite of his Granny, who spoils him and protects him somewhat from his father's stern criticism. His mother feeds him his favorite food, and we see that Adam is still a child, sheltered and petted by the women of the family. His father, Moses, is intimidating to Adam and points out that Adam has the physical size of a man but not the behavior of an adult. At first, Moses seems simply argumentative and difficult, but he becomes more sympathetic when he continues his harsh criticism on the village green, and we realize how justified he has been: Adam's careless preparation of his musket could cost him his life. Moses Cooper is trying to prepare his son for manhood.

Ruth Simmons, Adam's girlfriend, also tries to push Adam in the direction of greater maturity and self-understanding, as we see when they walk out together, that is, go courting. But it is only after the debacle on the village green, with his father dead and the British pursuing him, that Adam begins to receive the full guidance of others. He meets Solomon Chandler, an older man with white hair who calms him down, encourages him to cry and mourn, feeds him, and talks to him about the nature of cowardice and bravery. Solomon is a figure of experience, a former soldier in the French and Indian Wars, prepared and ready to do battle, and he serves as a mentor and guide to Adam. Along the Concord Road, Adam meets his cousin Joshua Dover, and then a whole group of men from Lexington, including the reverend and Cousin Simmons. They treat Adam with restraint and solemn formality. It is not simply that the loss of his father has changed him; it has also changed how he is viewed by others. Cousin Simmons becomes his final tutor, teaching him what to do in battle, leading him away from the most dangerous spots, and staying with him throughout the day.

When Adam finally returns to his home, he again meets with his mother, Granny, and Ruth, but with all three women he behaves differently, for he is now the household head and ready to face responsibility. Cousin Simmons raises the issue of leaving Lexington to fight in Boston. At the end of the novel Adam still has not made his decision, but we know from his mature demeanor that when he does decide, he will make the correct choice.

The other characters are well rounded and credible, even when their function, as with Solomon Chandler, is primarily to act as mentor and guide to Adam. Fast has them speak a convincing brand of English in which less is more: their restraint and lack of effusiveness even under extreme circumstances ring exactly true as the style of a less emotive age than our own. Biblical cadences, always apparent in older American dialects spoken in Protestant areas, echo in the speech of the characters; dignity and orderliness characterize even the dinnertime discussions around Moses Cooper's table. The ferment and chaos of revolution and political change are delivered in measured Augustan prose style, and Fast is careful to avoid even a hint of linguistic anachronism. *April Morning* is thus as valuable for its linguistic merits as for its political history.

THEMATIC ISSUES

Theme exists at three main levels in *April Morning*. Adam's maturation is the theme in the foreground, the putative justification for the plot. In the immediate background is the common Fast theme of agrarian inno-cence, here set against the intruding British rather than against the cor-ruption of the city or of aristocratic decadence as in other Fast protest novels. The third thematic level is incidental; like stage props or theat-rical flats, several themes come up in the discussion to set the stage and define the concerns of the period. The most important concern the tactics and strategies used by the colonials against the British.

Maturation

Adam Cooper at fifteen is halfway between a boy and a man, on the one hand enduring youthful conflicts with his father and seeking comfort from his grandmother, on the other trying to stay up late with the adults and appreciating being called "young man." Adam enjoys sweet carrot pie, his gun, and his innocent relationship with his girlfriend, Ruth. As we have seen, Adam comes of age under fire, and just as the horrors of combat force him into manhood, so too the whole colonial "army," not a real military organization at all but rather a collection of farmers and countrymen fighting with birdshot fired from ancient hunting pieces, comes together as the beginning of a fighting force.

The Horror of Battle

As is always true of Fast, the battle scenes are horrific but effectively written. They are brutally realistic, quite unlike the stylized images painted by Trumbull (*The Death of Dr. Joseph Warren at the Battle of Bunker Hill, The Death of General Mercer at Princeton*), Emanuel Leutze (*Washing-ton Crossing the Delaware*), or Currier and Ives, the creators of some of our most memorable Revolutionary War imagery. Adam's battles are loud, sweaty, frightening, exhilarating, exhausting, and emotionally dis-turbing. Among their best realistic characteristics are the humanizing touches given to the enemy, hated intruders though they are. Here, a dead redcoat turns out not to be a fearsome "lobster," as the colonials called the British, but "a young boy with a pasty white skin and a face full of pimples, who had taken a rifle ball directly between the eyes" (147). The reader inevitably thinks of Adam himself, about the same age. Both British and colonials are caught in an escalation of violence out of control, and while Fast clearly sees the future Americans as being in the right, he never shrinks from writing honestly about the true cost of war, paid for by the blood of innocents on both sides. Maturity is a painful business, whether for a young boy or a youthful nation, for it involves facing up to a world full of difficult choices, some of them evil ones.

Agrarian Innocence

A third theme is that farm life promotes simplicity and a connection to productive labor and nature that brings out the best in people. The Coopers live an idyllic country life that parallels that of Tom Paine's near-in-laws, the Rumpels:

> On Weekdays, we ate our meals in the kitchen. On the Sabbath, we ate dinner in the dining room, and Mother set the table with china and silver. We weren't rich, but Granny's mother had been rich enough for china and silver. On weekdays, we ate with plainware. (11)

Throughout Fast's work the perfect life is epitomized by families such as the Coopers. The location is never urban, not even the lovely San Francisco of *The Immigrants*, where Higate Winery serves as the rural utopia. Perfection is a farm or rural village, where the residents cluster in large extended families and live off the fruits of their own labor, enjoying their truck gardens, vineyards, and other farm products. The lifestyle is characterized by a rigorous simplicity, here based on Protestant severity. The particular religious faith is irrelevant, for Jews and Catholics can live this way too. The key is self-reliance, self-restraint, social equality of all community members, an antimaterialistic philosophy, and generalized spiritual faith. This agrarian radicalism is almost Edenic—what life would have been like if there had been no Fall.

From a Marxist perspective, urban life divorces the worker from the fruits of his or her labor, alienating the laborer from the elemental satisfactions of honest work and from the natural world as well. The representatives of urban life in *April Morning* are the British army, pushing arrogantly into Adam's Eden-like village on their way to Concord to uncover a colonial arms cache, forcing the committeemen who run the town and the local militia to choose between protecting themselves by force and heeding their religious prohibitions against violence. The British, mainly London street boys, are evil not because they are urban but rather because they are the arms of empire, of distant, European control bent on shaping the American continent into a mirror image of Old World aristocratic privilege. Face to face, the soldiers may look unsettlingly like Adam Cooper; as an armed force, they represent the status quo ante, a retrograde return to the ancient order of exploitation. The promise of a new start in America will be cut to ribbons by British bayonets if Adam's village fails to stand for the principle of self-determination.

Warfare and Brotherhood

Incidental themes in *April Morning* include numerous interesting historical questions, many of which come up at the dinner table in the Cooper household and in the discussions about possible revolution in the colonies. The most coherent and extended of these thematic details is important in Fast's other work; it comes up late in the novel and concerns the development of the Continental army's military tactics, a process we see examined in depth in an earlier Revolutionary War book and in a later one: "It makes sense. If we cluster together, the redcoats can make an advantage out of it, but there's not a blessed thing they can do with two or three of us except chase us, and we can outrun them" (*April Morning* 146). This is the lesson George Washington finally learns in *The Unvanquished* (1942) and applies to good advantage in *The Crossing* (1971): that the genius of the Continental army is to avoid direct confrontation, to retreat without panic, to avoid defeat, and to live to fight another day. As Adam says, "The most important thing I had learned about war was that you could run away and survive to talk about it" (142). The Continentals, after all, lived in America and were defending their own land; they could win by not losing, by simply outlasting the will of their distant enemy to fight. Fast's Revolutionary War books even suggest that the New World invented a new form of warfare, a "people's war" fought by citizen-soldiers, undisciplined and individualistic, who could retreat time and again yet never lose (though in fact this style of war is also characteristic of the Maccabee brothers in ancient Judea, in *My Glorious Brothers*).

Most significantly, Adam and his fellows learn that combat binds men together in a special brotherhood, one impossible to explain to those who have not experienced it. This common Fast theme had been best developed in two other Revolutionary War books, *Conceived in Liberty* (1939) and *The Proud and the Free* (1950). Along with the centrifugal force that makes soldiers scatter in pursuit of their own safety, there also comes a centripetal force—an emotional power pushing men together for their mutual good and occasionally prompting feats of amazing heroism.

Thus, like the youthful Continental Army, young Adam learns discipline and youthful manhood, how to retreat without panic and despair, how to turn and strike back, as did Washington in Fast's *The Crossing*, how to be that new thing on the face of the earth: a citizen-soldier fighting not for hire or out of dire necessity but because of principle and social conscience. Seen in this light, Adam, Tom Paine, George Washington, and all of Fast's other colonials are simply different facets of the same rough diamond, the unpolished colonials who would gradually become the best fighting force in the New World.

ALTERNATIVE READINGS: FREUDIAN/PSYCHOANALYTICAL AND FEMINIST INTERPRETATIONS

Two alternate readings may throw light on *April Morning*'s essential nature. A Freudian/psychoanalytical reading might focus on Adam's successful acquisition of maturity, a case of Oedipal conflict resolved. In contrast, current feminist thinking looks askance at male coming-of-age stories based on experiences in combat, as does Barbara Lavette in the novels that feature her in The Immigrants series.

The title character could be seen by a Freudian critic as a case of unresolved conflict with authority. Freudian/psychoanalytical critics find the keys to human behavior in early childhood experiences and, especially in the case of the immature male, in challenges to the authority of the father or father figure over the love of the mother. This Oedipal conflict is a normal developmental stage for most males, an episode of competition that is resolved and put behind them, but some are unable to come to terms with their ambivalent feelings of aggression and fear toward the father and remain in a permanent state of rebellion against all authority, even distant authority. This generalizing of a conflict with a specific parent also manifests itself in a conflict about women, with the adult male unable to maintain a normal and mutually satisfying relationship with a female.

In contrast to Tom Paine, whose battles with his biological father, rebellion against authority figures, and inability to sustain a relationship with a woman fit the Freudian pattern, Adam Cooper can be seen as successfully resolving a typical Oedipal conflict. At the start of the book, Adam is suffering the sting of his father's disapproval, with the elder Cooper looming large in the son's mind. Adam seeks comfort from the women of the family, his mother and grandmother. He is still childlike, resentful of his father's apparently absolute and arbitrary control, and trying through complaint and charm to move the women to his side. When the invasion of the British army is imminent, Adam never asks his father's approval but goes to the village green to sign on with the militia. In symbolic terms, his ready acceptance of the colonial cause is a revolt against both his father's authority and that of the ultimate distant father figure, the English king. Even Adam's challenges to the religious orthodoxy of his family could be seen as rebellion against the most powerful father figure, the Supreme Being.

The British attack, however, forces Adam into an accelerated maturation, and as a consequence he resolves his Oedipal conflicts. He comes to see his dead father as a human being, high-handed but concerned for his son's welfare and anxious to enforce obedience to promote Adam's survival. The British enemy is similarly humanized and made rational, and Adam, whatever his degree of future involvement in the war, will make his decision on political and philosophical grounds, not on the stirrings of adolescent emotional revolt against authority. He is also clearly on his way to a mature relationship with his girlfriend, Ruth, who will replace his mother and granny as the significant female figures in his life.

If a Freudian perspective on *April Morning* is approving, a feminist one is decidedly negative. Feminist critics refuse to accept male definitions of what is human and normal, arguing along with Simone de Beauvoir that "the categories in which men think of the world are established *from their point of view, as absolute*" (*The Second Sex* 257). A feminist perspective thus might reject the validity of male perspectives on maturation: half of the human population plays by different rules, and perhaps the male rules are wrong.

An interesting feminist perspective on the question is offered by one of Fast's most memorable characters, the protagonist of The Immigrants series. What would Barbara Lavette say about Adam's march to maturation? (She calls herself no feminist early in the series, but her criticism of war is certainly based on feminist reasoning.) In Karachi, she says that "war is for men and idiots. Or are they the same?" (*Second Generation* 370). About Bernie Cohen, long a soldier, she says, "This man . . . has only one profession. He has a competence in death. Why on God's earth am I sitting here?" (*Second Generation* 425). Her father, Dan, agrees, calling war the "filthiest, bloodiest, stupidest rotten game man ever invented. There are no good guys and no bad guys. It's a lousy, rotten scam" (*The Establishment* 43). Bernie remembers what Barbara once said: that wars "were games, politics were games—deadly, senseless murderous games of children in adult bodies. Glory, idealism, and courage were the three mindless labels" (*The Establishment* 72). Bernie's mission to Israel is even called a "Jesus syndrome," sacrificing one's self to save the world. Perhaps her strongest indictment of war is in *The Legacy*:

> The crux of it is war—the absolute definition of a man's world. They make us pregnant and there's the nine months of vomiting and trying to sleep with a belly that doesn't belong to you and screaming your guts out while you try to bring a new bit of life into this sorry world, and then these lunatics work out a solution for the whole thing in a place called Vietnam. (230)

Clearly Barbara Lavette would not subscribe to the notion that young men should find maturation through war; she believes just the opposite, that war is an addiction for males who have never grown up. Barbara's viewpoint is not uncommon among feminist thinkers. Many feminists have attacked the works of Hemingway and his imitators for their macho assumption that violence and war are ennobling masculine characteristics. Fast's own position, as the creator of both *April Morning* and of Barbara Lavette, is curious and perhaps shaded with some ambivalence. Barbara's philosophy is frequently close to Fast's own intellectual position, at least as shown when he writes in his own voice, but the evidence of his fictional protest books shows him, like Bernie, resigned to the reality of "just" wars. One would guess he would classify Adam's experience as an ugly historical necessity, but one to be avoided in the future at all costs.

7

The Immigrants Series
(1977–1985)

> I am a workman—all artists who are not dilettantes are workmen—
> and I know how and earn my daily bread. Sometimes a lot of bread
> indeed, sometimes less. I have done well. I have no complaints—
> except that I never wrote that book I go on dreaming of writing.
> —Howard Fast, *Counterpoint*

THE SAGA OF A CALIFORNIA FAMILY

When Howard Fast complained in 1964 that he had never written the
book he dreamed of writing, he had not yet begun to write The Immigrants series, a quintet of books that captures the author's version of the
American experience in a personally resonant way, yet which was also
enormously successful commercially. The family saga that began with
The Immigrants in 1977 has been one of Fast's most popular creations,
with each novel in the five-part series regularly on the best-seller lists,
the first work followed by *Second Generation* (1978), then by *The Establishment* (1979), next by *The Legacy* (1981), and finally by *The Immigrant's
Daughter* (1985). Together, the five books have sold over 10 million copies. The primary focus of this chapter will be on *The Immigrants*, since it
sets up all the major characters and themes. However, since all five books
can be read as an almost seamless whole, and since the story of Dan and

Jean Lavette is actually found in their influence on their daughter, Barbara, the plots and situations of the books that follow the first novel will
be covered as well. They provide the resolution for what begins with the
immigration of the main character's parents to New York City.

The saga spans a century, from the 1880s to the 1980s, and traces the
rise, interaction, and occasional decline of several families of newcomers
to California, some of them recent immigrants from abroad, others earlier
settlers to America seeking their fortune on the West Coast. As a consequence, each novel operates on a number of levels to intrigue reader
interest and loyalty. Readers of Fast's Revolutionary War and other early
novels will recognize some familiar themes and concerns: the leveling
effect of a frontier environment, in which no one can claim primacy
because of long-term residence; a struggle between those who wish to
create a new aristocracy to divide the classes, and egalitarians who try
to preserve the frontier spirit; and a "multicultural" emphasis on the
diverse peoples who inhabit the frontier. In this series Fast brings in a
new concern, the assimilation of different cultures into the culture of the
American majority, certainly an appropriate theme for California. But
essentially the series is about family, in the narrow sense of a nuclear
group and in the larger sense of an extended group bonded together by
self-interest, proximity, and happenstance. Family connections drive the
novels and create interest in the fates of the characters.

GENERIC CONVENTIONS

The Immigrants is primarily a family dynasty novel, as are the other
books in The Immigrants series, for they trace the fortunes of the extended Lavette family through several generations. *The Immigrants* focuses on the key figure of Dan Lavette, Italian on his mother's side,
French-Italian on his father's, orphaned by the San Francisco earthquake
of 1906 but becoming an archetypical American entrepreneur at the
tender age of sixteen. The fortunes of Dan Lavette's ample "family," a
family created by marriage, business partnership, and friendship, provide a good deal of the attraction of the first book and its sequels, as we
watch lives unfold in the best tradition of domestic sagas.

As a family saga, the books inevitably involve a series of romances,
mainly failed. The first is the romance of Jean Seldon and Dan Lavette,
which leads to a marriage troubled by the disparity of their two worlds:
Nob Hill and Fisherman's Wharf. Despite the birth of two children, Tom

and Barbara, the couple go their separate ways as Dan works to expand his shipping empire in the economic boom created by World War I and the children are left in the care of a nanny while Jean pursues new interests in modern art and the avant-garde. As the couple have less and less to say to each other, a restless Dan is ripe for a new romance. When he accepts an invitation by Feng Wo to meet his family, a courtesy Jean, who disdains Chinese, rejects contemptuously, Dan meets and falls immediately in love with Feng Wo's daughter, May Ling. She is aware of the impossibility of their affair but succumbs to his bluff honesty and guilty implications that he will eventually leave Jean and marry her. Dan provides May Ling with a house and spends much of his time away from work with her, leaving Jean to live her own life as a patron of the art world. May Ling eventually becomes pregnant and gives birth to a son, Joseph.

While Jean pursues desultory affairs with her society friends and continues to dabble in the art world, Dan takes May Ling on a leisurely trip to the Hawaiian Islands to scout tourist destinations his partners have proposed for development. He and May Ling sail alone from island to island in a romantic interlude quite different from their usual guilty behavior in San Francisco. At the same time, Jean travels in England and has a flirtation with an English lord, and then poses nude for a fashionable artist. Back in San Francisco, Dan Lavette refuses to act on an ultimatum from May Ling, and she leaves for a librarian's job at the University of California campus in Los Angeles, taking Feng Wo and Joseph with her. The heartbroken Dan becomes involved in a drunken brawl but is unable to free himself from his emotional and guilt-ridden relationship with Jean. The surface pattern is a conventional one of whirlwind romance, followed by conflict and alienation that lead to guilty affairs. The affair extends over several books, with added complications. For example, at one point, when Dan comes to Los Angeles to visit May Ling, using as an excuse his intention to start California's first big-time passenger air service, May Ling suspects he intends it as a means to continue their affair by commuting from Los Angeles. She rejects his rather pathetic attempts to continue the affair, insisting that he must choose between her and Jean. It is only after Dan's business begins to fail and his Hawaiian cruise ships lose all their bookings that he finally confronts Jean about a divorce—to which she readily agrees. Other romances in the series include that of Clair Harvey, the nearly abandoned daughter of the captain of the *Oregon Queen* and the virtually adopted

Since not all editions of The Immigrants series include a genealogy of the Lavette, Levy, and Cassala families, the version here may be helpful.

The Lavettes

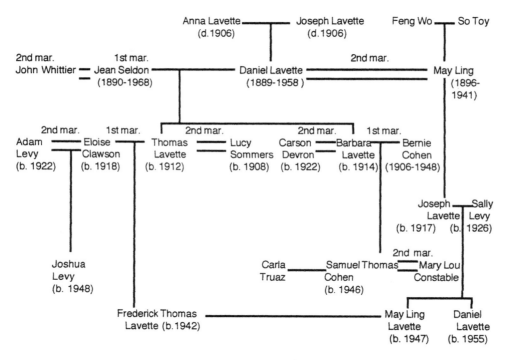

Anna Lavette (d.1906) — Joseph Lavette (d.1906)

Feng Wo — So Toy

2nd mar.
John Whittier — Jean Seldon (1890-1968)

1st mar.

Daniel Lavette (1889-1958)

2nd mar.

May Ling (1896-1941)

2nd mar.
Adam Levy (b. 1922)

1st mar.
Eloise Clawson (b. 1918)

2nd mar.
Thomas Lavette (b. 1912) — Lucy Sommers (b. 1908)

2nd mar.
Carson Devron (b. 1922) — Barbara Lavette (b. 1914)

1st mar.
Bernie Cohen (1906-1948)

Joseph Lavette (b. 1917) — Sally Levy (b. 1926)

Joshua Levy (b. 1948)

Carla Truaz

2nd mar.
Samuel Thomas Cohen (b. 1946) — Mary Lou Constable

Frederick Thomas Lavette (b.1942)

May Ling Lavette (b. 1947)

Daniel Lavette (b. 1955)

The Levys

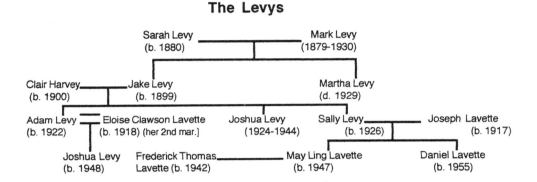

Sarah Levy
(b. 1880) ——————— Mark Levy
(1879-1930)

Clair Harvey _____ Jake Levy
(b. 1900)   (b. 1899)

Martha Levy
(d. 1929)

Adam Levy ___ Eloise Clawson Lavette
(b. 1922)   (b. 1918) (her 2nd mar.]

Joshua Levy
(1924-1944)

Sally Levy _____ Joseph Lavette
(b. 1926)   (b. 1917)

Joshua Levy
(b. 1948)

Frederick Thomas _____ May Ling Lavette
Lavette (b. 1942)   (b. 1947)

Daniel Lavette
(b. 1955)

The Cassalas

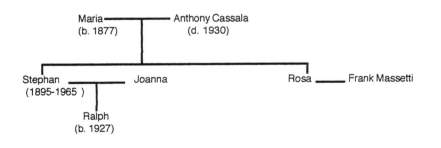

Maria ———— Anthony Cassala
(b. 1877)   (d. 1930)

Stephan _____ Joanna
(1895-1965)

Rosa _____ Frank Massetti

Ralph
(b. 1927)

daughter of Sarah and Mark Levy, who falls in love with the Levy's son
Jake; the unrequited love of Stephan Cassala for Jake's sister Martha,
who is too starstruck to take him seriously; and the assorted affairs of
Barbara Lavette.

The series also offers much more. There are capsule histories of the
important events of the time, from the San Francisco earthquake to the
Great Depression to World War II. The extended saga form offers Fast,
always a diligent researcher, the opportunity to present fascinating disquisitions on more mundane topics: the number of houses of ill repute
in the San Francisco Tenderloin District before and after the earthquake;
the development of the California wine industry in the Napa Valley; the
driving forces behind the airline and shipbuilding companies up and
down the state; the bloody longshoreman's strike of 1934. Such social
history is more limited and personally involving for many readers than
political history; its effect is to tie the characters of the saga to the larger
events, providing almost tangible tastes and feelings of life on the West
Coast from just before the turn of the nineteenth century to almost the
end of the twentieth. In doing so, it partakes of some of the conventions
of historical fiction, blending fact and fantasy to bring the past to life.
For instance, Jake Levy and Stephan Cassala, Anthony's son, serve in
France during World War I. Jake fights heroically and returns unscathed
but completely uninterested in the world of competitive business, while
Stephan is wounded seriously but survives to return to banking with his
father. Barbara Lavette's one-time lover and fiancé, Marcel Duboise, a
journalist for *Le Monde,* is wounded while covering the Spanish Civil
War, and Bernie Cohen, Rabbi Blum's assistant, fights in the International Brigade on the republican side and tries to save Marcel by swim-
ming a river with the wounded newsman on his back. The stock market
crash of 1929 destroys the Levy-and-Lavette empire, Barbara Lavette
goes to Berlin in 1939, and May Ling and Dan are caught in the Japanese
attack on Pearl Harbor while on a romantic sailing trip in *Second Generation.*

A good part of the fascination of the series lies in the historical detail:
the picture it gives of burgeoning California, the last great American
frontier, and therefore, for Fast, the last chance for America to live up to
its ideals of equality and justice. Fast is clearly intrigued by the newness
of the state and of its ethnic and racial mix, just as the younger Fast was
fascinated by the raw, newly formed civilization of Philadelphia and its
surrounding colonies in his American Revolution novels. The weight of
English and European culture finally degrades the purity of the revo-

lution, as social class differences and inherited wealth make their influence felt on the patriots. California offers one more chance to get it right, to let everyone—French-Italians, Chinese, Russian Jews, Chicanos, and others—compete on a level playing field and earn their place in society based on their efforts, not on their family connections or inherited wealth. San Francisco is the main arena for this contest, but the even newer, rawer, and less polite Los Angeles also figures in the plot. One example of Fast's portrayal of this process is his subplot about Jake and Clair Levy's buying Higate, an old winery in the Napa Valley, an operation crippled by the Volstead Act and prohibition, which made alcohol production and consumption illegal. Rabbi Samuel Blum, a character who will become significant later on, engages the young Levys, who have been growing table grapes in their struggle to get by, to produce sacramental wine for his association of synagogues. His driver, young Bernie Cohen, is a fervent Zionist who wants to study agricultural methods to use in the Israel of the future. The rabbi's offer leads to the survival and eventual success of Higate. Long and fascinating disquisitions on the production of California wine result from the rabbi's proposal. Thus, we can appreciate not just a simple soap opera of families in conflict, but rather a true epic picture of a whole society in the making, with characters transforming their environment even as their surroundings shape them. The Immigrants books have a page-turning urgency and characters with a kind of super-reality, the kind of sharply defined characters in long-running television series. In a way, the series is the most ambitious project Fast ever undertook, for it sets out to tell not just personal stories but also the history of the final settling of the North American continent.

In general terms, most of Fast's novels fit into the category of American realism in that they attempt to depict their worlds in straightforward, objective terms. Fast's prose is frequently "cinematic" in that it strives for clarity and transparency, avoiding self-reference, archness, lushness, or any of the other stylistic signatures of the writers of Fast's youth. Even the plain-and-simple paratactic prose of Hemingway, sometimes so lean as to be affected, is avoided. Fast is not afraid of adjectives or subordinated sentences, and the effect is like that of literate journalism, a clear, uncontaminated window into another world, with nothing calling attention to itself. If sentences sum up a worldview, then Fast's vision of his works is just that, the novel as a way of seeing clearly, with his old model writers Jack London and Theodore Dreiser brought up to date and made even more unadorned. Yet The Immigrants series is more than just plain

Puritan storytelling, for Fast also includes his own life and the lives of others.

The Immigrants is in some sections virtually autobiographical. Especially, but not exclusively, Barbara Lavette represents a version of Fast's own experiences. As he says in *Contemporary Authors Autobiography Series*, "While living in California, I decided to write a book about a woman whose life and experience would parallel my own, having her born the year and month of my own birth, namely November in 1914. . . . I called her Barbara Lavette" (18:184). (In fact, Fast misremembered: Dan and Jean move into their new house on Russian Hill in "*August* of 1914, *soon after the birth of their second child*," Barbara [emphasis added].) Looked at from this perspective, The Immigrants series is a thinly disguised—not disguised at all after *Being Red* came out—autobiographical novel. Autobiographical instances abound, for example, Barbara's experiences on Calcutta's "sleeping streets," where homeless refugees live, or her contempt citation by the House Un-American Activities Committee (HUAC), which Fast had written about in *The Pledge*. Barbara Lavette's blacklist struggles clearly reflect Fast's own difficulties, as do her infuriating attempts to write the screenplay for her own novel (as Fast did for *Spartacus*). Barbara's conflicts about her personal wealth certainly mirror Fast's own socialist reservations about amassing capital created from his writing.

Many other of Fast's habits and enthusiasms are reflected in The Immigrants. For Dan, Jean, and finally Barbara, walking in scenic places becomes a daily habit in old age; Fast is an indefatigable walker. As was Dan, Fast was a committed sailor whose wife was far less enthusiastic, and both Fast and Dan gave up sailing in their later years. Fast's enthusiasm for wine and wine making informs many of his novels. Barbara Lavette's politics and Fast's own, as reflected in *Being Red* and his other works, seem so close as to suggest she is often a spokesperson for his ideas. The criticism leveled at Barbara's novels is a direct reflection of the attacks on Fast's fiction.

Beyond the personal and autobiographical, the series is also a clear example of the roman à clef, a work in which fictional characters can be identified with real figures. As in Fast's excellent novel *Power*, a fictionalized biography of United Mine Workers president John L. Lewis, it is easy to see the historical parallels. Dan Lavette and his family are reminiscent of the founding fathers of California transportation, the Crocker-Huntington-Stanford-Hopkins combine that created the Central Pacific Railroad, which linked Sacramento and the rest of the United States, and then the Southern Pacific, which connected San Francisco and New Orleans in 1883. (The fictional Seldon bank and its associated family is frequently mentioned in the books in the same sentence as the very real Crocker Bank and family of San Francisco.) The Hearsts were powerful West Coast newspaper magnates. Another real-life parallel is the one between the Otis and Chandler families of the *Los Angeles Times* and the Devrons in Fast's Los Angeles. The gentlemanly Hungarian movie director Hargasey suggests the real director Michael Curtis, the man who made *Casablanca* and *King Creole*; Curtis, like Fast's Hargasey, was always a gentleman. Congressman Norman Drake, HUAC member, professional anticommunist, and California's Republican candidate for the vice presidency in the 1950s, at first makes us think of Richard M. Nixon, but then Fast slyly refers to the real Nixon as a colleague of Drake. Even Dan Lavette, when he works seven days a week on his shipbuilding activities and lives in complete isolation on Terminal Island near San Pedro, reminds us of Howard Hughes, the entrepreneur and aircraft tycoon famed for his productivity, eccentricity, and hermit-like work habits. It would be easy to multiply these examples, for the books include many such parallels—some very obvious, many much more obscure. Part of the enjoyment of reading such a roman à clef lies in identifying such connections to the real world, which brings a small shock of pleasure.

The genre of The Immigrants is thus difficult to classify neatly, combining elements of a number of genres, including the realistic novel, the autobiographical novel, and the roman à clef. It would not be inaccurate to say that Fast sometimes shifts briefly into a comedy of manners, closely observing the language and styles of, for example, Hollywood movie folk or southern California surfers, although this observation lasts only for a scene or so. Finally, Fast always writes novels of ideas—political, social, cultural, and even geographic ideas, the last, for example, when he plays off East and West Coast attitudes or San Francisco against Los Angeles.

PLOT DEVELOPMENT

The Immigrants

The Immigrants begins in 1888 in the steerage hold of a ship in the Atlantic, bringing Anna and Joseph Lavette to New York City from Marseilles, France, where Joseph had been a fisherman since he was ten years old. Joseph is French-Italian, his wife Italian, and they embarked on their adventure to the New World in hopes of a new life. What they find is a cold and inhospitable New York, where they are cheated out of their meager savings by predatory countrymen. Joseph, in despair about feeding and sheltering his pregnant wife, signs on as a worker building railroads in California, a distant and virtually unknown place to people ignorant of English and the geography of the American West. Anna gives birth to a son, Dan, in the freezing boxcar in which they are traveling west. Later, when Joseph saves a small amount from his salary, they establish themselves in the queen city of the West Coast, San Francisco, a proud, booming metropolis of 425,000, split between its pretensions to world-class elegance and sophistication on the one hand, and on the other its frontier heritage (the city was then just over fifty years old), of brawling roughnecks and immigrants searching for their main chance.

A loan from another Italian immigrant, Anthony Cassala, allows Joseph to buy his own fishing boat, and the entrepreneurial fortunes of the family begin to rise. However, the San Francisco earthquake of 1906 kills Joseph and Anna, and Dan, at sixteen the only child, inherits the boat and immediately begins ferrying panic-stricken refugees to Oakland, a highly profitable enterprise. He turns his profits over to Anthony Cassala, which constitutes the beginning of Cassala's Bank of Sonoma. Dan has his father's love of the San Francisco Bay fisherman's life, and, working out of Fisherman's Wharf in conjunction with ship's chandler Mark Levy and his wife, Sarah, he expands his fleet to several crab boats and a crew of workers. In the face of virulent prejudice against Chinese, Dan hires Feng Wo, an accountant who is having trouble supporting his wife and daughter, May Ling. Together, the incipient corporation buys an old iron lumber ship, the *Oregon Queen*. At the same time, young Dan, still only twenty-two, courts Jean Seldon, daughter of a wealthy San Francisco banker (her grandfather was a placer miner in the California gold rush in 1851). After a whirlwind courtship, Jean and Dan marry over the objections of her family, who see him, correctly, as still a roughneck, in spite of his movement toward respectability. At this point, at barely over a hundred pages, the stage is set for the thousands of pages of the Lavette saga. The respectable Seldon side of the family, originally California immigrants themselves and now made part of the establishment by wealth and careful marriages to Boston aristocracy, battle with Dan's more rough-hewn corporate circle: Italian Anthony Cassala as financier, Jewish Mark Levy as manager and executive officer, Chinese Feng Wo as accountant, Jewish Sam Goldberg as lawyer, and French-Italian Dan

Lavette himself as entrepreneur, guiding genius, and front man. This conflict between the respectable and the up-and-coming in San Francisco society drives the plot for the remainder of *The Immigrants* and for four more novels.

Dan Lavette, who flirts with Democratic politics but never becomes deeply involved, decides that cargo shipping will collapse after the war ends and has put his money into cruise ships to Hawaii. However, events move quickly to the stock market crash of 1929, which destroys the Levy-and-Lavette empire. Anthony and Stephan Cassala struggle to keep solvent their Bank of Sonoma, formed with Dan Lavette's initial loan after the San Francisco earthquake, but it too collapses in the panic. The old man dies as a result, and a financial prop of Dan's corporation disappears. Dan's cruise ships fail. In the meantime, Jean has taken control of the Seldon Bank, which she has inherited from her father and, as the first woman to control a bank of such a size, deals from a position of strength. Dan and Jean never bridge their class differences and drift apart. When he asks for a divorce, Dan surrenders everything to her, including the mansion he built for her on Russian Hill, taking only enough money to leave town for Los Angeles. We get a prophetic scene with Barbara Lavette: Dan's daughter fits in badly in the East Coast Ivy League college scene and is wistful about the divorce. Quickly cut scenes show us Mark Levy dying of a heart attack, Dan hitting bottom as a hobo in San Pedro near Los Angeles, and Dan being hired as a mackerel fisherman by a former employee. The novel ends in 1933, with Dan's self-respect recovered and his body toughened by the healthy life of a fisherman. After two years, he has contacted his long-time love, May Ling, and they have married; he becomes a real father to his son Joseph, a promising student. The final scene is a reconciliation with Barbara, who has come to see him in Los Angeles.

Second Generation

The plots of the novels that follow *The Immigrants* trace the lives of all the above characters, adding only a few new ones. *Second Generation* now moves Barbara Lavette on to the main stage, with Jean and Dan sharing the spotlight with their adult daughter. Barbara has dropped out of her exclusive East Coast college, Sarah Lawrence, and is living in her mother's house on Russian Hill. Jean has married John Whittier, the conservative financier and strikebreaker. In spite of the anti-labor environment at home, Barbara takes part in the San Francisco longshoremen's strike of 1934 against Whittier, working first in a soup kitchen and then as a nurse treating the wounds of beaten strikers. Barbara is next seen in Paris, where she is working as a correspondent for *Manhattan Magazine*, writing a column on social and cultural fashions in the French capital. However, the loss of her lover, Marcel Duboise, in the Spanish Civil War, makes a grieving Barbara ready to accept an assignment from old communist friends of his, Claude and Camille Limoget, to travel to Nazi Berlin to ascertain if a communist contact man is still alive.

Fearful of fascist Berlin in 1939, Barbara nevertheless agrees to go for humanitarian and journalistic reasons but is quickly in trouble when she interrupts Gestapo bullying of an old Jewish man on the street. Barbara is arrested briefly but escapes Germany with the aid of a Nazi aristocrat who has San Francisco connections and is attracted to her naive innocence. She returns to California, where she lives with Dan, May Ling, and Joseph as she writes a novel about her Berlin experiences. Barbara also travels to San Francisco to set up, through the legal services of Sam Goldberg, the Lavette Foundation, a humanitarian organization funded by the $14 million she inherited from her grandfather's interest in the Seldon Bank. She then travels from Los Angeles to New York to promote her novel, allowing the reader views of both the film and literary worlds. After Sam Goldberg dies, she buys his old Victorian house in San Francisco and settles there as a writer. During World War II, however, Barbara accepts an assignment to cover North Africa, Burma, and Ceylon, and in a closely described interlude, undergoes the experiences that Fast describes in *Being Red* of being taken to the "sleeping streets" where homeless refugees live, and learning of the famine allegedly coordinated by the British. Bernie Cohen, who has been on a kibbutz in Israel and in the British army in North Africa, appears again, and Barbara and Bernie become engaged in spite of their differences: Barbara's experiences in Europe, North Africa, and Asia have made her a pacifist, while Bernie is still a committed Zionist and a professional soldier.

Dan and Jean figure less importantly in *Second Generation* but nevertheless undergo major life changes. Dan works at mackerel fishing but begins to feel his middle age and turns to running a small boatyard that builds yachts for wealthy Hollywood movie folk, the only shipbuilding activity during the depression. With the threat of World War II, he begins to build cargo ships on government contracts, an enterprise so hugely successful it transforms Terminal Island near San Pedro and Long Beach, the two major port areas of Los Angeles, into the largest shipyard on the

West Coast and one of the largest in the world. With an odd lassitude about his life and career, Dan, a millionaire once again, takes May Ling on a romantic reprise of their Hawaiian sailing trip two decades earlier, but May Ling dies in Dan's arms on board their boat, a victim of the Japanese air attack on Pearl Harbor in 1941. Dan becomes totally withdrawn and reclusive socially; however, he enjoys enormous financial success at his shipbuilding work, actually living on the premises at Terminal Island.

Changes continue to occur in the lives of the characters. Two wives, Jean Lavette Whittier and Eloise Clawson, leave their husbands. Jean drifts away from John Whittier and, apparently tired of her career as a bank executive, begins to seek out family connections. By the end of the book, she is reconciled with Dan, who has traveled to San Francisco to receive a presidential award for his shipbuilding. She also befriends Eloise Clawson, the sweet but passive heiress who married Jean and Dan's son Tom. The marriage is doomed by Tom's sexual ambiguity, his occasional violence toward his long-suffering wife, and his ambition. Through her friendship with Jean, Eloise meets Adam Levy, the son of Clair and Jake, who were reintroduced earlier when they visited Barbara in Paris on a wine-marketing expedition to France. The Levy subplot is thus tied in again, notwithstanding the death of patriarch Mark Levy, Dan's old partner in L&L enterprises, when Eloise and Adam become a couple, and Jean, through her friendship with Eloise and rekindled romance with Dan, attends the wedding of Sally Levy, Adam's sister, to Joseph Lavette, Dan and May Ling's son. (Sally and Joseph have known each other through his summer work at Higate Winery.)

The Establishment

The Establishment moves further away from Dan and Jean Lavette and toward their daughter, Barbara. She has become an established novelist, married to Bernie Cohen, who now manages a garage in San Francisco. They have an infant son, Sam. Bernie is bored by domesticity and engages in a scheme to smuggle airplanes to Israel for use in the coming war for liberation, a plan financed by Dan Lavette. Meanwhile, Barbara is called before HUAC because of her forthright recounting of her trip to prewar Berlin on behalf of her Communist party friends, the Limogets. The experience is a direct parallel to Fast's own HUAC appearance: Barbara, like Fast, faces a contempt of Congress charge for refusing to name the contributors to a fund for refugees of the Spanish Civil War.

While Barbara is testifying, Bernie is killed in a roadside ambush in Israel, and her depression is relieved only by her son Sam and her relationship with Dan and Jean, who are now living together in the house on Russian Hill. Dan sells his son Tom the shipping company he founded with Stephan Cassala with the profits from his Terminal Island shipbuilding operation, and he lives in retirement with Jean, who is increasingly dependent on him emotionally. He suffers a heart attack but continues to keep up an active life of walking and sailing in San Francisco Bay. He and Jean help support Barbara emotionally in her legal fight over the contempt charge. Eventually Barbara is sent to jail for six months, ironically to a prison on the same Terminal Island that had been Dan's wartime shipyard. Though somewhat reminiscent of Fast's own jail term in West Virginia, this facility is more modern and oriented toward West Coast inmates, for this is a women's prison mainly for blacks, Chicanas, and poor white drug offenders. On her release, a depressed Barbara travels to Israel to visit Bernie's grave, and although initially highly repressed and ambivalent about the visit, she experiences a full emotional release in a small memorial building overlooking the gravesite.

Tom Lavette, Jean and Dan's ambitious son, marries Lucy Sommers, yet another heiress but, unlike the reserved Eloise, one with ambitions of her own. Lucy challenges Tom to be more aggressive and persuades Tom to reject the political hopes that his surrogate father, John Whittier, had encouraged in favor of the more powerful influence of backstage manipulation through wealth and business interests. Tom is invited to join an unnamed group he and Lucy term "the establishment," an unlikely collection of entrepreneurs in oil, electronics, banking, and the like. Tom has become the mirror image of Dan, not so much a hands-on entrepreneur interested in the game of power as a measure of machismo but rather a cold-blooded manipulator of capital and people. However, Tom refuses to use his influence to help Barbara escape the clutches of HUAC, enraging Dan.

The other main subplot follows Joseph and Sally Lavette. Joe works as a doctor in a free clinic in the Los Angeles barrio, while Sally, miserable as a housewife with a small baby (named May Ling after Joe's mother), becomes a successful movie actress. We see their marriage almost torn apart by the conflict between good works and Hollywood values, before they finally reconcile at Higate.

The Legacy

The Legacy begins around 1958, with Barbara Lavette in Los Angeles, working as a scriptwriter for a movie production of her first novel. She is disgusted with Hollywood and Los Angeles, but enjoys a passionate affair with newspaper magnate Carson Devron. After Dan Lavette dies of a heart attack, she marries Carson, whose powerful family, a southern California mirror image of her own, disapproves of the match. Conflicts over Barbara's son, Sam, her politics, and, most significantly, her dislike of Beverly Hills and southern Californian attitudes and values cause the marriage to end, with Barbara returning to San Francisco. Barbara begins a desultory affair with her lawyer, Boyd Kimmelman, undergoes psychotherapy for depression, and begins writing a novel, *The President's Wife*, which takes her to Washington to interview a former first lady. Young May Ling, the daughter of Sally and Joseph Lavette, falls in love with a young Chicano from Higate, but he is sent to Vietnam where he is killed in an enemy attack shown on television in the United States. The horrible scene prompts Barbara to start a feminist antiwar organization, Mothers for Peace.

Other subplots involve the next generation, the legacy of the Lavette and Levy founders: their grandchildren. Frederick Lavette, the son of Barbara's brother Thomas and his first wife, Eloise, leaves Yale with four friends to register black voters in Mississippi, where they are waylaid and beaten by white racists, and two of the students are killed. While scarred by the experience physically and emotionally, Frederick recovers, returning to Higate to focus on producing wine. He will eventually develop a relationship with the young May Ling.

Another important subplot of *The Legacy* concerns Sam, who, unsure about his Jewish identity, chooses Hebrew University in Jerusalem for his premedical studies. In the most powerful section of the novel, Sam is caught up in the battle for Jerusalem in the 1967 Six Day War against the Arab forces. The battle scenes are exciting and realistic, and Sam, a medic, survives to return to San Francisco and his mother, Barbara. Sam eventually will marry Carla Truaz, the sister of the young Chicano with whom May Ling was in love. The final event of the novel is the death of Jean Lavette at seventy-seven of cancer; she is the last of the founding generation.

The Immigrant's Daughter

The Immigrant's Daughter, as its title suggests, focuses entirely on Barbara Lavette, who is sixty years old at the beginning of the novel. Her lover, Boyd Kimmelman, has recently died, and Barbara is given a birthday party at Higate. We learn that the marriages of Frederick and May Ling and Sam and Carla are troubled. Josh Levy, crippled by Vietnam, commits suicide. Barbara runs for Congress against Alexander Holt (she had run unexpectedly well six years earlier, but had lost), occasioning some interesting satire on what Fast amusingly named *candidatitus* when he himself ran for office in New York—the conviction against all common sense that one can win. Barbara is ahead when Holt, with whom she has shared an amicable relationship, puts a red-baiting television commercial on the air, which wins the election. Sam divorces Carla and marries Mary Lou Constable, the daughter of anti-Semitic parents. Barbara's brother, Tom, from whom she has long been estranged, dies. Her nephew Frederick, who has worked in Barbara's campaign, divorces May Ling to marry Carla. Barbara, lonely and at loose ends, visits the Bernhards in Malibu, where she meets her ex-husband, Carson Devron, and becomes involved in a trip to El Salvador to cover the war for Devron's paper, the *L.A. World*.

Barbara interviews rebels in El Salvador and leaves after receiving death threats. Clifford Abrahams, her contact in that country, is killed just after she leaves. Back in San Francisco, she learns that Frederick, who has broken up with Carla, is having an affair with May Ling, his former wife. Clair Levy is dying, and Barbara travels to Higate to see her, meeting the remaining members of her extended family. Barbara and Sam establish a warmer relationship; Sam's wife is pregnant, and he seems more mature. Carson agrees to publish a column by Barbara, and they continue a mostly platonic relationship. Finally, Barbara becomes involved in the nuclear freeze movement, returning to active political involvement. She has survived her adventures and traumatic losses of lovers and has rejoined society.

STRUCTURE

The basic underlying pattern is chronological and geographical, moving forward in time and shifting around the Bay Area. As a saga covering a hundred years of family and American history, *The Immigrants* and the novels that follow it are unified by their characters' continuing histories, while divided into "generations," decades-long chunks of time focused on important incidents and current events. The first unit in the first novel runs from 1888, with Joseph and Anna Lavette in a steerage hold, to 1933, with Dan working as a mackerel fisherman out of San Pedro and living in Westwood with May Ling, her parents, and his son, Joseph. The next unit, in *Second Generation,* begins in June 1934 with Dan in the same job and his daughter, Barbara, having left Sarah Lawrence College. It ends with Dan Lavette's meeting the new man in Barbara's life, Bernie Cohen, at the wedding of Sally Levy and Joseph Lavette in 1946 at Higate. *The Establishment* picks up the story two years later, in 1948, with Barbara and Bernie and their son in uneasy domesticity. The final scenes are Barbara's epiphany on a mountainside graveyard in Israel and her return to San Francisco in 1958. *The Legacy* starts in same year, 1958, with the death of Dan Lavette and Barbara in Los Angeles to write the script for her novel, at which point she meets Carson Devron. It ends ten years later, in 1968, with Barbara and her old lawyer, Boyd Kimmelman, in San Francisco. The last book in the series, *The Immigrant's Daughter,* opens with Barbara thinking about her sixtieth birthday, in 1974. The series closes in 1982 with Barbara still involved in left-wing politics and living a full life at age sixty-eight. Seeing the years covered in chart form shows the structure of the five works:

Work	*Period*	*Characters Emphasized*
The Immigrants	1888–1933	Dan and Jean, Mark Levy
Second Generation	1934–1946	Barbara, Dan and Jean, Higate characters
The Establishment	1948–1958	Barbara, Bernie, Dan and Jean, Tom, Sally and Joe
The Legacy	1958–1968	Barbara
The Immigrant's Daughter	1974–1982	Barbara

The list makes Barbara's dominance of the five books clear, as it does the nearly seamless chronology: Barbara is virtually the only main character who appears throughout all five books, and there are almost no gaps in the chronology.

The structure within the novels is similar. The first three books (but not *The Legacy* and *The Immigrant's Daughter,* whose chapters or sections are untitled) are divided into parts. For example, in the first novel, after an introduction, "The Immigrants," comes Part One, "Fisherman's Wharf," Part Two, "Russian Hill," Part Three, "Sons and Daughters," Part Four, "The Vintage," Part Five, "The Wind," and Part Six, "The Whirlwind." Each part corresponds to an important event in Dan Lavette's life, from his setting up shop on Fisherman's Wharf to erecting a mansion for Jean on Russian Hill, from the birth of his and his circle's children to some of the children's creation of an independent life (at Higate Winery, in Part Four, "The Vintage"), from the beginning of troubles for the L&L empire to the whirlwind of the stock market crash of 1929. (Such tags are useful references, and one wonders why Fast dropped them in the last two books.)

Within parts there are usually several distinct scenes, much as in a film, with a complete change of characters and setting. Typically, the first sentence of a new part, and each new scene in the part, signals clearly the topic to be dealt with. Fast is always the model stylist, with prose so translucent it hardly ever calls attention to itself. Sometimes these topics are historical background, or a recapitulation of a situation or character. For example, "Fisherman's Wharf" begins, "Perhaps never before in history—or since for that matter—did a new city arise from the ashes of the old as quickly, as hopefully, as vitally as San Francisco" (*The Immigrants* 41). More often the opening sentence will set up the character and situation to be dealt with, as in the first statement of "Russian Hill": "It was in August of 1914, soon after the birth of their second child, that Dan and Jean Lavette moved into their new house on Russian Hill" (*The Immigrants* 106). The opening sentences often help the reader keep track of time, a necessary task given the scope of the books, with an initial phrase or clause: "Three days after the earthquake . . ."; "On Wednesday the eighteenth of April in 1906 . . ."; "At thirty years of age . . ."; "That night, at dinner in his home . . ." This is no more than good writing, of course, but Fast's consistency and discipline silently guide the reader through what might in other hands be a morass of characters and plots.

Thus the structure of *The Immigrants* and its progeny consists of single continuous strands woven together into a narrative rope, with some strands fairly thick and well developed—the strand of Jean and Dan, for example—and others merely brightly colored strings or even just threads, as in the less important characters of Stephan Cassala and Martha Levy or the even less visible Rosa Cassala, Stephan's sister. The function of this narrative weaving is that it moves the story relentlessly onward, keeping the reader turning pages in anticipation of events to come. There is little flashback used except for strategic reasons, for example, to explain how Barbara has come to know Carson Devron at the beginning of *The Legacy*, or to provide a quick sketch of the Napa Valley or a short disquisition on shipyards during and after the depression. Like the characters' lives, the narrative structure unreels continuously, but with continuous change of scene and subject as well.

KEY CHARACTERS

The Immigrants series has well over fifty characters, many of whom appear only briefly, and a host of others who receive treatment in a series of ongoing subplots but who remain minor. These include, for example, Martha Levy, the daughter of Mark and Sarah and the sister of Jake. Martha has ambitions in the theatrical world and moves to Hollywood to become an actress. Her appearance not only links the second generations of the Cassala and Levy families but also provides a location shift that allows Fast to depict Los Angeles and the Hollywood movie scene in the 1920s, a topic on which he writes elsewhere. After being cheated out of money supplied by Stephan Cassala for acting lessons and humiliated by a sleazy producer, Martha commits suicide by driving off Mulholland Drive.

In spite of its title, The Immigrants series is built around the character of Barbara Lavette. As previously noted, Fast says that while in California, he "decided to write a book about a woman whose life and experience would parallel my own, having her born the year and month of my own birth, namely November in 1914. . . . I called her Barbara Lavette" (*Contemporary Authors Autobiography Series* 18: 184). Even if Fast did get the month of her birth wrong, we can take him at his word that the novel began with his conception of Barbara, not with Dan Lavette, as the position of *The Immigrants* as the first in the series and as the author-character gender identity would suggest. There is very little of Fast in Dan Lavette, and even less in the circle that surrounds Dan, but as we have seen, there is a great deal that is similar between Fast and Barbara. Fast said about his motivation for creating Barbara, "I enjoy writing about women," and, in fact, before starting *The Immigrants* he had a decade's worth of experience, more than one novel a year in the 1960s, each titled with a woman's name, from *Sylvia* in 1960 to *Millie* in 1973, twelve in all. Unlike the historical novels of his early career, which focused on the experiences of men and had few important women characters, the 1960s books validate the truth of Fast's claim about enjoying writing about women, for they are generally excellent and sensitive depictions of female experiences.

While it is instructive to see the genesis of Barbara Lavette as Fast experimenting with a female version of himself, this fact does little to explain the appeal of Barbara and her family for 10 million purchasers of the books in the series, and perhaps untold millions more readers. The student of Fast's work can see much of his life and times in *The Immigrants*, but such insight was not available to readers who bought the first book and were motivated to continue buying and reading four more. It is tempting to find the appeal of the series in the neat pattern created in the initial novel—the pattern formed by Dan, Jean, and Barbara Lavette. The triumvirate certainly work together to form a satisfying resolution to a common American conflict: the struggle between old established wealth and brash new energy. From colonial times to our own, new immigrants have challenged the established order, rocking the ship of state and infusing new ideas and approaches. As the title suggests, this is what the series is about—the continual flow of new citizens to California and the resolution of the struggle in a new order: in Hegelian terms, thesis, antithesis, synthesis.

Jean Seldon, although the product of her grandfather's immigration to California in search of wealth during the gold rush of 1851, is herself a synthesis of the rough-and-ready frontier settlers and the establishment propriety of the Boston branch of the family, which brings the Seldons respectability. She, in turn, is attracted to Dan, not simply because he is handsome but because of her own rebellion against propriety. Dan is her "fisherman," a breath of fresh air in the stuffy Victorian surroundings of Nob Hill. Dan is raw ambition, pure potential unrealized and offering untold possibilities; he is a life force full of the energy symbolized when he and Jean race up the San Francisco hills as if they were flat land. The spoiled rich girl, however, discovers that she wants only so much fresh air, and the marriage soon sours. Barbara, who combines Dan's seriousness, energy, and creativity with Jean's elegance, sense of style, and dignity, can thus be seen as a very satisfactory resolution to this conflict, one that can be seen as a continuing phenomenon of life in an immigrant nation.

While this neat pattern certainly is present, it does not fully explain Barbara's appeal, for she is a more complex character than either of her parents. Fast is fond of the word *strange* as an explanatory concept for the Lavettes (and for the Levys as well), repeating it frequently, but neither Dan nor Jean seems particularly strange. Dan's enormous drive to escape new immigrant poverty is confirmed by direct observation of any U.S. immigrant community: new Americans work as hard as Dan does and frequently skew the shape of their lives to ensure success, sacrificing family life and other pleasures for the sake of the next generation, but sometimes losing contact with their children as a result of their enormous efforts. Dan's love of the competitive game is also very familiar, as both an immigrant characteristic and a masculine one; indifference to money for its own sake is not unusual among some high achievers. For all May Ling's Chinese culture, Dan's liaison with her is clearly a return to the familiar immigrant and social class values her family represents, paralleling Jean's withdrawal from Dan and movement back toward her family and society friends.

Jean is not particularly strange either. Her early rejection of Dan seems cold and heartless to the reader but is easily seen as the end of youthful exploration and experimentation; Jean turns to the mildly bohemian San Francisco art community, once posing in the nude and even dabbling with a lesbian relationship, before, typically, returning to the socially conservative fold of her circle. Her one continuing rebellion is her promotion of modern art to an unreceptive San Francisco, but this is hardly eccentric behavior. Jean's increasing appreciation of family and her attempts to reconcile with Dan make sense after her marriage to the bloodless and prissy John Whittier; her attempts to nurture her emotional life in the face of what Fast calls her Protestant restraint are affecting but clearly understandable.

Barbara remains the key figure in the series, for most of the other important characters, though well rounded and interesting, provide few psychological mysteries. The men of action, including the Levy and Lavette team of Feng Wo, Dan's Chinese accountant, Mark Levy, his Jewish partner, Sam Goldberg, his Jewish lawyer, and Anthony Cassala, his Italian banker, are just that—a supporting cast of actors who get the things done that Dan thinks need doing. They are interesting because of their distinct heritages and well-shaped personalities, but their motivations are for the most part clear. More problematic and interesting psychologically are Tom Lavette, a somewhat shadowy figure forever lurking on the edge of the Lavette threesome of Dan, Jean, and Barbara, and Bernie Cohen, the idealist turned professional soldier.

Tom Lavette can be seen as a mirror image of Barbara, always choosing propriety and respectability, wealth and power, discretion and a secret life, where Barbara chooses their opposites. In terms of what Dan and Jean represent, Tom would therefore be Jean's dutiful and proper child rather than Dan's rebellious one, and in fact that orientation runs throughout the series: Dan loses all contact with Tom, while Jean is constantly lunching with him and striving to maintain contact. The drive to conform, even to the point of denying or hiding personal eccentricities, is a fascinating one, and Fast is clearly interested in the wellsprings of Tom's behavior. His marriage to Lucy Sommers suggests that Tom has never shaken his mother's influence and must reject the passive Eloise in favor of tough-as-nails Lucy, who will dominate him and define his purpose in life. The other interesting man-child in the series is Bernie Cohen, who, at least in Barbara's eyes, cannot resist playing soldier even in his forties. Here we see several of Fast's themes located in one character: the conflict between joining a band of brothers dedicated to a cause and living a normal domestic life, a theme seen in the Revolutionary War books; and the conflict between joining a just war or maintaining pacifist principles. Bernie's behavior offers no simple answers, but the questions are defined clearly.

Two of Fast's female characters in *The Immigrants* reflect his own interest and experience in theater and film as well as the deep longing for movie stardom that Fast explored in his novel about the film business, *Max*. Martha Levy is a victim of Hollywood's allure, acting out theatrical parts for Clair's benefit and ultimately succumbing to the pull of the bright lights; she represents the thousands of young women anxious for fame who come to a bad end in the jungle of deceit that is Fast's recurrent portrait of the movie capital. Sally Levy Lavette, Martha's niece and Joe Lavette's wife, is a success story in that she too gives up family, Joe and her baby May Ling, for Hollywood, but manages to reject its blandishments and return to the town of Napa, where she lives as a mother and wife. We see in Sally an extreme version of Barbara. Both are liberated women who choose careers but still crave domesticity; Sally, however, lacks Barbara's basic restraint and good sense and swings, pendulum-like, from being Joe's wife to being a Hollywood star, and back to being Joe's wife again. She is an interesting character because of her extreme emotionalism; almost a counterpoise to Jean, she exhibits no restraint whatsoever and will say or do whatever is on her mind at the moment. Interestingly enough, this complete lack of an emotional censor is what makes her a natural actress, in Fast's description, since she is able to lose herself completely in the part she is playing. Such facility comes at a huge price in her relation with others, and Sally, to her credit, is unwilling to pay the price for fame and wealth.

Barbara Lavette thus remains one of the few complete characters among the dozen or so who figure importantly in the series. Dan, Jean, Tom, May Ling, Mark Levy, Anthony Cassala, Martha Levy, Bernie Cohen, Sally Levy, Joe Lavette are all bedeviled to some degree by interior demons or an inability to adjust to unfortunate circumstance. Only Barbara has a secure emotional and philosophical center of gravity that returns her, like a weighted children's toy, to a more or less upright position after being pounded by life's forces. (Dan and Jean recover their equilibrium, but only in the last stage of their lives; Sally survives Hollywood, but at the cost of her career.) Barbara is thus truly a key figure, for she represents Fast's best answer to the central question of the novels: how to react to life's rewards and punishments.

Barbara represents the golden mean. She is, after all, the amalgam of Jean and Dan's genes, and we are told repeatedly that she has her father's height and her mother's coloring, Dan's strength and Jean's lyrical beauty. But unlike either of her parents, Barbara can strike a happy medium between work and home life, between being rich and being normal, between parenthood and professionalism, between radical politics and conservative good sense. She is no feminist—the women's movement did not come into full existence until the time of the final novels—but she is fiercely independent and self-defining. Her solution to the problem of wealth, which corrupts her brother, Tom, is to give it away, and her response to the beauty that defines but sometimes limits Jean is to ignore her own attractiveness. She balances home and family with her career as a writer, appreciating Spode bone china, to Jean's shock, but also writing a piece on Spode china for *Woman's Home Companion* magazine. Through such selective domesticity and professionalism she avoids the alienation from family that Dan fell into when he became consumed by work. Barbara bounces back from the deaths of her fiancé and husband, both dead because of chance events; even Jean, after Dan dies, suddenly realizes that Barbara has suffered the death of a husband twice. As a writer, Barbara is not original or brilliant so much as honest, a truthful and dutiful recorder of events and emotions. She can be sentimental and emotional, sometimes shooting from the hip when confronted by a severe injustice, yet she disciplines her feelings with a lifestyle and a restraint that would make a Puritan father proud. This amalgam of contradictory characteristics, of emotion versus reason, of the grand gesture (summed up by her refusal to bend to HUAC) versus her conventional and moral way of life, constitutes the way Fast thinks a life should be lived, and echoes the way he himself has lived his own life.

THEMATIC ISSUES

America as Second Chance

The larger theme of *The Immigrants* is a central one in American literature: America as a new Eden, a new chance for the European and other immigrants who have overpopulated and despoiled their native countries with war, pollution, and greed. The East Coast was always the direct inheritor of European custom and European philosophy. However much radicals like Tom Paine or the soldiers of the Pennsylvania Line from Fast's *The Proud and the Free* tried to throw off the mental shackles of social class, family privilege, and wealth, they always ended up tied down by the old ways, however ameliorated from their brutal European models. With California, everyone with the courage to immigrate—even from Boston or Baltimore—could compete equitably without the advantages of social class and inherited wealth. Fast makes us feel how new and unspoiled California was at the end of the nineteenth century. True, the original Mexican land-grant holders were pushed out, as we are reminded in *The Legacy*, but their numbers were small. The opportunity of the new land was theoretically open to anyone, for, as Sam Goldberg muses, California was the "only place on earth where a Jew was not a Jew but simply an immigrant in a world of immigrants" (*Second Generation* 94–95). He recognizes Dan and Barbara as pure products of the state, unbiased and ready to accept people for what they are, not on the basis of race, religion, class, or ethnic background. Even the prejudiced Jean comes to accept Jews, and we see in the story of Feng Wo and May Ling that the virulent hatred of Chinese turns into tolerance. Anthony Cassala is the first important Italian banker in San Francisco; Dan, whose French-Italian ethnic background is mixed to begin with, apparently retains only enough Italian to order in a restaurant, and even gives up his Catholicism in order to marry Jean. The melting pot is alive and well in California.

Cities and Lifestyles in Contrast

A related theme is the competing visions of San Francisco and Los Angeles. This theme is played mostly for comedy—Los Angeles is wonderful if you're an orange, says Jean in *The Legacy*—but there is a serious point as well in the literal and figurative coolness of the northern city in comparison with the sprawling, overheated, and sometimes vulgar style of Los Angeles, in no small part a product of the dream-factory nature of the movie business. Fast clearly votes for restraint and chilly summers, but he is open to the argument that Los Angeles too offers opportunity for those who have failed everywhere else: the dispossessed, the unwanted, the eccentric. The magic of southern California, as Sally Levy Lavette discovers, is that dreams sometimes do come true.

The Entrepreneurial Frontier

An interrelated thematic concern is the welcome that California gives to entrepreneurs like Dan Lavette. For all San Francisco's pretensions, it is still a frontier, and there is room for large visions and massive gambles on the future. However, the "second generation," as Fast calls them in his title, can become the establishment—the Tom Lavettes working in conjunction with the John Whittiers, men no longer risk-taking gamblers who create whole new industries but rather managers and money men who operate behind the scenes to grasp power and control. For all his socialist beliefs, Fast clearly depicts Dan Lavette as a positive force, a creator of industries and jobs rather than a mean-spirited Whittier squeezing the last dime of profit out of the miserable longshoremen. Capitalism, in other words, can be used as a positive force, though in the long run it is taken over by the worst of men and, in the case of the young Jean taking over the Seldon Bank, the worst of women.

Fast's fascination with the effects of power and money is evident throughout the series. Dan's various enterprises hire thousands of workers, and Anthony Cassala's Bank of Sonoma serves small business and immigrants unable to find credit elsewhere. Dan, as a shipbuilder on Terminal Island near San Pedro, slaves to meet his payroll and to keep his workers employed during the depression. World Wars I and II generate huge profits for the shipping business and enormous guaranteed contracts for Dan's shipbuilding operation. The series traces the busts and booms created by the San Francisco earthquake, the world wars, and the social and technological changes in between.

Troubles in Paradise

No credible Garden of Eden can exist without a snake or two, and the later books bring up problems in the California paradise. *The Legacy* in particular tries to capture the chaotic social changes that characterized the 1960s, with its divisions over the Vietnam War, social and sexual experimentation, violence over civil rights, and use of drugs. Each of these changes is encapsulated in a character or situation, as the third generation of Lavettes and Levys escapes from the ways of life that characterized their elders. The Vietnam War and the protests against it are summed up by the battlefield death, captured on television, of Ruby Truaz, the fiancé of young May Ling. The tragedy echoes Barbara's own loss of a fiancé in the Spanish Civil War. Her response, the formation of Mothers for Peace, calls to mind the Mothers Strike for Peace and a number of other women's antiwar organizations. The protests and divisions on the home front are summed up when her brother's wife, Lucy, arranges for the torching of Barbara's house. We see the use of drugs among the third generation of Lavettes and Levys, the self-described "wolf-pack," when marijuana is passed around casually at their fireplace overlooking Higate; May Ling even comments on how common drug use has become in her school. The events of Frederick Lavette's trip to Mississippi to register black voters parallel the murder of civil rights workers James Cheney, Andrew Goodman, and Michael Schwerner in that state in 1964. Finally, we see chaos in the families of the 1960s, with Samuel and Carla divorced, and Frederick and May Ling also divorced but as people of the time said, "living in sin," that is, living together without benefit of clergy. Again, Fast wisely shows us that modern life tends to reinvent the wheel, for divorce has been common among the older generations as well, and Jean and Dan lived together without benefit of marriage after their later unions ended. Each generation expresses its behavior in highly individualistic ways, but the behavior itself is not new. Despite the apparent familial chaos in *The Immigrant's Daughter*, family life continues, although even Barbara, who has lived with Dan, Jean, and May Ling, does not seem to completely recognize the parallels.

Immigrant Adjustment

Another California problem is assimilation. This theme occurs early in *The Immigrants*, with the prejudice against Feng Wo and later against

May Ling, both Chinese culturally but far more American than Asian in all but appearance. This prejudice fades quickly in San Francisco, and only minor suggestions of discrimination against Asians come up in the later books. There is a recurrent assimilation theme involving Mexican-Americans. Fast carefully uses the term *chicano,* meaning a U.S.-born person of Mexican descent, but the term alone does not change the reality of their unassimilated status. We see Ruby Truaz drafted, apparently unfairly, and Carla, his sister, expresses many Chicano complaints about bad treatment by Anglo society, especially in her anger over the limited number of Hispanic parts available to her as an actress. The parallel situation concerns Sam, Barbara's son with Bernie Cohen, who combines the Protestant/French-Italian-Catholic background of Jean and Dan Lavette with the Jewish heritage and Zionism of his father. Sam's confusion drives him from a snobbish and prejudiced New England prep school to premed studies in Israel. His exciting episode as a medic in the Six Day War gives him a sense of Israeli identity, but there is no simple resolution to the larger problem of assimilation—not for Sam, for Carla, or for any other hyphenated American anxious to keep elements of the old culture alive in the New World. The heavy emphasis on identity in the 1960s led to a new emphasis on ethnic heritage, and this concern runs counter to what Dan Lavette found in California, a chance to jettison all the cultural baggage of Europe—language, ethnic cuisine, religion—and to start over. Assimilation is a torturous issue, and Fast is careful to avoid a simplistic answer.

Universal Human Concerns

Finally, even in the West Coast paradise, people grow old. In the last books of the series, Dan, who has been the definition of energy and vigor, ages, weakens (though he can still handle the muggers in Golden Gate Park), and ultimately dies. Jean's loss of her beauty is nearly fatal for her self-image, for she is of a time when appearance was the ultimate definition of a woman, and she must construct a new identity as a somewhat crotchety old lady. Barbara, at age forty-five, looks at herself in the mirror and sees too that her youthful good looks have gone. The last book, *The Immigrant's Daughter,* shows Barbara facing the other problems of old age: the loss of her lover, Boyd Kimmelman; a feeling of uselessness; conflicts with her adult son and daughters-in-law. She adjusts to a cooler sexual fire with Carson Devron, to an accommodation with Sam's new wife, to her own lack of direction, and to the loss of old friends and relatives. She allows herself to be drawn into politics and returns to her writing, not young again certainly, but with a new understanding that life must be lived fully.

But readers did not buy 10 million copies of The Immigrants series simply to read economic and historical/sociological treatises. Much of the pleasure of the books comes from seeing the large thematic concerns affect the more homely domestic situations of the characters. The series is full of family themes and issues as well: marriages, births, separations, divorces, and finally deaths. The thousands of pages of exposition allow us to come to know the characters intimately, to predict their reactions, and to be surprised by their interconnections. Fast knows the secret of all effective family sagas: to give us heroes and villains, people to root for and people to hiss at. Dan and Barbara are especially vulnerable as characters, and watching them move through the major passages of life gives the story an elemental thematic interest that transcends simple storytelling.

ALTERNATIVE READINGS: SOCIALIST/MARXIST, FEMINIST, AND AUTOBIOGRAPHICAL INTERPRETATIONS

The economic, political, and sociological elements of The Immigrants series tempt the reader to see it from a socialist perspective, an approach surely legitimized by Fast's leftist background. Given his early training, how could he not formulate the hundred-year saga in Marxist terms? Socialist/Marxist theory postulates that the key to human behavior is the economic relationship between individuals and groups, the alienation of capital and labor from their immediate fruits, and the inevitable division of humanity into socioeconomic camps, with a consequent oppression of laboring groups by the moneyed class and a struggle by the oppressed for liberation. A Marxist reading would focus on issues of social class, with the central division lying between Dan and Jean; on uses of capital, focusing again on Dan and on Tom, John Whittier, the Seldons, and the establishment of the third book; and on economic forces in general at work in society, as in the sections on the world wars and the depression.

All the elements for a socialist/Marxist reading are present, yet the series does not in any way read like a manifesto; rather, it has the quirkiness of real history. For all his unrestrained defense of socialist values,

Fast was never a disciplined ideologue, and in fact when he was a party member, he was continually in trouble for allowing his artistic instincts to overrule the party line. The Immigrants series gives cold comfort to strict economic constructionists, for though economic forces clearly rule, the directed efforts of single individuals—Dan, Barbara, Feng Wo—have enormous influence as well. Economic forces create the Lavettes, but the Lavettes make history as well, and much of the pleasure of the books is in Fast's refusal to sort things out neatly into oversimplified cause and effect.

In fact, a recurring theme is Barbara's attempts to escape the Lavette money. She sets up the Lavette Foundation with the $14 million she inherits, hoping to avoid, perhaps, what she sees as the unhappiness of her mother's life and certainly to avoid being like the despised John Whittier. Barbara is indifferent to money, dressing in plain clothing and living in her tiny San Francisco house. Jean has a fling at capitalism when she heads the Seldon Bank but mainly cares about money as freedom to buy expensive modern paintings. Dan explicitly denies any love of money, seeing it only as a way to keep track of how well he is doing; he makes and loses a fortune with equanimity. The Cassala clan and the residents of Higate seem to have a healthy attitude toward wealth, the latter finding pleasure in making wine and in the beauty of the Napa Valley, rather than in considering their winery a new business empire. Sally Levy gives up Beverly Hills and a career in movies almost as quickly as Barbara does, making a life in Napa as a doctor's wife and nurse. Only John Whittier and Tom Lavette look like conventional capitalists as viewed through socialist eyes: they are both repressed and mean-spirited, and Tom turns into a lonely and aloof figure atop a San Francisco skyscraper, more pathetic than villainous.

Thus, though The Immigrants series looks ripe for socialist plucking, a Marxist reading of it probably distorts rather than elucidates. Rather than a scientific socialist formula, we get a humane, modernized medieval lesson: money need not be the root of all evil if there are other things that matter; good values are easier to practice on a farm/winery but can exist even in San Francisco, as Barbara shows. Even robber baron capitalists can do some good if imbued with the basic decency of a Dan Lavette.

A more productive reading may be to look at the series as a feminist work, with Barbara Lavette overcoming the expectations of her society and the people around her to find her own way. As we have seen in the feminist alternative reading of *April Morning*, feminists refuse to take male versions of the world as the ultimate reality and seek to obviate male definition and control of female behavior. A feminist reading of the series would examine Barbara's relationships with John Whittier, her false stepfather, and with Dan, her true mentor, with Marcel Duboise, her colleague and lover who helps her become sophisticated, and with Bernie Cohen, who struggles against her pacifism and her domesticity. Barbara's attempts at charting her own course in life begin when she leaves college, participates in the San Francisco dockworkers' strike, and rejects John Whittier as a controlling stepfather. Her successful efforts to bring Dan back into her life but on a mature and equal basis show her strength in avoiding all patriarchical relationships rather than in exchanging one for another. Throughout, Barbara continues to be self-defining. Giving away her inherited millions through the Lavette Foundation allows her to escape the fate of her brother, who finds wealth ultimately constricting rather than liberating. In her work, Barbara's attempts to become a professional in a literary world that severely constricted the territory available to women, and her triumph as a war correspondent would also be relevant to a feminist reading. Her independent life and her conflict over keeping it that way are classic feminist issues. With Carson Devron, for example, she exchanges an uneasy and unhappy marriage for a loosely structured friendship; her attitude toward marriage is ambivalent, since she recognizes that the compromises that lead to a successful union also will limit her freedom.

Yet Barbara is not clearly a feminist in the early books, at least not in her own description of herself, and even in the later ones, when she begins Mothers for Peace and runs for office, she is more feminist in her behavior than in her ideology. Barbara is, in fact, anti-ideological throughout the long saga, finding her values in moderation and simplicity. Here we do have a return to an earlier Fast theme: the purity of life on a farm or in a small community, as with the Rumpels' homestead in *Citizen Tom Paine,* for example. But Fast has progressed beyond such romantic simplicity, and Barbara would be bored with life at Higate, just as Sally chafes at small-town life in Napa. She is a modern woman, living freely in San Francisco and answering only to the demands she puts on herself. A feminist reading would stress her constant struggle to be self-defining, and the subtle, not always badly intended attempts to rein her in. Carson Devron, for example, seems genuinely puzzled that Barbara cannot make her interests secondary to his own, mainly because he never formulates the problem in those terms. Instead, he is a victim of male assumptions about the proper role of wives and, in his particular case, about the behavior appropriate for a good hostess and member of the Devron clan.

Whether The Immigrants series can be read as a feminist work thus depends on what one means by the term, for though there is an absence of ideology and consistent patterns of male oppression, there is a strong emphasis on female independence, self-definition, and power. Jean, May Ling, Sally, and Barbara all take charge at crucial points and decide on the direction of their own lives. Even Eloise finds her strength. Though sometimes victimized, none is a perpetual victim, and in fact they sometimes control the men in their lives. The only women in the series who might be considered weak are the traditional, still foreign, wives of the first-generation immigrants who practice the traditional feminine role, So-toy, May Ling's mother, and the Cassala women. In the larger sense, then, the series can be seen as a model of how women came to find their independence and power in California society.

Finally, we can easily see the series as autobiographical. Although the Fasts officially lived in California for only a half-dozen years or so, the author visited the coast and had long been fascinated by its geography, climate, and frontier spirit, as is clear from *Max* and some of his detective stories. Barbara is to some degree Fast's stand-in, credited as "a woman whose life and experience would parallel" Fast's own, born in the same year and undergoing the same passages through life. A biographical reading thus has a great deal of credibility.

That Barbara and Fast should be seen as parallels goes beyond the author's testimony. I need not repeat here the many incidents on which Fast drew to create Barbara's character, but one question remains unconsidered: what led Fast to depict some of his own experiences—as a reporter in India, as a novelist, as a scriptwriter in Hollywood—in the person of a female character? True, he says he "enjoys writing about women," but he had, after all, already recounted the India story in *The Pledge*, along with a number of other experiences, including his crucial appearance before the House Un-American Activities Committee and his experiences in jail. Why retell a well-told story yet again, and through the eyes of a female character?

The creation of Barbara Lavette surely says much about Fast—not about the events of his life, but rather about his creativity and even daring as a writer. His series of novels titled with women's names begin with *Sylvia* in 1960, and, as with this first one in the series of twelve, focus on strong, complex, interesting female characters. In the next decade, when the writer was in his sixties, he hit on the notion of reprising his own experiences through Barbara's eyes. Fast had never shied away from the challenge of a very different point of view, looking at the world as a freed American slave with Gideon Jackson in *Freedom Road*, as a gladiator through Spartacus and David in *Spartacus*, and as a revolutionary in *Citizen Tom Paine*. Barbara Lavette's perspective was just another leap for a writer curious about how life seems to others, and it is in this context that The Immigrants series can truly be read as autobiographical novels—works that show us Fast's unique perspective on events.

Seven Days in June
(1994)

So much of our early history is pure invention, pure lies.
                    —Interview with Howard Fast, 1995

With *Seven Days in June*, Fast returned to the Revolutionary War material that had sustained his interest for so much of his career. His most recent Revolutionary War books had been published more than twenty years earlier—*The Crossing* in 1971 and *The Hessian* in the next year. Even earlier, in *The Unvanquished* (1942), Fast had described Washington's retreats from Long Island, from Manhattan Island, from one New Jersey town after another, virtually chased by the British in a humiliating series of defeats. *The Crossing*, a scholarly, well-researched novel, completes the story, with Washington discovering that retreat complemented by a sudden, unexpected attack could be a strategy against the superior forces of the British army. The novel contrasts sharply with its predecessor in its more distanced, less emotional style. We feel we are reading a historical document brought to vivid life rather than a narrative based on history. In turn, *The Hessian* is a fine, melancholy look at a seemingly trivial engagement at the end of the war, a bare footnote to history that nevertheless sums up all the brutality and inhumanity war creates.

Seven Days in June has connections to both novels: to *The Crossing* in its explicit reliance on historical research and to *The Hessian* in that it shares the same protagonist as *Seven Days*, Evan Feversham. Fast's style changes over the years, from the luminous characters and heightened emotions that were his signature as far back as *Two Valleys* (1933), his first book, to a flatter, less romantic style in the books of the 1960s and after. The early style is more lush, somewhat comparable to that of F. Scott Fitzgerald; the later style is more in the tradition of American realism, of writers as diverse as Ernest Hemingway, James Jones, and Norman Mailer. In the early style, historical research provides an authentic backdrop; it may be integrated into the plot and characterization, but it serves mainly to heighten the effect of character and theme. In the later works characters are more human sized and realistic; they are very much products of their times, and the research tends to flatten and distance them, although also giving them more scholarly credibility. It is in this latter vein that *Seven Days in June* is written.

Evan Feversham, the shared protagonist of *The Hessian* and *Seven Days in June*, results from what is known in film criticism as a prequel, a useful if maligned term for a film produced after a successful work, a sequel, but set in an earlier time, and thus a *prequel*. *The Hessian* is set in the waning years of the Revolutionary War; it takes place on the Connecticut High Ridge, far from the Continental and British armies in the south, with Feversham as a burned-out army surgeon who is doubly alienated: he was brought up British, though we learn he fought on the American side, and he is a Catholic in a bigoted Protestant area of Connecticut. He is still an outsider, "a recipient of the dubious and grudging grace that Connecticut extended to Quakers, Papists, Jews and others of the damned" (*The Hessian* 23). Doctor Feversham is dour and sour, appalled by the human cost of war and by the way it forces complex moral issues into opposing categories of right and wrong. In fact, he is attracted to the nonjudgmental Christianity of some local Quakers but is opposed by Squire Abraham Hunt, the head of the local militia, a commanding man who never hesitates about moral decisions and is convinced of the rightness of his behavior.

The conflict of the plot concerns a Hessian contingent of sixteen soldiers offloaded from a British ship and marched through the pacific and essentially demilitarized Connecticut countryside, apparently on some reconnaissance mission. They hang a mentally disabled man who might give the alarm, and in one of Fast's memorable and gory battle scenes, the local militia—"farmers, storekeepers, a blacksmith and his two helpers, two carpenters and a cooper, and Biddle, the fuller, and Saxon, the undertaker," ranging in age from fourteen to ninety-one (*The Hessian*

38)—hide behind two Connecticut stone walls lining the path the Hessians will take, and spring up on signal to massacre the Germans with a withering crossfire. Only the drummer boy leading the contingent escapes, taking refuge with Quakers. The squire leads the chase after the wounded drummer, who is surreptitiously treated by Feversham; the boy is captured and court-martialed at the village tavern, with the historical General Packenham brought in to preside. The drummer, pathetically, gives a Nuremberg defense: "I am good soldier, I obey orders" (163), but the verdict is predictable, given local fear and hatred: the boy is hanged.

Feversham's struggle with Squire Hunt over the drummer boy is both personal and philosophical. Feversham says he knows too much about war, while "Hunt knew too little" (39). The squire is a respected judge, while Feversham is a nonjudgmental healer of both sides, of whoever the sick may be. The squire has contempt for men who will not defend their own and says to Feversham, "In your eyes [the Quakers who sheltered the Hessian drummer] have done nothing. In my eyes . . . they've betrayed our cause" (166). The squire says to Feversham, "I know how to hate, and you don't, and hate is a lovely thing" (170). The squire is specific in his belief in the Old Testament dictum of an eye for an eye.

The surgeon's own morally sophisticated stance is complex, with Feversham disturbed by "Puritan righteousness"; when challenged to name a cause more just than the American, he suggests Oliver Cromwell's, pointing out ironically that as a Catholic he cannot be expected to view that Protestant radical leader objectively. When this leads to a charge of having no side, Feversham at first answers with a kind of moral relativism, saying his wife, house, and patients are all American, thereby creating his sympathy, while the British had behaved abominably in general and toward Catholics in particular. But he also says he does not admire neutrality and truly respects the Quakers for being "on the side of mankind" (106).

The argument between the squire and Feversham is the debate we see in different forms throughout Fast's canon: should I take sides or simply withdraw and follow my own personal interests? What circumstances demand that I violate principles of peaceful coexistence and the golden rule, or perhaps even stricter dictates of religious dogma? The moral compasses of Tom Paine, of Washington, of all the Revolutionary War characters in Fast's works, tend to point firmly in one direction, but Feversham's swings in a number of directions. He has his own Catholic values, though he is a nonpracticing religionist, and he has his wartime experiences, which convince him of the futility of choosing the "right" side, since all end up in slaughter. He recognizes the rigor of the Puritan way, understanding that Americans are not "Englishmen two or three or four generations removed from Europe" (169–170), having fought for and tamed the new land, not through mercy but through toughness and endurance. A running observation throughout *The Hessian* is that the Puritans used millions of stones to build hundreds of miles of stone walls, a dedication to hard work and seriousness that gives them clear title to the land they tamed. They are not without tolerance and an awareness of the virtues of difference, but Feversham finds their uncompromising stances ultimately inhumane, even in his own dearly loved wife. On the other hand, the Quaker practice of providing food and shelter to both sides in the war has made them despised, but even in these partisan times, there is a grudging respect for their practice of Christian values. When challenged as to his own beliefs, Feversham answers that he finds the Quaker way of life "interesting—and often admirable" but that he lacks "both the courage and the desire to turn the other cheek" (104).

The road from Tom Paine to Evan Feversham is a long one, from youthful confidence in the redemption provided by revolution, even bloody revolution, to doubt about war and violence as solutions, and it is significant that Fast recreates the earlier experiences of the surgeon in his novel about Bunker Hill. Even a war like the Revolutionary War, one we think of as justified if only because we cannot imagine our present identity without it, raises doubts. Like Tom Paine himself, Fast does not give up his principles but, rather, moderates his views. Means and ends must be looked at together, something the loutish Packenham and the severe and righteous Squire Hunt would never consider seriously. Feversham's insight in *The Hessian* is that the Quaker formula for serving humanity provides the model of true morality, of "being on the side of mankind," but Quaker restraint in the face of passion may never be possible for most people. Feversham, himself a passionate man, struggles with the question of involvement in righteous action in the microcosm created in *The Hessian*. In *Seven Days in June*, Fast creates a much larger arena for his agonized attempts to serve humanity without taking up a partisan position.

PLOT DEVELOPMENT: TWO SIDES TO THE BATTLE OF BUNKER HILL

Seven Days in June is just that: a description of the five days leading up to the Battle of Breed's Hill, later known as the Battle of Bunker Hill, of the events on the day of the battle, and of the following day. The narrative begins with the flogging to death of a British sailor on a man-of-war in Boston Harbor, a punishment for the adolescent trick of putting a dead rat in the officer's soup. The scene then shifts to the next day, June 13, and the four British army leaders: Sir William Howe, sent from England to deal with the colonial rebellion; his two seconds in command, Major General Henry Clinton and Major General John Burgoyne; and General Thomas Gage, nominally in command and the only one of the four with a real understanding of America but out of favor because of his failures at the battles of Lexington and Concord. (Clinton had extensive knowledge of America but a very British point of view.) The four are unsure about how to handle the situation in Boston, which has been largely abandoned. The American patriots now hold it under siege with an "army" made up of fifteen thousand farmers and other civilians. After the fiascos at Lexington and Concord, the British officers are reluctant to trigger a true war by overreacting to the colonial challenge, yet their instinct as professional soldiers is to sweep the Americans aside with their three thousand British troops, the best soldiers in the world. The immediate interest of the British newcomers, however, is the Tory (British loyalist) women remaining in Boston, and Clinton makes an immediate conquest of Prudence Hallsbury, the wife of an older Church of England minister.

The second chapter or "day," June 14, shifts the scene to Evan Feversham, the former British military surgeon living in Connecticut who has volunteered his services to the rebels. He is accompanied by Dr. Benjamin Church, an incompetent physician who has insinuated himself onto the Committee of Safety, the group nominally in charge. We see that the American forces are mostly groups of amateur soldiers, village militia groups, many of them boys out for a lark. Feversham meets Dr. Joseph Warren, another medical man who has been named commander in chief of the militia. Then, in a letter to his wife, Feversham writes about the events of the day and his personal doubts as to why he has put himself at risk.

June 15 shifts back to the British, with Sir William Howe beginning his notorious affair with the even more notorious Mrs. Loring. Halfway through this section, the scene turns to Feversham and Warren, whose relationship of mutual respect has cemented their common belief that invisible living things cause infection, a radical theory at the time. Feversham, the most experienced military surgeon among the continentals, shocks his fellow physicians by insisting on the painful application of rum to sterilize battlefield wounds.

By June 16 Clinton is already nervous about the scandal that Howe's affair with Mrs. Loring will create, and Howe pays off her estranged husband with the position of officer in charge of colonial prisoners. The remainder of the chapter treats Feversham's preparations for battlefield surgery, introduces us to the various American commanders, reinforces the perception that the colonial forces are jolly but ill prepared, and reemphasizes the difficulty of deciding how to respond to the British challenge.

June 17 is the day of the battle, and the section is divided into alternating scenes of the British and American preparations for conflict. Throughout the previous days and on this day, we learn of the counterpoising strategies. The colonial forces have decided to occupy Breed's Hill and Bunker Hill overlooking Boston, adjacent high points on the peninsula facing Boston but separated from it by a half-mile of water. From this high ground, cannon captured from the British at Fort Ticonderoga could command the harbor and drive out the British navy, returning Boston to its citizenry. They build a redoubt, or small fortress, near the top of Breed's Hill, and raise an earth and stone entrenchment down to the Mystic River—both provocative actions. The alternative would be to continue the siege in the hope that enough troops would remain to deter the British; however, it is hay-cutting time, and even the American farmers who did not return home would still face the problem of diminishing food and supplies. Most of the population of Boston is camping out in the surrounding towns, and Feversham sleeps on the floor with dozens of others.

From the British perspective, the military problem is complicated by ignorance of American strength and intentions. The humiliation suffered at Lexington and Concord requires a forceful response, but the limited number of troops Howe has available creates the possibility of another embarrassing defeat if the Americans do indeed stand and fight. Howe originally planned to push the rebels off Breed's and Bunker Hills on June 18 but instead orders an attack on the afternoon of the seventeenth when a British ship begins to shell the redoubt on its own initiative.

The next sections are also titled "June 17," but each has a time attached. "9:00 A.M." describes the American uncertainty over whether the redoubt will be an easily flanked death trap and American leader Artemus Ward's cowardice or treachery in refusing to reinforce the weakly defended entrenchment position. Howe is still obsessed with Mrs. Loring. In "June 17, 11:00 A.M." Mrs. Loring and Mrs. Hallsbury are given chairs on a British man-of-war from which they can see the victory that Howe has promised his mistress. The Americans continue to beg for reinforcements. Anticipating his own death, Feversham writes a long letter to his wife; he also proves invaluable to the American forces because of his experience of war and his understanding of British thinking. Generals Gage and Howe debate the propriety of burning Charlestown, the abandoned village on the same peninsula as the two hills, since snipers are killing British troops from its cover; Howe orders the village burned. Mrs. Loring and Mrs. Hallsbury are bored at the lack of action.

The attack begins in the next section, "June 17, 2:00 P.M." The British, wearing full uniforms and packs on a sweltering day, march slowly up Breed's Hill. American riflemen jump up from behind their entrenchments and cut the light infantry to pieces. The British retreat. Farther down the line, Howe leads his beloved grenadiers into the teeth of the American fire and loses most of his officers, drummer boys, and front ranks; by his final charge, 90 percent of his grenadiers had been killed or wounded.

In the next section, "June 17, 4:00 P.M.," Clinton and Burgoyne bring up a handful of reinforcements and with Howe lead another charge. The Americans again cut down the front ranks but are so low on gunpowder they must retreat to Bunker Hill. Mrs. Loring, devastated at an impending British loss, faints. The Americans retreat from the peninsula to the safety of their own lines. The final two sections, "June 17, 5:00 P.M." and "June 18, 8:00 A.M.," describe the wrapping up of the battle. The British occupy the two hills, and Clinton, who will write the report, remarks that it is a victory; London will not ask or care about the more than 50 percent casualties they have taken. Colonel William Prescott, who has heroically led the defenders on Breed's Hill, confronts Artemus Ward, the cowardly head of the militia. The next day Feversham agrees to treat the Americans taken prisoner, but the British refuse to acknowledge them as prisoners of war, arguing that they are only bandits and criminals. Feversham writes a long letter to his wife, elucidating his feelings about the heroism of Warren, who has been killed, and the other patriots who have stood for an ideal without expectation of recompense. Feversham also expresses his hatred of war, telling his wife he will return to Connecticut.

Fast appends a brief afterword, which explains subsequent events in the lives of the historical characters.

STRUCTURE

The structure of *Seven Days in June* is to alternate views of British and American characters involved in the battle, with a concomitant alternation in point of view and perspective. While Fast's sympathies are firmly pro-American, we nevertheless see the colonials through British eyes, and vice versa. It is perhaps not surprising that the British should find their colonial cousins hard to understand. In European eyes, they are farmers and bumpkins living at the edge of the world, but Fast also shows us how little the Americans understand British thinking and attitudes. The Americans, as characters point out in the novel, have lived in the New World for 150 years and have developed a distinct and unique culture. Feversham, a renegade Britisher, is the bridge character who can explain his former countrymen's thinking to his new compatriots.

The following list makes the structure somewhat clearer:

Date/Section	Events	Effect
June 12	whipping of sailor	British brutality
June 13	British generals meet	Confusion about rebels
	party for generals	British decadence
June 14	Feversham meets Church	Corrupt colonial
	Feversham meets Warren	Heroic colonial
June 15	Howe and Mrs. Loring	Decadence
	Feversham and Warren	Altruism

| June 16 | Howe appoints Loring jailer | Corruption |
| | Feversham tempted but continues his duty | Honor, integrity |

The events of June 17 become very complex, with scenes shifting back and forth too rapidly to outline, but it should be clear from this brief listing how Fast, like a playwright, contrasts adjacent scenes to make moral points. Howe and the British are shown as brave but arrogant and obsessed with conquest, whether of women or of the enemy. Feversham and the Americans have their faults and weaknesses but are basically honorable and serious. A series of scenes in the June 17 section provide almost comic views of Howe and his mistress, in contrast to the argumentative but hard-working American officers: Howe making love to the fleshy Mrs. Loring before going off to war, Howe eating to excess at breakfast with Mrs. Loring in attendance as hostess, Mrs. Loring viewing the battle from shipboard, as if reclining on a cruise ship's deck chair.

Apart from some final recapitulation scenes, the later June 17 sections bring the alternation to an end when the two forces meet in battle. There is no resolution to the differences in point of view: neither side knows clearly if it has gained a victory, with Clinton anxious to write a self-serving history of the battle but other British officers denying to Feversham that a battle has even taken place (only a police action against bandits, they say). The Americans have been driven from the two hills, but they have killed or wounded more than half the British troops. However, the Americans are themselves divided, with Prescott contemptuously throwing accusations of cowardice and treachery in the face of Artemus Ward. Feversham is given the last word in his letter to his wife, telling her that there has been no victor and that "precious reason and compassion, which are all that make us human, have been cast aside" (187). War solves nothing; Fast points out in his afterword that the entire conflict might have been avoided had it not been for General Gage's intransigence.

Another structural technique is repetition. With more than two dozen characters in action and with the scenes alternating, the potential for confusion and chaos is high, yet the novel becomes clearer as it goes along in spite of the increasing complexity of the battle. A number of devices allow the solidifying of character identifications and justify the repeated explanation of who is who and what is going on. For example, Feversham's letters to his wife (he writes three times) tell her, and us, about the people he has just met, and the repetition from another perspective is a clever way to keep the discussion interesting. Another device is to provide a dramatically appropriate explanation, as, for example, when Lieutenant Threadberry explains to Mrs. Loring and Prudence Hallsbury what they can expect to see in the battle.

GENERIC CONVENTIONS

Seven Days in June is similar in approach to Fast's earlier research-based Revolutionary War book, *The Crossing*. The earlier work quoted contemporary documents, which were identified as such (actual letters and reports, as well as Dunlap's *History of the American Theater* on Hessian and continental uniforms) and provided well-drawn maps, endnotes, and two pages of bibliography. *Seven Days in June*, in contrast, supplies only two maps and never breaks the narrative to include documentation or research sidebars. Nevertheless, research is evident in every scene, and there is no question that we are reading a historical account, modernized in its language, to be sure, and fictionalized as far as the conversations between characters go, but still a painstaking representation of how events must have transpired. In fact, Fast may well be too accurate for readers sensitive to what he calls the coarse language used by the characters, who speak with the earthiness familiar to readers of the popular works of the time.

Historical novels, of course, describe a history as it might have been, not history as it truly happened, which is beyond the ken of any writer, novelist or historian. In a sense, though, this make-believe version of the past must meet the very strict standards of fictional credibility and representation in that the demands of literary coherence, order, and motivation must be met. We can only ask that the author not violate the spirit of the record in shaping characters into believable figures. Thus complaints that Howe's affair with Mrs. Loring surpasses understanding would do well to blame history, and not Fast; the narrative shows a coherent picture of a middle-aged man besotted by a very loose woman, which is entirely consistent with the historical record. Fast, a strict constructionist in his use of research, resists the temptation to supply speculative motivation. About the only legitimate complaint is that the narrative is so orderly that it defies the messy realities of battle, but the bird's-eye prerogative of the novelist permits us to suspend disbelief, and no reader would wish for a confused story line.

KEY CHARACTERS

Evan Feversham is the key character in *Seven Days in June* and, to some degree, a stand-in for the author. Although there seems little similarity in their biographies, Feversham reflects Fast in philosophy and perspective. Both were betrayed by the organizations to which they had devoted their lives—Feversham the British army, Fast the Communist party. Both have lived as outsiders in the Puritan land of Connecticut, and both have tried to serve their societies. Both are fascinated with war, in spite of themselves (Feversham even leaves his medical aid post to watch the battle begin); both are appalled at its human cost, its irrationality, and its denial of religious and human values. Both recognize that some wars may be seen as justified, though they decidedly do not share that view. This conjunction of attitudes between writer and character is, of course, unsurprising, especially since Feversham is the only fictional character in the novel. He is also, apart from George Washington, the only protagonist to appear in two of Fast's Revolutionary War novels. As such, we can view him as the novelist's voice and final position on the war.

As the only major fictional figure, Feversham is carefully shaped to make a number of points. In the main he is set against Sir William Howe, and to a lesser degree the other British generals. He is, after all, originally one of them, as he is reminded regularly by his American compatriots, so the distance he has traveled from his background in the British military is significant. Feversham is also compared and contrasted to the Americans he is now serving with. Finally, as the main spokesperson for Fast's view in the novel, he serves as a narrative voice throughout.

Feversham is the war hater in the novel. His experiences in three campaigns in the British army in Europe have convinced him that war solves nothing. The loss of his first wife in childbirth because of incompetent medical care motivates his self-abnegating generosity as a doctor—for example, when he enters the shelter of a youth thought to be contagious with smallpox. Feversham's love for his wife is touching; readers of *The Hessian* will note that he is decidedly more articulate in his letters than he was speaking to his wife in the earlier book. He resists the temptation of the willing serving wench on the road to Boston, and in fact his only conflict is over participation in the battle. His knowledge is sorely needed, but he is committed to "serving mankind" as a medical officer, the same conflict he underwent in *The Hessian*.

Howe, in complete contrast, is the war lover. He has learned nothing from his life of campaigns except the efficacy of extreme aggression, in life as in war. Howe has no interest in serving others; he memorizes the names of the doomed drummer boys because the troops like such personal touches and will thus fight harder. He exhibits no sorrow or pain at the loss of his men or officers, identifying the destruction of "his grenadiers" as a reflection on himself as a general but never considering human agony. He shows no loyalty to wife or family, and even his passion for Mrs. Loring lacks any emotional quality. He regards the mounds of her flesh with the same lust for conquest as he regards Bunker and Breed's hills.

The other British generals, Gage, Clinton, and Burgoyne, are paler, less driven versions of Howe. Gage has spent the most time in America, but what understanding he has gained is undercut by his insensitivity and hamhandedness, as evidenced by the disastrous decisions that triggered the battles of Lexington and Concord. Clinton has some insight into and even reluctance to burn Charlestown village, but his competitive nature and egotism effectively tamp down what decent impulses he has. Burgoyne is a fop and another egotist, interested in conquest to promote his own status. Feversham's contempt for the British officer class is well justified by the contrast with the American defenders.

The American characters fare much better (there are virtually no sympathetic British in the novel), but Fast is careful to balance heroism and decency with their opposites, showing fallen human beings among the colonials as well. The contemptible Mr. Loring, whose "corruption defies description" (190), is a perfect example of egotism and self-interest, virtually selling his wife to Howe for a British uniform and the chance to brutalize the fellow Americans taken prisoner by the British. Dr. Benjamin Church is no better, serving on the Committee of Safety but reporting all the colonial plans to the British. Artemus Ward, the head of the militia, has more mysterious motivations, for it is not clear whether his failure to support the soldiers on Breed's Hill is caused by cowardice or treachery.

In sharp contrast are the American heroes, men Feversham is proud to serve with. Dr. Joseph Warren loses his life for the cause, giving up his honorary position as commander to fight as an ordinary soldier; he is generous to a fault about the squabbling of his officers and is a model of decency and rational good sense. The odious Church is balanced by young Johnny Lovell, a spy because of personal conviction, risking the love of his family for an ideal. Dr. Joseph Gonzalez is a Jew living in Rhode Island, an American for generations who is accepted for what he is—a brave physician and an honorable colleague to Feversham. Colonel William Prescott, Major Thomas Knowlton, Colonel John Stark of the New Hampshire Riflemen, Major General Richard Gridley, a resourceful engineer, Captain Abel Nutting, a brave forward observer, and Colonel Moses Little of the Ipswich Volunteers are all model colonial officers, many becoming famous for their courage and honor in the conflicts that followed. Even crotchety old Israel Putnam, for all his temper, finally does the right thing and comes to the aid of the undermanned defenders.

For all these well-drawn historical characters, it is Feversham who remains in the imagination. He is the author's voice and our guide to what to think about the others. He sums up Fast's ambivalence toward war, fascinated, as the author is, with its violent drama and evocation of legitimate heroic action yet repulsed by the way it negates all that we value in humanity. Feversham is a memorable character, and it is clear why Fast resurrected him from the honorable retirement he enjoyed in *The Hessian*.

THEMATIC ISSUES

The two main thematic threads that run through the alternating scenes of *Seven Days in June* concern the contrasting motives of the British and American armies and Evan Feversham's antiwar philosophy. In each case, Fast builds his theme by accretion, as scene after scene is added to sum up the final point.

British Arrogance and Oppression

British ways are never treated kindly in Fast's Revolutionary War novels. As we saw with *Citizen Tom Paine*, ordinary folk in eighteenth-century England had few rights and fewer prospects: young Tom is beaten and left for dead by the squire's son, and he faces a miserable existence as an apprentice. Fast begins *Seven Days in June* with an inoffensive British sailor beaten to death for a child's prank and continues the portrait of arrogance when Clinton has his private parts washed by his male servant, an act Fast classifies as the epitome of dehumanization in *Being Red*, where he describes World War II British officers so treated in India. Then Clinton, frustrated by Mrs. Hallsbury, has sex with his servant's wife, who is hoping for a promotion for her husband and perhaps a useful illegitimate son by a distinguished British general. Her husband is aware of the debauchery and thus becomes a pimp for his wife.

Coupled with Howe's affair with Mrs. Loring is the buying off of Mr. Loring and then Clinton's later affair with Mrs. Hallsbury, apparently with her husband's tacit approval. This combination quickly makes the theme evident: the ancient right of first night taken by the British aristocracy when their subjects were married is not simply a historical curiosity but a living fact, as aristocratic and powerful men feel free to indulge their appetites any time they see fit. Burgoyne too is a sexual predator. Only Gage seems interested in making war apart from making love. Even worse, the sexual aggression of the British generals prostitutes the women involved and turns their husbands into pimps. No better metaphor for the conquest of America could be imagined, with military ambitions conflated with erotic ones into an urgent need to overcome, with no rational philosophy involved. This is not simply a fanciful literary conceit. Howe's eagerness to attack Breed's Hill is inextricably interwound with his need to show off for Mrs. Loring, and the illogicality of his attack is evident in his complete ignorance of the strength of his enemy behind the entrenchments. In much the same way, Clinton and Burgoyne exhibit an almost physical need to become involved in the attack, racing down to support the repulsed charge like young attack dogs on the scent of blood. British society is a predatory one, where might makes right and the strong rule by their power alone.

American Egalitarianism

American society, too, is far from perfect, having its corrupt Dr. Churches and Artemus Wards. Feversham sees the divisions of social class along the road to Boston when he stops to treat the victim of the pox, and Fast does not romanticize life in the New World. However, classic outsiders like Dr. Gonzales, the Jewish doctor from Rhode Island, and Feversham himself are accepted as equal contributors to the movement, and heroes like Warren and Prescott far outnumber the traitors and rogues. The colonials do withhold support for the defenders on Breed's Hill, but the absence of fanatical courage that characterizes the British soldiers in fact reflects the value of their lives. The Americans fight well behind stone walls and see no purpose in bloody sacrifice to the interests of empire. The men led by Warren and Prescott are on their way to becoming true citizen-soldiers—warriors who calculate self-interest against the interests of the group and will refuse pointless orders. In contrast, the British soldiers are automatons, trained and disciplined past the point of refusal; any hesitation will lead to instant death at the hands of their fellows.

The contrast between the two societies, both English speaking and predominantly Protestant, both linked by similar tastes in clothing, furniture, and style, could not be greater. America has become a new cult ire during the one hundred and fifty years of its existence, a wild and somewhat woolly place, perhaps, but one characterized by respect for the individual. The exploitation of others practiced so casually by the British officers is unthinkable on the American side of the lines. The colonials may argue and even betray each other, but they do not use each other as slaves or, worse, as tools and furnishings. The battle is a conflict of philosophies, not simply of men, and after Breed's Hill, the American way of seeing life begins to take political and national shape.

The Antiwar Message

The other great theme of *Seven Days in June* is Evan Feversham's perceptions about the uselessness of war as a means of solving problems. As we have seen, the novel presents a variety of points of view about war, with the British generals representing the professional war lovers, the few Americans with experience in the French and Indian Wars having doubts about the wisdom of the course they are undertaking, but with the majority of the Americans viewing the Boston siege as a lark, an escape from women, children, and the responsibilities at home on the farm. The twelve members of the Independent and Loyal Third Company of Mounted Artillery, who have no artillery, pass Feversham on the way to Boston; they are dressed in outlandish uniforms of yellow, green, and pink, and the doctor asks himself, "What could be more fun than riding through the countryside on a delightful June day in their wonderful uniforms?" (42).

More somberly, Feversham considers his own motives. Has he come

to Boston to escape his wife and the responsibilities of his medical practice? He thinks to himself, "Men were a race of children . . . and war was
a child's game until death and horror brought maturity. And then the
young were old, and there was no interval to mark the passage of time"
(41). Even women, in the characters of Mrs. Loring and Mrs. Hallsbury,
partake of the war as entertainment, at least until the possibility of danger to Howe crosses the mind of his mistress.

Feversham's view prevails in the novel, and it is a mixed one. Although he writes to his wife that he has seen "such nobility and courage
on the part of plain people as [he] has never known," he has also been
"witness to a terrible display of the madness we call war" (186). There
has been no victor. Feversham retreats to his home in Connecticut.

ALTERNATIVE READING: A HISTORICIST INTERPRETATION

Historicism questions whether literature written in an earlier time can
truly be understood by modern readers. The historicist points out that
the modern reader's framework of reference is shaped by contemporary
philosophies and understandings, which are different from those of the
earlier period in which the literature was written and that these color
the reader's evaluation and interpretation of the work. Historicism thus
deals with the question of whether the literary experience of the past is
retrievable by modern readers, and if so, how much of the original is
accessible and by what means.

The same question arises in regard to the creation of historical fiction
by the modern writer. Any serious historical novelist must confront this
question and submit to judgment of how accurately the attitudes, emotional responses, sensibilities, and textures of the past have been created
in his or her work. Re-creations of linguistic and stylistic conventions, of
ideas, even of events must inevitably be seen through the frame of reference of the present, if only because we already know the outcome of,
for instance, the Battle of Breed's Hill/Bunker Hill. Despite the historical
research and trappings, the modern writer of historical fiction and the
modern reader cannot escape a twentieth-century mind and outlook.
Does this fact make the historical novel impossible to write?

Fast's American Revolutionary War works face this problem. Fast has
sometimes been criticized for indulging in historical anachronism, that
is, attributing to his historical characters modern attitudes, responses, or

language that would have been uncharacteristic of people of that time. Historicism suggests that such anachronisms are inevitable in an attempt to recreate the past and that they are at best controllable only to a degree by the writer. To some degree the writer who hopes for a wide readership must cater to the needs of a modern reader if understanding is to be achieved. For example, Fast has taken considerable pride in his research into the language spoken and written in eighteenth-century America; he has always been concerned that his characters' language reflect the actual usage of the time. As he admits in a number of his books, however, a certain level of modern usage is necessary for the modern reader's understanding: spellings must be made consistent with modern usage, archaic idioms should be simplified or avoided, and in general the language needs to be made accessible.

As in his successful novel *The Crossing*, about the Revolutionary War, Fast relies heavily in *Seven Days in June* on contemporary materials to create a sense of period and to establish the factual base for his fictional characters. Perhaps to answer critics who little appreciated his research, he included references in *The Crossing* to Dunlap's *History of the American* [Military] *Theater* about Revolutionary War uniforms, maps, texts of actual letters written during the war, and military reports from the period. Endnotes and two pages of bibliography complete the scholarly apparatus. *Seven Days in June* has no such academic superstructure (although it does include maps), but it nonetheless gives much the same sense of historical realism. In an opening note, Fast even apologizes for the coarse language used by the characters, explaining that the usage is in complete accord with the letters and manuscripts of his sources. A quick reference to a standard history reveals that the larger events of the battle followed the order that Fast gives them and that, apart from the actual conversations of the historical characters in the novel, the characters' motives and general outlooks reflect historical record. Evan Feversham's surgical techniques, instruments, and philosophy, too, reflect the practices of the late eighteenth century. But even if the historicist is right—that despite period details, literature speaks to the time in which it was written—this is not necessarily a negative message, for if Fast's excellent historical recreation speaks to us about the present, it has met its creator's goal.

Inevitably, an investigation of the history contained within the historical novel must not only examine that part of the novel that remains fixed in the period in which it was created but also that part that reflects the nationalistic perspective of the narrator. A southerner and a northerner will never write about the Civil War from the same perspective.

They will call attention to very different details and will interpret the facts in different ways that lead to quite divergent conclusions. As in *April Morning*, Fast tells *Seven Days in June* from the American point of view. However, it is of historical value to realize that in every war there are two perspectives, and in this case, it might be interesting to examine the British view of this historical event, a view that questioned the legality of the American actions. From the British view, the British troops at Lexington were simply exercising their legal prerogative by challenging the armed farmers in the middle of the night; in their view too, Howe's grenadiers had every legal right to push the armed civilians off the hills overlooking Boston. There was no Continental army at the time, and the Americans themselves were often confused about who their own leaders were. The Continental Congress in Philadelphia had appointed Dr. Warren as supreme commander, but since the Congress was a self-appointed body, the British questioned its legal authority, especially in the far distant state of Massachusetts. Nor did the colonials have a standard uniform, a single flag, or a single purpose in confronting the British. Even among the colonial forces, many still considered themselves subjects of the king.

The moral argument about the sexual corruption of the British generals would also be subject to question by British historians. Mrs. Loring and Mrs. Hallsbury are in fact Americans and certainly share in the responsibility for the behavior of their lovers. The ribald language and earthy behavior of the British generals are actually more consistent with general American behavior than the repressed and straitlaced values of the Boston-area Puritans, whose name, then and now, evokes a too-strict, too-judgmental perspective on sins of the flesh. The sophistication of British civilization was becoming known world-wide as the British empire expanded; in contrast, as Clinton remarks to himself, Yankees were acting as if the whole world "were theirs without doubt or question; and suddenly he was aware of the seat of his disquiet and misgiving—the arrogance of these people, not guts or gallantry but simply an astonishing and righteous arrogance" (23). Such a reversal of perspective may seem to American readers as simply deconstructive contrarianism (see Chapter 4), but historical criticism would speak to the importance of ensuring a balanced view by considering opposing historical frameworks, however far any such balance might be from capturing an elusive "the way it *really* was."

In Fast's novel, the British officer Gage points out that it is "inconceivable that they [the Americans] want to make a war with us. There's no reason for war. Their complaints are petty, and we've given into one demand after another" (20). Gage sees the Americans as Clinton does: "They are a stiff-necked, ignorant, and vulgar people—and righteous. They are the most righteous folk on the face of this earth. I know, gentlemen . . . I married one of them," he sighs (20). We learn no more of Gage's thoughts about the "devilish Puritan strain," for his wife has come in and overheard him, but these remarks alone are enough to create another perspective on the events that follow. In other words, through such characters, Fast has done his duty as a historian; though his history is fictionalized, he has built into his text the British perspective in opposition to the American. No one perspective can be final, but the role of the historical novelist is to make us understand the dialogue that took place in the past, as well as the dialogue we engage in with our own history.

The Bridge Builder's Story
(1995)

"It is not the length of love that matters, but rather the quality of it, and in my love for you I found a quality that was all I had ever dreamed of."
—Fast's fictional Jane Austen, in *The Novelist*, subtitled "A Romantic Portrait of Jane Austen" (1992)

NO MAN IS AN ISLAND

In 1995, Fast published *The Bridge Builder's Story*, an affecting novel that looks forward in its daring mixture of genres and chronological leaps of narrative, but also looks back in its reliance on previous Fast themes. If *Seven Days in June* returned to the familiar territory of the historical novel set during the Revolutionary War, *The Bridge Builder's Story* takes us back to the personal and spiritual themes explored in The Immigrants series and in Fast's later works.

The Bridge Builder's Story takes a good deal of risk in the narration of its hero's story. While Fast himself has rejected the academic label "experimental" for his prose, preferring to practice a skilled craftsmanship which avoids self-consciousness and authorial intrusion into the narrative, he has nevertheless experimented frequently with innovative ways of structuring his work. Always a rational and orderly writer, he has a fondness for logical episodes that unravel like scenes in a play, each distinct and purposeful. Yet he has felt free to devise new and interesting narrative approaches for such episodes and scenes, for example by tracing Gideon Jackson's journeys in each chapter of *Freedom Road* or by introducing a stageful of characters in *Spartacus'* Villa Salaria and then following individuals and groups as they part on different travels. *The Bridge Builder's Story* begins as a conventional first-person narrative, a report on an adventure in Nazi Germany, but jumps forward unpredictably in time and place, unsettling but also intriguing the reader. The sense of genre is also toyed with, for what initially is an adventure story becomes a psychological investigation, a romance, and a retrospective. One must admire Fast's courage as a writer in taking such risks with his material.

For all its innovation as a narrative, *The Bridge Builder's Story* returns to familiar themes and territory, including Europe in the 1930s and New York City in the 1950s. *The Bridge Builder's Story* will inevitably remind knowledgeable readers of previous romantic episodes in Fast's work, and especially Barbara Lavette's first and deepest love affair with Marcel Duboise in pre–World War II Paris. She too enjoys heady times in the French capital, visits Berlin and is arrested by the Gestapo, and loses her lover to Hitler's violence. Although Fast's canon returns frequently to the theme of romantic obsession, in *The Bridge Builder's Story* the situation and setting suggest an autobiographical relevance beyond the simple dedication. Dedicated to Bette Fast, "wife, companion and lover for fifty-seven years," the novel overtly struggles with the complex emotions involved in grief, and the attempt to find an appropriate psychological niche for a deceased lover while moving on with life. This is not, of course, Fast writing autobiography, but rather using fiction to wrestle with common life problems, just as he has done throughout his career. Barbara Lavette's attempts to mourn her lost lovers arise out of Fast's empathy, not his own experience; in this novel, his own loss must have deepened his creative sympathy for his hero, but *The Bridge Builder's Story* should be read as just that, a story developed from the author's imagination and enriched by his own experiences, both happy and sad.

PLOT DEVELOPMENT

The novel begins as a straightforward first person narrative: "My name is Scott Waring" (3). This first section is "Berlin," and the time is 1939. We learn that Scott is an engineering student who has married his schoolmate Martha, and whose wedding trip to Europe included stays in Paris and Berlin. Scott had been given a Webley 30-calibre automatic pistol by his grandfather, a retired military man, and unaccountably takes the pistol on his honeymoon. Scott's facility with the German language he has studied for seven years leads him to insist on completing the Berlin stage of the trip, even though Martha would prefer to stay in Paris because of her fears of Hitler's Germany. Though not a practicing Jew, her great-grandfather was a famous Jewish member of the Civil War Confederacy. An added complication is that Scott's father Charles was an ace in World War I, shooting down twenty-three German fighter planes. Charles is now an adviser to President Roosevelt, working from the White House to develop new aircraft to counter the burgeoning Nazi threat. Scott, confident in the pacifist sentiments he has developed in opposition to his family's military and anti-German history, sees little threat in visiting Berlin, though Martha is uncomfortable, noticing the interest accorded Scott's background by a German official they meet on the HMS *Queen Mary*.

After a blissful stay in Paris, the couple moves on to the German capital. Scott takes Martha to a rally at the Reichstag (the building housing the German national legislature), at which Hitler will speak, and again unaccountably, puts his grandfather's pistol in his pocket. At the rally the young couple is pushed to the front of the audience, and just as Hitler emerges Scott places his hand on the gun. He is immediately gripped by two plain-clothes Gestapo officers, who take him and Martha into custody. Their interrogation is all the more severe since Scott can provide no reason for bringing the gun to the rally, and since the secret police agents have recorded his hotel room banter with Martha about shooting Hitler. The Gestapo has been waiting for him to compromise himself, and he has walked into their hands. In a horrific and unexpected scene, Scott is forced to watch through one-way glass as Martha, her dress torn away, is beaten and punched by two agents, who have stripped to the waist to keep her blood off their clothes. To stop the beating Scott invents a patently ridiculous story about his involvement in an assassination plot. The unconscious Martha is removed and Scott is put in a car to be driven to a Gestapo headquarters outside Berlin.

On the dark, rainy highway the Gestapo car swerves to avoid a truck and Scott attacks the driver with his manacled hands. The car plunges into a river and after a terrifying struggle Scott escapes. Soaked, freezing, and completely lost, he finds refuge in the nearby town of Coburg, at a brothel run by Berthe Baum, who, thanks to Scott's excellent German,

quickly understands his predicament. Berthe, who is Jewish, hates the
Gestapo who have sent her husband to his death. She runs her house of
prostitution only to save herself and her son Paul from a similar fate.
Scott is given food, clothing, money, and a ride to the train station. Back
in Berlin, the U.S. Embassy provides refuge, but he learns Martha has
been reported dead in a street assault. The Gestapo wishes to avoid an
international incident, and drops its charges against Scott in return for
releasing Martha's body. Scott, who realizes his irrational behavior with
the gun has caused his wife's death, returns to the U.S., where he talks
little about what has happened and finds cold comfort in the stiff funeral
ceremonies for his wife.

Scott returns to MIT to complete his engineering degree. He is the
protégé of Professor Hans Bauman, a Jewish emigré from Berlin who
also lost his wife to the Nazis. Although Scott is still a pacifist, Bauman
convinces his former student to join him in the Army Corps of Engineers,
where their joint skills at bridge building (and, of course, their knowledge of how bridges can be destroyed) will help the completely unprepared U.S. Army meet the challenge of fighting the Nazis.

The next section of the novel is "New York," and the time period has
jumped forward twelve years, to 1951. Scott is living a sterile, limited
life in the city, working profitably as a designer of bridges but remaining
unmarried and unattached to any woman, even as a friend. He has
abused alcohol and drugs. He dines occasionally with his mother and
sister but has no other social life. He is, however, in therapy with Dr.
Lieberman, a former surgeon turned psychoanalyst. Scott's analysis is
focused on his inability to come to terms with the loss of Martha; his
obsession has put his life in a holding pattern. Dr. Lieberman turns the
discussion to another of Scott's emerging obsessions. During his Army
service in Europe he was among the first Americans to enter the concentration camp at Buchenwald, but is unable to talk about what he saw.
The psychoanalyst also learns that Scott visited Berthe Baum in Coburg
on an Army leave, and attempted to make love to the former madam,
who apparently serves as a mother figure. Later, in New York, Scott had
himself circumcised for no reason that he is able to explain.

Dr. Lieberman forces Scott to confront his guilt about Martha's death.
He has turned her into an icon of perfection, even though she was still
a young college girl at the time of her death, her identity incomplete.
The episode with the gun cannot be explained away, and Scott cannot
forgive himself. Scott's father has died and his mother has remained a
distant, privileged figure. The only nurturing he has received in his life
has been from Professor Bauman, his teacher and mentor, and Berthe,

who saved his life with no expectation of reward. Bauman lost a wife to the Gestapo; Berthe's son Paul was sent to a concentration camp. Thus Scott, his psyche wounded, and his identity arrested by his wife's death, finds himself mysteriously drawn to and involved with Jews who have suffered similar outrages at the hands of the Nazis, outrages he can never share with his Christian family and coworkers. Dr. Lieberman, who is also Jewish and has been a battlefield surgeon, has insight into Scott's difficulty. By forcing him to confront and articulate the issues involved, he brings the engineer to greater acceptance of himself.

By 1953 Scott is thirty-five, successful at his work and emotionally more stable but still socially isolated. He meets Janet Goldman, a would-be Broadway dancer who works as a waitress in the restaurant Scott frequents. They quickly fall in love—part of Scott's courtship is to describe the engineering innovations of the George Washington Bridge—but Scott learns she has her own tortured emotional history. Janet is a Dachau survivor, kept alive in the concentration camp where all her family was killed only because a prison guard repeatedly raped her and kept her as his servant and slave. Janet and Scott's love for each other overcomes their fears of intimacy, but then Scott thoughtlessly takes her to meet his mother, who has also invited Scott's sister and her banker husband. Scott's insensitivity to how Janet will feel in the posh surroundings of his mother's apartment, located on 72nd Street between Fifth and Madison avenues in a milieu completely alien to the dancer-waitress, leads Dr. Lieberman to suspect that Scott has an unconscious desire to destroy their relationship. Has Scott introduced Janet to his mother simply to measure her against Martha, who did fit in with this rarefied environment?

Scott keeps repeating how little he really knows, understands, or even likes his mother, but what becomes apparent is that he also knows little and understands even less about himself. Janet points this out, and accuses him of wanting a "ménage à trois with a ghost!" (150), referring to Scott, herself, and Martha, whose photographs are prominently displayed in both Scott's apartment and in his mother's as well. Scott sulks, gets drunk, and is beaten up in a bar. Dr. Lieberman suggests that Scott has so little self-awareness that he has accepted the myth that there is no class structure in America, and that his coddled early life offered him no challenges to toughen his thinking and accept unpleasant realities—as a result, he simply denies their existence.

The final part is "Munich," and continues the chronology of the previous section, "New York," with only a few days interruption. Scott puts his pictures of Martha into a drawer and takes Dr. Lieberman to dinner, and relates to him as an equal rather than as a patient. He then flies to Munich to "try to enter the soul of a little girl who had been put into Dachau at age eleven" (184). He enters the barracks at Dachau and pretends to be Jewish noting the Germans' elaborate formality and extreme politeness. Finally, he drives to Coburg and is reunited with Berthe, who is about to emigrate to Israel. They eat and drink together, and she advises him to "leave the dead alone" (203), since only the here and now is meaningful. Taking the advice of this tough survivor, an earthy woman who has lost a husband and a son to the Nazis but has held on and prevailed, Scott feels a sudden release. He returns to New York where Janet waits for him. They are reconciled, and Scott is finally free of his obsession.

STRUCTURE

The novel contains three parts, "Berlin," "New York," and "Munich." The first two parts are almost equal in length, about eighty pages each. "Munich" is half as long, and wraps up the loose ends of the plot as Scott finally finds the courage to face his past and accept who and what he is.

Each part is subdivided into chapters, and each chapter is for the most part focused on one episode or scene. In outline, the structure is as follows:

Part One "Berlin": 1939–1940

    Chapter 1. Honeymoon trip on HMS *Queen Mary* to Europe

    Chapter 2. Paris and Berlin up to the arrest

    Chapter 3. Interrogation

    Chapter 4. Journey to Coburg and escape

    Chapter 5. Return to Berlin

    Chapter 6. Return to U.S.: Martha's funeral, MIT, Army Corps of Engineers (1940)

Part Two "New York": 1951, April and May of 1953

    Chapter 1. Psychoanalysis with Dr. Lieberman (1951)

    Chapter 2. Scott meets Janet (7 week affair, 1953)

    Chapter 3. Scott loses Janet

    Chapter 4. Scott gets drunk/is beaten up

    Chapter 5. Scott consults Dr. Lieberman again

Part Three "Munich": June 1953

The part and chapter structure shows how tightly focused and logically organized the novel is, yet the reader's experience of this unified and coherent structure is likely to be somewhat different because of jumps in the narrative that confound our expectations and because of shifts in the style and in our sense of the narrator's lack of trustworthiness.

The reader may feel somewhat frustrated at the end of "Berlin" since, after the straightforward narration of the Paris and Berlin events, we anticipate the continuation of Scott's life; instead, we have a kind of coda describing his entrance into the Army Corps of Engineers. Next, since the genre seems to be that of an adventure story, we might expect descriptions of battles in Europe, possibly involving Scott's revenge on the Nazis, Scott coming to terms with his anger, and perhaps resolving these emotions with the pacifism he expressed earlier. We get none of this. Also, the first-person narrative has represented Scott as a reliable and credible narrator, one whose version of events can be trusted. The only hint of a problem with Scott concerns why he takes the pistol to the Hitler rally; he provides no understandable explanation, and the reader may even perceive his action as a clumsy plot device.

In "New York" the narrative unexpectedly jumps forward in time, leaving out the war years. The reader hears nothing of Scott's life during and after the war. We see him in therapy with Dr. Lieberman, the only other major character in chapter 1. We suddenly realize that the genre has changed from an adventure story to a psychological analysis, and with this perception comes the realization that Scott's version of himself—and therefore of the events around him—is not necessarily reliable. Rather than the open, frank narrator he has seemed to be, in the confines of Dr. Lieberman's office he seems a closed, tortured soul who acts impulsively. His voluntary circumcision as an adult shocks even the doctor; his inability to talk about the barracks at Buchenwald puts a different perspective on his taking the gun to the Hitler rally since he himself doesn't know why he does things. His descriptions of Martha are also suspect, given his obsession and inability to see the world clearly.

Chapters 2 through 5 of "New York" also confuse our expectations. Scott seems well after his treatment by Dr. Lieberman, yet we note that he has no real social life, a telling symptom of his unresolved obsession

with Martha. Seen through his eyes in the first-person narration, however, his courting and winning of Janet seem to confirm his new mental
health, and Fast's fine descriptions of springtime in New York City seem
to turn the story toward romance. When Scott takes Janet to meet his
mother, however, we suddenly see how trapped he is in the role of
dutiful, privileged, upper-class son. He claims to be obligated to his family, yet even he comes to recognize how dependent he is for a supposedly
independent thirty-five-year-old man. Unable to deal with Janet's accu-
sation that he still worships Martha and that he has no idea who he is,
Scott reacts immaturely, by getting drunk and involved in a barroom
fight that puts him in the hospital. His return to Dr. Lieberman signals
that he is not well at all, for all the brave front he puts up as narrator.

It is only in "Munich" that we finally see the mature, well-integrated
Scott emerging. He allows himself to put away his pictures of Martha
and to visit a concentration camp. His farewell to Berthe, who is herself
leaving the site of her sorrows, shows us he is ready to love Janet as a
mature individual. The final New York chapter is abbreviated since there
is little left to say.

GENERIC CONVENTIONS

Just as the narrative of *The Bridge Builder's Story* shifts in each of its
three parts from straightforward in "Berlin" to the painful admissions
of a tortured psyche in "New York," to the finally integrated reflections
of a healing mind in "Munich," so the reader's sense of genre shifts. As
noted earlier, "Berlin" at first reads like an exciting adventure tale, with
a handsome young couple caught by the Gestapo in 1930s Berlin, an
escape from the clutches of the secret police, an unexpected rescue by
an unlikely ally, and a risky train ride to Berlin and the American Embassy. This is territory established and mastered by the writer of political
thrillers Helen MacInnes, with a nod to Eric Ambler as well. But our
sense of genre comes crashing down with the completely unanticipated
death of Martha and Scott's ignominious return to the United States. We
might expect Scott to return to Europe as an avenger, given the extent
of his grievance, but in fact he is still wrestling with his pacifist beliefs
even as he joins the U.S. Army Corps of Engineers. "Berlin" ends not
with the bang we might expect from its apparent genre, but rather with
a whimper from the wounded Scott.

In "New York," the true genre of *The Bridge Builder's Story* becomes apparent: it is a first-person portrait of a damaged soul, an innocent gone abroad who has encountered raw evil with no preparation. As we appreciate just how unreliable a narrator Scott is, we come to understand just how vulnerable he was, and how often this story has been told in other times and guises: the untested American emotionally flattened by the horrors of European war. Even Ernest Hemingway's wonderful Jake Barnes of *The Sun Also Rises* fits this psychological profile. Yet *The Bridge Builder's Story* does not simply leave its central character a walking wounded survivor; rather, we see the path back to sanity.

Fast had made this kind of psychological adventure/detective story his own turf earlier on, with its finest expression the novel he published under the pseudonym Walter Ericson, *Fallen Angel*, in 1952. (It was republished as *The Darkness Within* in 1953 and again as *Mirage* in 1965 under Fast's real name; the film version was also titled *Mirage*.) In this eerie and evocative work, a successful New Yorker loses his memory and struggles to make sense of the odd and violent situations in which he finds himself. While *Mirage*'s detective/mystery genre makes it quite different in plot and texture from *The Bridge Builder's Story*, the search for identity, the wonderful descriptions of New York City in the 1950s, the focus on psychology—all constitute the same kind of territory, a struggle by an unreliable narrator to find the truth of his own identity.

Finally, *The Bridge Builder's Story* is also in the tradition of Fast's works about love and romance. In the 1950s Fast became more and more proficient at creating attractive, credible, strong, and highly individualized female characters, a proficiency illustrated by his series of novels titled with women's names, beginning with *Sylvia* in 1960. *The Bridge Builder's Story* has two female protagonists, Martha as the illusory woman loved in youth, Janet as the utterly practical soul-mate of the male hero's maturity. In both cases the descriptions of the lovers in Paris and New York, though brief, are particularly well drawn, evoking a nostalgic and bittersweet ache of time irrecoverable.

KEY CHARACTERS

The most important character is of course Scott, the narrator, confusing us with his seemingly straightforward rendition of events, and then allowing us to see his shame, guilt, torment, and final acceptance. He is the bridge builder of the title, a competent designer of connecting structures at the literal level, but a near incompetent at building metaphorical bridges between himself and other people. Scott's narrator's voice is friendly and attractive, with the appealing openness sometimes seen among successful and protected American young people. For all of the harrowing experiences he shares with us in "Berlin" we would like to spend more time with him, and most readers are probably a bit disappointed by the questioning and unhappy voice of "New York." In fact, it is only when we hear Dr. Lieberman's doubts about Scott, and later Janet's, that we begin to see how narrowly circumscribed and even incomplete his view of reality actually is. Fast suggests that Scott's privileged background leaves him vulnerable and untested, a prime candidate for psychological meltdown.

Dr. Lieberman expresses the idea directly: Scott and Martha are the "golden children of two well-educated white Protestant families" (162). They had been coddled, protected, and nurtured, to the extent that Scott is unable to respond to the evil that destroys Martha, her "bloodless" white Protestant funeral (68) providing no "screams of sorrow and anger and curses flung at the men who did this" (68). On this count, Irish or Jewish funerals provide outlets for the living, and guidelines for future behavior. Scott's father remarks that Martha's mourners lack not emotion but the means to express it. Such means are provided by Dr. Lieberman, for the young bridge-builder has internalized and repressed not only his rage, guilt, and grief about Martha, but also his feelings about the concentration camp he helped liberate. For all his high-priced education, Scott lacks emotional knowledge, the learning provided by life to Berthe Baum and Janet Goldman.

It is tempting to search for a repudiation of an "engineering" mentality in *The Bridge Builder's Story*, an easy playing off of the technical against the humanistic, with Scott representing what thinker C. P. Snow called the technological "culture" and Dr. Lieberman and Janet standing for the humanistic and artistic. In fact, Fast seems to have no such intention of oversimplifying human thinking, and an engineer named Ammann, the designer of the George Washington Bridge across the Hudson River to Manhattan, is given credit for the most creative act of thinking in the book. The design of the bridge places stress in a manner that suggests it should, according to conventional engineering philosophy, collapse; however, an arrangement of crisscrossing beams buttresses the bridge's supporting towers and distributes the weight back to its point of origin. Scott calls this the bridge's "indeterminacy," for it is "eternally falling but never falling." (126). Scott's enthusiasm for this daring design, and the emphasis given its description in the book, suggests it is a metaphor for what Scott learns about the human condition: like the bridge he so admires, he must learn to accept the possibility of collapse and simultaneously brace himself against its effect, distributing the weight back to its point of origin rather than trying to carry it all himself. Berthe, Janet, and Dr. Lieberman have all suffered strains that should have destroyed them, but have survived and even prospered. This is the lesson Scott must learn.

In fact, it is mostly the women in Scott's life who are the key characters who affect him. Martha Pembroke at first seems the seminal influence on his character, but by the time we get to "New York" she is long dead, and we begin to see that her influence is symbolic rather than actual. Scott's guilt and emotional incapacity lead to his arrested development and alienation from society; his idealization of and obsession with Martha are revealed as a pose, for she too was unfinished and incomplete, only a sophomore in college. She may well have been more "sensible" than Scott, but even her own father opposed the marriage, not because he disliked Scott but because he felt his daughter was too young. She is, in terms of both plot and Scott's psychology, more of a symbol than a well-rounded literary character. His love for her is the "utter adoration of first love . . . never tested by living or working or suffering together . . . pure and romantic and apart from reality" (57). She is Beatrice to Scott's Dante, the stimulus to his imaginings rather than a fully realized participant in events.

Scott seems at first to have been deeply influenced by his grandfather and father, both of whom he talks about frequently in "Berlin," but apart from choosing pacifism in response to the family's military tradition, the male influence is as misleading as everything else in Part One. In fact, we increasingly see Scott's mother as the real problem, cold, aloof, correct, demanding without seeming to be. Scott repeatedly stresses her distant beauty; she is never warm, loving, or understanding. Even anger from his mother might have served Scott better, for it is only when he takes Janet to meet her do we appreciate how much she controls him without ever raising her voice. Scott is powerless to argue effectively because, as his father has said about Martha's funeral, he lacks the language in which to couch emotion. Scott's sister plays only a small role in the book, but she is a version of her mother, and she too uses Scott's guilt to control his behavior.

The two women in Scott's life who influence him positively are Berthe and Janet. Berthe should be contrasted with Scott's natural mother, for as a surrogate maternal figure she, as Dr. Lieberman points out, gives

Scott life and sustenance when no one else in Germany would. Berthe, a madam in a house of prostitution, understands human nature, and is as direct and practical in her dealings with Scott as his mother is distant and inscrutable. Though brooking no nonsense, Berthe is also warm and grateful, in contrast to Mrs. Waring's icy propriety. Scott's real mother has lived insulated from life by her money and social class; Berthe has survived Nazi betrayal, the deaths of her husband and son, the shelling of her house, and the famine of postwar Germany. She is a survivor, but has nevertheless preserved her humanity, as evidenced by her love of good food and fellowship. Her final message to Scott is that it is the here and now that matters, not the past: "leave the dead alone, Herr Waring," (203), for we must live in the present and future.

Janet Goldman should be contrasted with Martha as having the final positive influence in Scott's life. She occupies only a limited space in the book, but she is the counterbalance to Martha, real where Martha was illusory, actualized while Martha was simply youthful potential. Like Berthe, Janet is a survivor, having overcome the loss of her family, rape, beatings, and life in a new society. A practical manifestation of Berthe's advice about living in the present, she is completely focused on physical expression through dance; she has no "tricks of enticement or flirtation" (121); she has no plans for the future or agendas to pursue, only the immediate living of her life. Set against his obsession with Martha, she is exactly what Scott needs.

The final key influence on Scott's life is Dr. Lieberman. A former Army battlefield surgeon and a practical rather than theoretical analyst, he is at pains to distance himself from orthodox Freudians. He freely casts doubts on his own approaches to analysis, and promises only to help Scott talk through all the walls he has built up around himself. One of the main walls, besides the obvious obsession with Martha and the brake it has put on his development as an adult, concerns Scott's inability to talk about his experiences with the liberation of Buchenwald and his identification with Jews. Scott's voluntary circumcision, his sexual impotence, his possible Oedipal focus on Berthe—all these confused and interconnected issues have become compartmentalized in Scott's mind, so that he is unable to explain even to himself how one is related to the other. Dr. Lieberman's approach is to provoke, to bully, to show kindness, to challenge, to constantly push Scott to articulate and explain himself. Though unconventional, the approach works, and the reader can see how a committed therapist can force a patient into self-awareness.

The breakthrough is finally Scott's, but the character of the doctor is the means to eventual self-understanding.

THEMATIC ISSUES

The Bridge Builder's Story includes numerous themes, but three dominate in each part and in fact are recurrent themes in Fast's canon: (1) The role of a committed pacifist in a just war; (2) The role of Jews as minorities in hostile societies; (3) The nature of romantic love, and especially obsessive love.

Pacifism

Although Dr. Lieberman equates Scott's pacifism to his sheltered, coddled background, the young man's antiwar sentiments seem deeply held. The problem comes when such sentiments collide with thugs such as the ones who beat Martha to death in Berlin: what is the proper course of action under such circumstances? Again, when a year later Hitler's armies are rampaging through Europe and Professor Bauman asks Scott to join him in the Army Corps of Engineers, the issue of pacifism arises. Bauman argues that pacifism has become almost impossible under the circumstances and that Scott, who says he could not kill another human being under any circumstances, has in fact killed the two Gestapo men in the car. Scott ultimately joins the Army Engineers, and destroys bridges as well as builds them, a compromise with his principles that may contribute toward his later problems. In *The Establishment* we see Bernie Cohen fight in World War II and again in Israel's war for independence. His son by Barbara Lavette, Sam Cohen, is a medic in Israel's 1967 war. Yet Fast clearly feels uncomfortable even about such righteous causes, and the moral justification for participation remains murky.

Scott suffers from what seems to be, in the jargon of psychology, "cognitive dissonance" about a number of issues—that is, he is torn in two directions and is unable to resolve his feelings. His problems begin with his acceptance of the gun from his grandfather, even though he has no interest in weapons and disapproves of them in principle. Again, he jokes with Martha about shooting Hitler and for no understandable reason puts his hand on the pistol when Hitler appears. These actions, so strange as to seem failures at first of the author to create a consistent character, in fact reflect Scott's ambivalence and confusion as he struggles to resolve the conflicts between his family's military past and his own peaceful preferences. The novel suggests that such ethical confusion and inconsistency are not Scott's alone; they are the general problem of any anti-war champion trying to maintain the principle in a world so dangerous and hostile, so intolerant of the idealistic and peaceful.

Jewish Survival in Hostile Christian Cultures

The second theme involves existing as a minority in predominantly Christian settings which, to a greater or lesser extent, are hostile to Jews. Germany is obviously the extreme case in the novel, but anti-Semitism also surfaces in the New York bar in which Scott is beaten up, in the genteel propriety of Scott's family when it reacts to Janet Goldman, and even in Scott himself, who is confused about whether he thinks of Dr. Lieberman mainly as a doctor or mainly as a Jew. Scott, of course, sometimes identifies himself as Jewish, for example when he travels to Germany at the end of the book, but he has acquired enough honesty to recognize the mixed messages he receives from his environment. He discovers that Jews are treated with an excessive politeness in Germany, as if such false courtesy could erase the past; instead, he sees that it continues the policy of exclusion and creating difference.

The theme is not new in Fast's work. Sam Cohen, the son of Bernie Cohen and Barbara Lavette, decides to take his premedical studies in Israel in order to straighten out his confusions about identity. Assimilation, while an indication of lowered prejudice and barriers, also means a watering down of the powerful forces that have kept the Jewish community lively and unified in the face of so much hatred and violence. Having Scott, the ultimate "bloodless" white Anglo-Saxon Protestant, experience anti-Semitism and identify empathetically with Janet's concentration camp experience, provides an original and interesting viewpoint. Fast offers no easy solution to the problem of discrimination and prejudice; however Professor Hans Bauman and Janet find protection in refugee status and work, and even Berthe, the supreme survivor, plans to emigrate to Israel. As with pacifism, reality tends to break down the best intentions of theory, and individual consciences must make private decisions about how to react to particular situations.

Obsessive Love

The main theme of *The Bridge Builder's Story*, however, is love, especially the obsessive love Dr. Lieberman equates with the old notion of possession as domination by an evil spirit. Fast has always been a romantic at heart, and his works have often soared when they turned to the subject of youthful infatuation and romance. Barbara Lavette and Marcel Duboise's shattered union in *Second Generation* has already been mentioned, but Barbara's parents, Dan Lavette and Jean Seldon provide another example of two lovers unable to recover from their first passion. Dan and Jean divorce only to reunite until parted by death many years later. Fast's works, though admitting of the pleasures of the flesh, tend to promote monogamy and spiritual union with a true soul mate as lover; his novels sometimes have romances and marriages destroyed by circumstance, but as in this one, the surviving lover remains true for an extended period of time.

In *The Bridge Builder's Story*, Fast seems to play two themes against each other, themes as old as literature: youthful passion versus the calmer pleasures of mature love. Scott's love for Martha did not have time to endure the tests of real life, of the pressures of work, of suffering, of time simply passing. Dr. Lieberman points out that Martha was too young when she died to have established a record of living through which she could be loved, though Scott has heightened her reality in his imagination. No real person could compete with such a perfect image, as the women Scott dates soon learn, and Janet survives in Scott's regard only because of the help of Dr. Lieberman, Berthe's sensible advice, and Scott's cleansing trip to Germany. The movement from the illusory Martha to the real Janet suggests the way romantic love gives way to what Shakespeare knew as love of understanding, a deeper and more solidly based emotion than the passion that drives the adolescent lovers of, for example, *A Midsummer Night's Dream*. It is not, of course, that one kind of love is superior to another, but rather that they constitute normal human stages of life, stations that must be left behind in the conduct of a life. Scott has become derailed at an early stage, and must learn to part from passion in order to move on to a deeper, mature love.

ALTERNATIVE READINGS: FREUDIAN/ PSYCHOANALYTICAL AND AUTOBIOGRAPHICAL INTERPRETATIONS

Two main interpretations suggest themselves here, the first a reaction to Dr. Lieberman's protestations about not being a Freudian, the second an inevitable conclusion based on Fast's own recent experiences in life. Neither interpretation, however, can stand much critical/analytical pressure, for each is merely a guidepost pointing to a direction rather than a road map explaining the details of the territory.

Freudian/Psychoanalytical

Despite Dr. Lieberman's protestations that he is not a Freudian but rather an eclectic practicing a common-sense therapy that his colleagues might not even care to label as psychoanalysis, what emerges from his sessions with Scott is heavily Freudian. The followers of the Viennese analyst, of course, find psychological problems rooted in early sexuality, in inabilities to progress beyond infantile emotional attachments to parents of the opposite sex, and in such problems being repressed into the subconscious mind.

Scott, for all his innocence and his peculiar "compulsion" about taking his grandfather's gun with him to the Hitler rally, seems to have been progressing normally. He left home and married, and apparently established a satisfactory sexual relationship with his wife. When Martha is killed, a Freudian might argue, Scott reverts back to more infantile behavior: he is unable to form an attachment with another woman; he subconsciously attempts to subvert his relationship with Janet by allowing his mother to compare her to Martha. He forms a psycho-sexual attachment to his surrogate mother, Berthe, who saved his life when he was helpless, nurtured him with food, and protected him like a mother. He attempts to have sex with Berthe, an Oedipal urge so obvious that even Scott seems to recognize it, but finds he is impotent. He attempts to cure his impotence by undergoing circumcision, a symbolic way of pleasing his Jewish "mother."

Scott's breakthrough comes, on his final trip to Germany, when he is able to relate to Berthe as a friend and confidant rather than as a helpless child, as in his first encounter, or as a potential lover, as in his second. He returns to New York to a satisfactory sexual relationship with Janet in the final pages of the book. He has overcome his fixations with Martha, with his mother, and with Berthe. The Freudian overtones to these occurrences seem obvious, and though they do not necessarily follow a strictly orthodox pattern, a Freudian interpretation certainly illuminates Scott's motives and difficulties.

Autobiographical Interpretations

The autobiographical resonances of *The Bridge Builder's Story* also may serve to clarify the idea of obsessive love. The novel is dedicated to Bette Fast, whose death in 1994 separated Fast from his "companion and lover" of fifty-seven years. Such a lifetime with another person is the antithesis of Scott's few years with Martha as suitor and a few weeks with her as a husband. As Dr. Lieberman observes, they have no experience working, suffering, or living together. Scott's illusion of Martha is psychologically real, and his obsession may be perfectly comparable to the grief felt by someone who has lost a companion of more than half a century. That one is illusory and the other real makes no different in effect; the guiding or balancing force in life has gone, and the lover is left empty, without direction, inconsolable. Scott's grief is guilt, of course, but it is also the grief of the survivor.

Such an autobiographical interpretation does not find Fast's particular circumstances in *The Bridge Builder's Story*, but only notes that he has frequently written out of his personal experience, and that his experience while he was creating this work involved grief for his wife, an emotion, given the length of their marriage, impossible for outsiders to fully imagine. Fast also clearly paid tribute to Bette's beauty, grace, and talent in the exquisite short play, written in 1976 but performed in 1991 and reprinted in 1992, *The Novelist*, "A Romantic Portrait of Jane Austen." It is therefore not too difficult to see at least a little of Fast, the careful craftsman, in Scott Waring, the excellent engineer. Certainly their life stories and backgrounds are different, but their emotional pain and obsession with a luminous woman, now deceased, are comparable. If we permit ourselves this interpretation, then Dr. Lieberman (literally, Dr. "loveman") becomes a side of Fast himself, working through obsessive grief and finding the strength to go on. The novel would thus be a form of therapy, a reflection on grief and obsession, on love cut short and love that goes on forever. As such, it is informed by the novelist's pain and his struggles to carry on in the face of a personal disaster. It is a completely appropriate book to write at this point in his life and career.

Bibliography

Note: This bibliography has been compiled from various published sources on Fast. Be aware that the large number of works Fast produced and his need to work under several pseudonyms during the period of his blacklisting have led to some confusion in listings of his works. The best is the bibliography in the *Contemporary Authors Autobiography Series*, Volume 18, pp. 185–187, on which I rely heavily.

References to page numbers given in the text of this book are to the original editions as listed in the bibliography, with the exception of *Freedom Road*, where page numbers are from the Pocket Book edition of February 1962; *April Morning*, with page numbers from the Bantam Books edition of 1987; and *The Immigrants* (1977), *Second Generation* (1978), *The Establishment* (February 1987), and *Immigrant's Daughter* (February 1987), all from the Dell editions.

WORKS BY HOWARD FAST

Novels

Agrippa's Daughter. Garden City, N.Y.: Doubleday, 1964.
The American: A Middle Western Legend. New York: Duell, 1946.
April Morning. New York: Crown Publishers, 1961.
The Bridge Builder's Story. Hampton Falls, N.H.: Thomas T. Beeler, 1995.
The Children. New York: Duell, 1947.
Citizen Tom Paine. New York: Duell, 1944.

Clarkton. New York: Duell, 1947.

Conceived in Liberty: A Novel of Valley Forge. New York: Simon and Schuster, 1939.

The Confession of Joe Cullen. Boston: Houghton Mifflin, 1989.

The Crossing. New York: Morrow, 1971.

The Dinner Party. Boston: Houghton Mifflin, 1987.

Freedom Road. New York: Duell, 1944.

The Hessian. New York: Morrow, 1972.

The Hunter and the Trap. New York: Dial, 1967.

The Immigrants series:

    The Immigrants. Boston: Houghton Mifflin, 1977.

    Second Generation. Boston: Houghton Mifflin, 1978.

    The Establishment. Boston: Houghton Mifflin, 1979.

    The Legacy. Boston: Houghton Mifflin, 1981.

    The Immigrant's Daughter. Boston: Houghton Mifflin, 1985.

The Last Frontier. New York: Duell, 1941.

Max. Boston: Houghton Mifflin, 1982.

Moses, Prince of Egypt. New York: Crown, 1958.

My Glorious Brothers. Boston: Little, Brown, 1948.

The Outsider. Boston: Houghton Mifflin, 1984.

Place in the City. New York: Harcourt, 1937.

The Pledge. Boston: Houghton Mifflin, 1988.

Power. Garden City, N.Y., 1962.

The Proud and the Free. Boston: Little, Brown, 1950.

Seven Days in June. New York: Carol Publishing Group (Birch Lane Press Book), 1994.

Silas Timberman. New York: Blue Heron, 1954.

Spartacus. New York: Blue Heron, 1951.

The Story of Lola Gregg. New York: Blue Heron, 1954.

Strange Yesterday. New York: Dodd, Mead, 1934.

The Tall Hunter. New York: Harper, 1942.

Torquemada. Garden City, N.Y.: Doubleday, 1966.

The Trial of Abigail Goodman. New York: Crown, 1993.

Two Valleys. New York: Dial Press, 1933.

The Unvanquished. New York: Duell, 1942.

The Winston Affair. New York: Crown, 1959.

Works under the Pseudonym of E. V. Cunningham/Detective Fiction

Alice. Garden City, N.Y.: Doubleday, 1963.

The Assassin Who Gave Up His Gun. New York: Morrow, 1969.

The Case of the Kidnapped Angel. New York: Delacorte, 1982.
The Case of the Murdered Mackenzie. New York: Delacorte, 1984.
The Case of the One-Penny Orange. New York: Holt Rinehart, 1977.
The Case of the Poisoned Eclairs. New York: Holt Rinehart, 1979.
The Case of the Russian Diplomat. New York: Holt Rinehart, 1978.
The Case of the Sliding Pool. New York: Delacorte, 1981.
Cynthia. New York: Morrow, 1968.
Helen. Garden City, N.Y.: Doubleday, 1966.
Lydia. Garden City, N.Y.: Doubleday, 1964.
Margie. New York: Morrow, 1966.
Millie. New York: Morrow, 1973.
Penelope. Garden City, N.Y.: Doubleday, 1965.
Phyllis. Garden City, N.Y.: Doubleday, 1962.
Sally. New York: Morrow, 1967.
Samantha. New York: Morrow, 1967. Published as *The Case of the Angry Actress,* New York: Dell, 1985.
Shirley. Garden City, N.Y.: Doubleday, 1963.
Sylvia. Garden City, N.Y.: Doubleday, 1960.
The Wabash Factor. Garden City, N.Y.: Doubleday, 1986.

Novels under the Pseudonym Walter Ericson

Fallen Angel. Boston: Little, Brown, 1952. Published as *The Darkness Within,* New York: Ace, 1953. Published under the name Howard Fast as *Mirage,* New York: Fawcett, 1965.

Short Story Collections

Departure and Other Stories. Boston: Little, Brown, 1949.
The Edge of Tomorrow. New York: Bantam, 1961.
The General Zapped an Angel: New Stories of Fantasy and Science Fiction. New York: Morrow, 1970.
The Last Supper and Other Stories. New York: Blue Heron, 1955.
Patrick Henry and the Frigate's Keel and Other Stories of a Young Nation. New York: Duell, 1945.
Time and the Riddle: Thirty-one Zen Stories. Pasadena, Calif.: Ward Ritchie Press, 1975.
A Touch of Infinity: Thirteen Stories of Fantasy and Science Fiction. New York: Morrow, 1973.

Nonfiction

The Art of Zen Meditation. Culver City, Calif.: Peace Press, 1977.
Being Red. Boston: Houghton Mifflin, 1990. (autobiography)
Goethals and the Panama Canal. New York: Messner, 1942.
Haym Salomon, Son of Liberty. New York: Messner, 1941.
The Incredible Tito. New York: Magazine House, 1944.
Intellectuals in the Fight for Peace. New York: Masses & Mainstream, 1949.
The Jews: Story of a People. New York: Dial, 1968.
Literature and Reality. New York: International Publishers, 1950.
Lord Baden-Powell of the Boy Scouts. New York: Messner, 1941.
The Naked God: The Writer and the Communist Party. New York: Praeger, 1957.
The Passion of Sacco and Vanzetti: A New England Legend. New York: Blue Heron, 1953.
Peekskill, U.S.A.: A Personal Experience. New York: Civil Rights Congress, 1951.
The Picture-Book History of the Jews, with Bette Fast. New York: Hebrew Publishing, 1942.
Spain and Peace. New York: Joint Anti-Fascist Refugee Committee, 1952.
Tito and His People. Winnipeg, Manitoba: Contemporary Publishers, 1950.
War and Peace: Observations on Our Times. Armonk, N.Y.: Sharpe, 1993. (essays)

Plays

Citizen Tom Paine. Produced in Washington, D.C., 1987. Boston: Houghton Mifflin, 1986.
The Crossing. Produced in Dallas, 1962.
David and Paula. Produced in New York, 1982.
George Washington and the Water Witch. London: Lane, 1956.
The Hammer. Produced in New York, 1950.
The Novelist. Produced in Williamstown, Mass., 1987.
The Novelist: A Romantic Portrait of Jane Austen. New York: French, 1992.
The Second Coming. Produced in Greenwich, Conn., 1991.
Thirty Pieces of Silver. Produced in Melbourne, 1951. New York: Blue Heron, 1954.

Screenplays

The Ambassador. 1974.
The Hessian. 1971.
The Hill. Garden City, N.Y.: Doubleday, 1964.

Spartacus, with Dalton Trumbo. Directed by Stanley Kubrick. Produced by Universal Studios. 1960.
21 Hours at Munich, with Edward Hume. 1976.
What's a Nice Girl Like You? (television play based on *Shirley*), 1971.

Films Produced from Fast's Works

Freedom Road. 1980. (television miniseries)
The Immigrants. 1979. (television miniseries)
Jigsaw. 1968. (based on *Mirage*)
Man in the Middle. 1963. (adapted from *The Winston Affair*)
Mirage. 1965.
Penelope. 1966.
Rachel. 1948.
Spartacus. 1960.

Anthologies of Fast's Work

The Call of Fife and Drum: Three Novels of the Revolution. Secaucus, N.J.: Citadel, 1987. (*The Unvanquished, Conceived in Liberty*, and *The Proud and the Free* collected in one volume.)
A Howard Fast Reader. New York: Crown, 1960. (includes *The Golden River*)

Edited Anthologies of the Works of Others

Best Short Stories of Theodore Dreiser. Cleveland: World, 1947.
The Selected Works of Tom Paine. New York: Modern Library, 1946; London: Lane, 1948.

For Young Readers

April Morning. New York: Crown, 1961.
The Romance of a People. New York: Hebrew Publishing, 1941.
Tony and the Wonderful Door. New York: Blue Heron, 1952 (illustrated by Imero Gobbato); New York: Knopf, 1968; published as *The Magic Door* (illustrated by Bonnie Mettler), Culver City, Calif.: Peace Press, 1980.

Poetry

Korean Lullaby. New York: American Peace Crusade, n.d.
Never to Forget the Battle of the Warsaw Ghetto, with William Gropper. New York: Jewish People's Fraternal Order, 1946.

Other Work

Contributor to Richard Burrill, *The Human Almanac: People Through Time.* Sacramento, Calif.: Sierra Pacific Press, 1983 (includes Fast's *The Trap*).
"Revising the Record: Did Washington's Wisecrack Tip the Balance?" *Americana* 20 (December 1992):6–7.

Unpublished Materials

Fast's manuscripts, University of Pennsylvania Library, Philadelphia, and University of Wisconsin, Madison.

WORKS ABOUT HOWARD FAST

Despite his long and colorful career, no critical or analytical book has been written about Fast. His works received numerous reviews when they were published, however, and a selection of typical critiques follows. In general, reviewers over the years have praised Fast's passion and emotional intensity, as well as his technical skill at creating good characters and gripping stories. His ability to capture the spirit of a past time and to relate it to present interests received particular notice. He was most often criticized for oversimplifying historical situations and characters to make a political point: for being "tendentious," or one-sided in support of liberal or leftist causes. After the late 1940s, when Fast's radical politics became more widely known, some reviewers were hostile simply because of his beliefs. Over the long term, however, Fast seems to have been treated fairly enough by newspaper and magazine reviewers, who often identified his strengths and weaknesses with great precision. Rather, it is the academic world that has slighted this phenomenally prolific writer of popular fiction. The only serious extended study of his work is this one.

General Information

Campenni, Frank. "Fast, Howard (Melvin)." In *Contemporary Novelists,* 291–294. London: St. James Press, 1986.

"Fast, Howard (Melvin)." In *Current Biography*, 200–202. Bronx, N.Y.: H. W. Wilson, 1943.

"Fast, Howard (Melvin)." In *Current Biography*, 206–210. Bronx, N.Y.: H. W. Wilson, 1991.

"Fast, Howard." In *Something about the Author*, 7:80–82. Detroit, Mich.: Gale Research, 1975.

"Fast, Howard Melvin." In *Who's Who in America, 1980–1981*. Bloomington, Ind.: Macmillan, 1981; *Who's Who in America*, 1995. New Providence, N.J.: Reed Reference Publishing Company, 1994.

"Howard Fast." In *Contemporary Authors*, 185–186. New revision series. Detroit, Mich.: Gale Research, 1981.

"Howard Fast." In *Contemporary Authors Autobiography Series*. Vol. 18, 167–187. Detroit, Mich.: Gale Research, 1994.

"Howard Fast." In *Contemporary Literary Criticism*, 23:153–161. Detroit, Mich.: Gale Research, 1983.

"Howard Fast." In *International Who's Who*. London: Europa Publication, 1994.

"Howard Fast." In *Twentieth Century Authors* [First Supplement]. London: St. James Press, 1955.

Macdonald, Andrew, and Gina Macdonald. "Fast, Howard (Melvin)." In *Twentieth-Century Romance and Historical Writers*, 219–223. Detroit, Mich.: Gale Research, 1982.

Macdonald, Gina. "E. V. Cunningham." In *Critical Survey of Mystery and Detective Fiction*, 437–444. Pasadena, Calif.: Salem Press, 1988.

Manousos, Anthony. "Howard Fast." In *Dictionary of Literary Biography*, 9: 277–281. Detroit, Mich.: Gale Research, 1981.

Newquist, Roy. "Interview with Howard Fast." In *Counterpoint*. Chicago: Rand McNally, 1964.

Petrov, Anatolii. In " 'Ekh Govard!': Istoriia odnogo neotpravlenogo pis-ma." *Znamia: Literaturno Khudozhestvennyi i Obshchestvenno Politicheskii Zhurnal*, 163–186. Moscow, Russia, August 8, 1992.

Biographical Information

Buckley, William. "Mr. Fast Explains." *National Review*, February 24, 1989, 62–63.

Gross, Ken. "Howard Fast." *People Weekly*, January 28, 1991, 75–79.

Howe, Irving. Review of *The Naked God*. *New Republic*, December 16, 1957, 18.

Rothstein, Mervyn. "Howard Fast in a New Mode with Latest Novel." *New York Times*, March 10, 1987, C16.

Russo, Francine. "Cameos: The Novelist." *Village Voice*, October 29, 1991, 100.

Tescott, Jacqueline. "Interview with Howard Fast." *Washington Post*, March 3, 1987, D:1.

REVIEWS AND CRITICISM

Being Red

"Biography: 'Being Red.' " *Library Journal*, October 1, 1990, 96.

Isserman, Maurice. *New York Times Book Review*, November 4, 1990, 14.

"It Seemed a Good Idea at the Time." *New York Times Book Review*, November 4, 1990, 14.

Kanfer, Stefan. *New Leader*, December 10–24, 1990, 21.

McBride, P. W. *Choice* 28 (April 1991):1368.

Meyer, Gerald. "Howard Fast: An American Leftist Reinterprets His Life—'Being Red' by Howard Fast." *Science and Society* 57 (Spring 1993): 86.

Nash, Charles C. *Library Journal*, October 1, 1990, 96.

"Party Time." *New York*, November 5, 1990, 124–125.

Radosh, Ronald. *Commentary* 91 (March 1991):62.

Richler, Mordecai. "Red Writer." *Gentleman's Quarterly* 60 (October 1990):145–150.

Citizen Tom Paine

Booklist, May 15, 1943, 368.

Bookmark 4 (March 1943):18.

Cleveland Open Shelf (April 1943):8.

Cross, J. E. *Library Journal*, April 15, 1943, 327.

Fadiman, Clifton. *New Yorker*, May 1, 1943, 73.

Feld, Rose. *Weekly Book Review*, April 25, 1943, 3.

Mayberry, George. *New Republic*, May 10, 1943, 646.

Neville, Marion. *Book Week*, May 9, 1943, 2.

Nevins, Allan. *Saturday Review of Literature*, May 1, 1943, 8.

W.K.R. *Christian Science Monitor*, May 3, 1943, 14.

Rice, Elmer. *New York Times*, April 25, 1943, 1.

Trilling, Diana. *Nation*, May 8, 1943, 676.

Weeks, Edward. *Atlantic* 172 (July 1943):121.

Freedom Road

Booklist 41 (September 1944):21.

Catholic World 160 (October 1944):92.

Cleveland Open Shelf (June 1944):12.

Commonweal, October 20, 1944, 21.

E.M.B. *Springfield Republican*, August 27, 1944, 4d.

Evans, John W. "Freedom Road." In *Masterplots*, 2779–2782. Pasadena, Calif.: Salem Press.

Horn Book 20 (November 1944):499.

Kirkus, June 1, 1944, 236.

Mayberry, George. *New Republic*, August 14, 1944, 196.

McNaught, Eleanor. *Canadian Forum* 24 (October 1944): 165.

Moon, Bucklin. *New York Times*, August 27, 1944, 5.

New Yorker, August 19, 1944, 58.

Powers, J. M. *Boston Globe*, September 6, 1944, 17.

Prescott, Orville. *Yale Review* 34 (Autumn 1944):192.

Reddick, L. D. *Library Journal* 69 (August 1944):650.

Rice, Jennings. *Weekly Book Review*, August 20, 1944, 2.

Rothman, N. L. *Saturday Review of Literature*, September 23, 1944, 11.

Spectorsky, A. C. *Book Week*, August 13, 1944, 1.

Trilling, Diana. *Nation*, August 19, 1944, 219.

Weeks, Edward. *Atlantic* 174 (September 1944):127.

Spartacus

Heath, Melville. *New York Times*, February 3, 1952, 22.

Roth, C. J. *Library Journal*, March 1, 1952, 437.

Saturday Review, March 8, 1952, 17.

Sharma, K. N. " 'Spartacus': Variations on a Theme." In R. C. Prasad and A. K. Sharma (eds.), *Modern Studies and Other Essays in Honour of Dr. R. K. Sinha*, 261. New Delhi: Vikas Publishing House, 1987.

Sheehan, Henry. "The Fall and Rise of Spartacus." *Film Comment*, March 1991, 57–63.

Swados, Harvey. *Nation*, April 5, 1952, 331.

London Times Literary Supplement, November 7, 1952, 271.

April Morning

Booklist, May 15, 1961, 571.

Donelson, Ken. "Coming to Manhood, All in a Few Hours." *Virginia English Bulletin* 36 (Winter 1986):3.

Fearing, Kenneth. *New York Times Book Review*, April 23, 1961, 38.

Gentry, Curt. *San Francisco Chronicle*, April 23, 1961, 26.

Glauber, R. H. *New York Herald Tribune Lively Arts*, May 7, 1961, 34.

Kirkus, March 1, 1961, 229.

Mitchell, Julian. *Spectator*, October 6, 1961, 472.

Nyren, Dorothy. *Library Journal*, April 1, 1961, 1476.

Scoggin, M. C. *Horn Book*, December 1961, 568.

London Times Literary Supplement, October 27, 1961, 777.

Ver Steeg, C. L. *Chicago Sunday Tribune*, April 23, 1961, 4.

The Immigrants Series

Leedom-Ackerman, Joanne. *Christian Science Monitor*, November 7, 1977, 18.

Nelson, Barbara. *Library Journal*, September 1, 1977, 1760.

Newlove, Donald. *New York Times Book Review*, October 2, 1977, 22.

Riaume, Jean-Marc. "Les Sino-Americains dans 'The Immigrants' (1978) et 'Second Generation' (1970) de Howard Fast." In *Seminaires 1985*. Talence: Centre de Recherches sur l'Amer. Anglophone, Maison des Sciences de l'Homme d'Aquitaine, 1986: 105–115.

Salisbury, Stephan. *Saturday Review*, September 17, 1977, 41.

Sheppard, R. Z. *Time*, November 6, 1977, 120.

VanLaan, James R. "Second Generation." In *Magill's Literary Annual, 1979*, 648–651. Englewood Cliffs, N.J.: Salem Press, 1979.

Seven Days in June

Michaud, Charles. Review. *Library Journal* 119 (July 1994):126.

Publisher's Weekly, July 11, 1994, 66.

The Bridge Builder's Story

Hall, Linda. "The Bridge Builder's Story." *New York Times Book Review*, October 22, 1996, 37.

OTHER SECONDARY SOURCES

Borklund, Elmer. *Contemporary Literary Critics*. London: St. James, 1977.

de Beauvoir, Simone. *The Second Sex*. New York: Bantam Books, 1952.

Fowler, Rober, ed. *A Dictionary of Modern Critical Terms*. New York: Routledge & Kegan Paul, 1987.

Groder, Michael, and Martin Kreiswirth, eds. *The Johns Hopkins Guide to Literary Theory and Criticism*. Baltimore: Johns Hopkins University Press, 1993.

Harris, Wendell V., ed. *Dictionary of Concepts in Literary Criticism and Theory*. Westport, Conn.: Greenwood Press, 1992.

Lancaster, Bruce, with J. H. Plumb. *The American Revolution*. New York: American Heritage Publishing Co., 1971.

Lynn, Steven. "A Passage into Critical Theory." *College English* 52 (1990): 258–271.

Makaryk, Irena R., ed. *Encyclopedia of Contemporary Literary Theory*. Toronto: University of Toronto Press, 1993.

Thacher, James. *Eyewitness to the American Revolution*. Stamford, Conn.: Longmeadow Press, 1994.

Weisberger, Bernard A. *The American People*. New York: American Heritage Publishing Co., 1971.

Index

About the Author

ANDREW MACDONALD is associate professor of English at Loyola University in New Orleans. He has published widely in the areas of popular culture, mystery fiction, and science fiction. He is co-author, with his wife Gina Macdonald, of *Mastering Writing Essentials* (1995), a text for bilingual writing students. His interest in Howard Fast began during visits to the former Soviet Union and Russia, where Fast's works are widely read and popular.